T0318220

International Money and
Capitalist Crisis

International Money and Capitalist Crisis

*The Anatomy of
Global Disintegration*

E.A. Brett

Routledge
Taylor & Francis Group

LONDON AND NEW YORK

To my colleagues and students

First published 1983 by Westview Press, Inc.

Published 2018 by Routledge
52 Vanderbilt Avenue, New York, NY 10017
2 Park Square, Milton Park, Abingdon, Oxon OX14 4RN

Routledge is an imprint of the Taylor & Francis Group, an informa business

British Library Cataloguing in Publication Data

Brett, E.A.
    International money and capitalist crisis.
    1. International finance—History—20th century
    I. Title
    322.4'5   HG3881

    ISBN 13: 978-0-367-01646-3 (hbk)
    ISBN 13: 978-0-367-16633-5 (pbk)

Library of Congress Catalog Card Number: 82-51289

Contents

List of Tables and Figures

Tables

Figures

Preface

This book emerged accidentally, though not fortuitously, out of a more general work on theories of development which I was working on in the late 1970s. While tempting to look at the effect of theory on practice, I was confronted with the increasingly active policy-making role of the IMF in deficit countries. I therefore found myself investigating both the content of its policies and the structures and forces that allowed it to occupy so pivotal a role. As the increasing importance and politicisation of its role had not escaped attention, I was then asked by the International Foundation for Development Alternatives in Geneva to extend the original chapter into a general background paper on the role of the IMF in the third world as a contribution to their 'Third System Project'. This study then served both as a contribution to the debate that eventually materialised in the Arusha Conference on the IMF held in July 1980 (whose results were published in *Development Dialogue*, 1980(2)), and also as the basis for this book. I am very grateful for the support given me by IFDA in this project, and for their permission to use the material to be found in the original paper.

In attempting to understand the growing importance of the monetary problem for deficit countries, I found myself drawn into more and more abstract and general problems of economic theory and institutional change. My starting point here was the fact that the IMF itself makes constant use of general and highly orthodox economic theory to justify its own existence and the nature of its actions. It was therefore impossible to evaluate these without acquiring at least the partial knowledge of this theory set out in the first part of this book. Yet doing this merely created another theoretical problem—the correspondence between orthodox explanations and the actual evolution of the system in reality was imperfect to say the least. While orthodoxy presented an equilibrium world where automatic market mechanisms produced a process of stable, equitable and even development, the most cursory inspection of reality revealed a crisis-ridden world dominated by the unstable and inequitable results of a process of uneven development. Over the past decade my primary intellectual concern has been in the development of a Marxist political economy capable of providing an understanding of problems of inequality, domination and class conflict at the national level more adequate than the categories provided by the orthodox disciplines of economics and political science. Developing these categories (Part II of this work), and applying them to the international monetary and financial history of the post-war period (Part III), seemed to me to produce a far more convincing explanation for the major changes which have occurred in post-war monetary history and therefore justified the attempt to publish this book.

The outcome of these various redraftings has been a shift from a limited concern with the nature of the IMF and the development problem to a very general, theoretical concern with the contradictionary nature of the development of the world capitalist economy as a whole. Here, however, one important omission must be noted. This world is confined to its capitalist component, and entirely excludes any consideration of the monetary or financial relations that prevail between it and the socialist bloc, increasingly important though they may be. Centrally planned monetary and trading relations involve different mechanisms and therefore require different explanations from those determined predominantly by market exchanges. Their implications should certainly be incorporated in any complete study, but as I have not had the resources I therefore ignored them entirely.

This work has benefited greatly from the assistance I have received from both students and colleagues at Sussex and elsewhere. David Evans, in particular, provided incisive comments on the whole of the firt draft which led to a substantial clarification of basic arguments. Rob Eastwood and Tony Venables made important contributions to the development of Chapter 3. More generally I have developed a number of my general ideas on the problems of international money in conversations with Mike Hall, Robin Murray and Fred Bienefeld, and on the development of financial and monetary problems in the third world with Sarah Bartlett, Stephany Griffith Jones and Carlos Fortin. Finally I owe a particular debt to the librarians of the Institute of Development Studies at Sussex, the resources of which provided the basis for most of the substantive material in this book.

E.A. Brett
Sussex University

Introduction

The Bretton Woods system, which provides the core of this work, was, in the words of its master builder, established to end the 'chaotic competition, monetary disorders, political disruptions, and ... wars within as well as among nations'[1] which had characterised the preceding thirty years. This system, created in 1945, appeared to achieve this objective over the following twenty-five years (if both the arms race and the wars stemming from the attempt to contain the spread of communism in the third world are excluded from consideration). But the US brought this period of apparent stability to a close in August 1971 by unilaterally separating the dollar from gold and introducing controls that violated many of the obligations that had sustained the system over the whole period. During the subsequent decade crisis has succeeded crisis. In 1973 continuing pressure on the dollar forced a change from fixed parities to 'managed floating'. In 1974/5 the oil price rise induced a depression deeper than any experienced since the 1930s. In the last three years (1978-81) the revolution in Iran, the invasion of Afghanistan, the renewed oil price rise and the onset of a depression which must be far deeper than that of the mid-1970s have completed the transition from stability to cumulative disintegration. Currency unrest and inflation make effective intervention in economic management impossible and are, in the words of the Bank for International Settlements 'symptomatic of deep-rooted underlying problems'.[2]

This economic impotence of the ruling class manifests itself in rising unemployment and increasing exploitation at the national level, and in intensified international competition as each country attempts to solve its own problems by increasing its exports to the rest. The general liberalisation of monetary and tariff arrangements which has taken place during the post-war period now makes it possible for the strongest countries to adopt 'beggar-thy-neighbour' strategies by using their economic superiority to destroy the weaker industries in deficit countries and thus to undermine the viability of the system as a whole. In self defence the weak are forced into protectionism which may allow them to save at least some of the most vulnerable sectors of their productive capacity, but which makes it

impossible for the international trading system to be effectively managed on the basis of the liberal principles which have dominated the
operation of all of its key agencies during the post-war period. Thus
the intensification of the crisis both increases the pressures on the
governments of the nation states responsible for maintaining the
relations between capital, which is increasingly threatened by the
intensification of competition, and labour which is increasingly exploited and insecure, and also on the viability of the international
structures which have been created to sustain the enormously complex
system of international economic transactions which are essential to
the survival of everyone. Unless this process of disintegration can be
understood and brought under control there is little doubt that the
future of civilisation as we know it will be put at risk.

The possibility of a return to these conditions of endemic crisis
were consistently denied by bourgeois theorists[3] during the long prosperity when the real contradictions built into the system could be
concealed through its ability to provide something close to full employment and growth. The resulting social compromise found its
characteristic theoretical expression in Keynesian interventionism
which guaranteed capital the maximum utilistion of its producitve
capacity and labour the right to work and to a progressively increasing
standard of living. These conditions, of course, only existed in their
pure form in the advanced industrial centres as huge numbers were
excluded from their benefits in the third world. But even there the
prosperity created through rapid economic growth could be passed
on to a broad enough spectrum of the population to guarantee their
increased integration into the hegemonic international economic
order which was being created. During this period, too, the creativity
of critical thinking on the left was severely curtailed by the repressive
effects of Stalinism which, combined with the apparent failure of
Marx's predicted crisis of capitalism, led to a period of stagnation.

The return to crisis, however, has overturned both this optimism
and the dominance of Keynesianism. The combination of inflation
and intensifying recession has produced a return to the sternest
principles of neoclassical orthodoxy embodied in the monetarist
teachings of the Chicago school. Although many practising economists are dismayed by the results, there can be no doubt that this
return to the old orthodoxies is the authentic expression of the views
of the dominant fractions of the international capitalist class.[4] It is not
simply an irrational attack upon the working class, but a strategy
which is deeply repressive yet 'both coherent and the best available to

the ruling class'.[5] More than forty years after Keynes had 'proved' that unemployment could be eliminated through state intervention, the governments of the western and most of the third world are engineering an increase in unemployment and a reduction in state intervention as the only means of breaking the inflationary spiral and restoring capitalist prosperity. This view's most dedicated adherents are in the international agencies and most especially in the IMF where it serves as the basis for all the advice which it imposes upon member countries forced to ask for its assitance because of balance of payments problems. Thus any book concerned, as this is, with understanding the nature of the real options open to the ruling class in its response to the crisis must now come to terms with the nature of the political assumptions and the analytical and policy tools which monetarist and more especially international monetarist theory has put at is disposal. This will be directly attempted in Part I of this book through an examination of the principles on which the Bretton Woods system was based and of the theoretical and policy assumptions of the orthodox understanding of international economic relations.

The destruction of the consensus has also generated a massive increase in political activism among classes and groups that had been rendered quiescent by the favourable conditions of the boom years. This activism has both produced major political crises in the third world – notably in Iran, Nicaragua and South Korea – and a growth in militant political and industrial action in the industrial centres. It has also opened the way for a resurgence of Marxist political economy which questions the long-term viability of the capitalist system itself and finds in the renewed monetarist emphasis on repression both a validation of Marx's original thesis that the system could not effectively incorporate the working clas into a democratic political order, and the opportunity to build an effective political movement committed to a transition to socialism. This work is located directly in this tradition, and is concerned to develop a more adequate understanding of the international dimension within it.

Classical marxism formulated a clear understanding of the nature of the function of the capitalist mode of production, and much of the recent work has been concerned to integrate this with an understanding of the functioning of the modern nation state. This study, following the tradition established by Lenin and taken up again more recently by Mandel, Robinson and the editors of *Monthly Review*,[6] is concerned to re-establish the significance and the complexity of the international dimenson for both the functioning of the mode of production and of the nation state system itself. The post-war period has completed the internationalisation of capitalism: production at any point now depends directly upon a multitude of relations with producers at an infinite number of others. These interactions depend upon the existence of monetary and trading arrangements organised and supervised by international institutions which have to attempt to perfom many of the functions at the international level which are performed at the national level by the nation state. To understand both their potential and their limitations it is therefore essential that we develop a political theory of the functioning of capitalism as an international system of economic interaction and social control. Thus Chapter 1 attempts to set out the essentials of a theory of international economic and most especially monetary organisation, while the substantive chapters deal concretely with its evolution and subsequent disintegration.

Although this study takes the monetary system as its central focus and is therefore concerned directly with circulation rather than production, it does not assume that the problem of crisis emerges directly out of that sphere as the monetarist theorists do. Instead, it sees production and circulation as an integrated whole, with a crisis the outcome of the inability of the system to maintain the two in balance over the long term. At the international level this manifests itself in imbalances between production and consumption in different countries which take the form of disruptions in the flows of goods and of credit. These are registered as disequilibria in the balance of payments which exert direct pressures upon the monetary relations through which the exchanges are mediated. Thus to understand the nature of these relations it is essential that we consider the underlying tendencies at the level of production and exchange which determine the ability of particular countries to compete internationally and therefore produce positive or negative effects on the balance of payments and on monetary relations. These problems have to be looked at in terms of trade theory, and more especially through a theoretical approach which links trade theory with the differential development of productive capacity in the various countries in the system to produce what we can summarise as the process of 'combined and uneven development' characteristic of capitalism as a global system. An understanding of the relationship between accumulation in particular locations and capitalist exchange as a whole is essential if we are to grasp both the integrated nature of the system as a totality and intensely uneven nature of the growth of productive capacity at the local level.[7]

It is this process of internationalised accumulation, and more especially the uneven form which it must take under capitalism, which ensures that the system cannot remain indefinitely in equilibrium and that the crisis must necessarily affect the whole capitalist world when it comes. To deal with this problem this study has attempted to theorise the nature of international trade by demonstrating how the addition of the Marxist notion of the rising organic composition of capital, or even the less complex bourgeois conception of increasing economies of scale, makes the neoclassical orthodoxy based upon Ricardian assumptions of comparative advantage untenable. By doing this it shows that capitalist accumulation cannot be seen as a purely cyclical phenomenon as the usual equilibrium based analyses imply, but must lead to deepening structural differentiations which will, in the long term, make it impossible for a stable relationship between supply and demand, production and consumption to be sustained. Thus while Chapter 3 deals with the underlying dynamic which produces uneven development, Chapter 4 attempts to show how this must inevitably lead to crisis as a result of the inability of a system based upon individualistic competition and accumulation to control the balance between supply and demand and therefore plan the relationship between what can be produced and what can actually be paid for.

Chapter 5 and 6 attempt to concretise these theoretical assertions by examining the stages through which the system has evolved during the post-war period. Here we can identify three major periods by relating the change process to the rise and fall of American hegemony over the system as a whole. Thus an initial period of apparently stable growth up to the early 1960s was based upon a clear situation of American dominance sustained by the overwhelming superiority of its productive and military power. This was succeeded by ten years in which that superiority was increasingly challenged in both the economic and military spheres, but where it was still sufficiently strong to hold the system together, although not strong enough to forestall a recognition of the need for reforms which would lessen its dependence on American resources. Finally we have the period of disintegration ushered in by the separation of the dollar from gold and the growing recognition that the old hegemony had collapsed and that no adequate alternative can be found to replace it. What these chapters attempt to demonstrate is the intimate connection between the costs of sustaining American imperialist dominance internationally, the relative decline in the superiority of American productive capacity, and the ability of capitalism to sustain itself as an expanding yet stable system of production and consumption.

Having done this the study concludes by returning to Lenin's classic analysis of the breakdown of the earlier expansionary phase in capitalism's history, and attempts to show both why it was possible for it to return, however briefly, to another such phase, and why the limits of this attempt have now been reached. It does not attempt to set out any detailed strategy for a working-class response to the problem which this creates for them. That must now become a central problem for their political practice.

Notes

1. The words are taken from H.D. White's US memorandum setting out the principles on which the IMF was eventually to be established. 'Preliminary draft proposals for a United Nations Stabilisation Fund', in J.K. Horsefield, ed., *The international monetary fund, 1945–1965*, vol. III, *Documents*, Washington, IMF, 1969, p. 37.
2. Bank for International Settlements, *Annual Report*, 1979, p. 3.
3. This term is used, for want of a better one, to cover the broad spectrum of thinkers from the neoclassicists to the Keynesian who operate within the limits set by the capitalist system and are therefore primarily concerned with its reproduction or partial reform.
4. For a coherent statement of these views see Confederation of British Industry, *The road to recovery*, London, CBI, 1976.
5. A Glyn and J. Harrison, 'The common sense of monetarism', *New Statesman*, 27 June 1980, p. 962.
6. Notably the relevant chapters of E. Mandel, *Late capitalism*, London, Verso, 1978, and his earlier *Europe vs. America*, New York, Monthly Review, 1970, Chapter 8; H.L. Robinson; 'The downfall of the dollar', *Socialist Register*, 1973; and the Editors, 'Emerging currency and trade wars', *Monthly Review*, 29 (9), 1978; and H. Magdoff, 'The US dollar, petrodollars, and US imperialism', *Monthly Review*, 30 (8), 1979.
7. For an early and powerful formulation of this process see L. Trotsky, *The history of the Russian revolution*, London, Pluto Press, 1977, Chapter 1.

Part I
The Organisation and Theory of International Stability

1 The Political Theory of International Money

The more inflation spreads and is prolonged, the less owners of commodities and holders of credit notes can be obliged to accept inconvertible paper money outside the borders of a single state. In the final analysis, a world paper money of obligatory usage presupposes a world state, a world government, that is, the disappearance of inter-imperialist competition, that is, superimperialism. We are further from that than ever. (E. Mandel, *The generalized recession of the international capitalist economy*, Brussels, Imprecor, 1975, Chapter 1.)

Organising Internationalised Production
Capital now operates globally, shifting goods, services, investments and credit from place to place with little concern for 'local and national seclusion and self-sufficiency'.[1] It is dominated by the power of the transnational corporations (TNCs) which, as citizens of the world, do business wherever there is money to be made and have created privileged circuits for the international flow of capital, trade, technology and profits.[2] Their control over the productive resources of the world grows constantly because their scale of production and global reach enables them to outcompete small national capitalists at the local level, and because of the existence of the liberal trading and monetary system created by international agreement in the post-war period. This system, together with the network of financial and trading intermediaries which have grown up to service it, provides

productive capital with the political and economic conditions which are essential for its smooth operation and constant expansion.

But while capital operates globally, the space it occupies is divided politically into territorially limited nation states exercising sovereign rights over domestic and foreign economic policy. Thus the global system can only function as it does because most nation states have accepted treaty obligations through the IMF and GATT which limit their right to impose monetary or tariff constraints on their external economic relations, and because the Bretton Woods system has provided it with a workable form of international money through which the necessary transactions can be conducted. The continued viability of this system and of the international capitalist class which sustains it therefore depends upon the extent to which the bulk of these nation states can be persuaded to accept these constraints, and on the continued acceptability of the international monetary unit. How, then, are we to understand the relationship between national and global levels in the resolution of these problems?

Bourgeois theory has characteristically dealt with this problem by evading it. It presents the international economy as a system of atomised individual exchanges regulated by the operation of the world market which enforces the principle of economic efficiency and comparative advantage through the effects of free competition. It therefore defines these activities as economic and not political, thus excluding the problem of sovereignty from the analysis, and viewing the creation of the system of global regulation as the outcome of a series of freely negotiated agreements between independent nation states. This view, with its individualisitic bias, necessarily excludes both the possibility that any particular country can impose a deter-minate tendency upon the trajectory of international development, or that the system as a whole can function to extend the social power of one class over any other. As a result imperialism disappears from view, as does any understanding of class struggle, as the motivation of historical processes. Theory is then reduced to a concern with me-chanisms for maximising the level of international exchanges whose universal benefits are taken to be virtually self-evident.

The global crisis has now decisively displaced this complacent viewpoint by bringing into the open both the hierarchical and the integrated nature of the contemporary economic and political order. Inflation, recession and unemployment have been carried right through the system as effectively as the plague was carried across medieval Europe. The TNCs, as the primary instrument of this process, continue to expand and profit as more and more governments solicit their services, while their activities intensify the overall level of domestic and international inequality and undermine the ability of the system as a whole to sustain its integrity and legitimacy. And while they constantly extend an authentically international structure of economic management, the operation of the IMF, GATT and the EEC – the leading agencies of international economic regulation – is increasingly determined by the need to provide them with the framework of rules and controls required to sustain the openness and the flexibility of the world system within which they operate. This combination of private and public control has now clearly produced something which is beginning to approximate an internationalised state system which has appropriated key areas of economic sovereignty from the previously dominant nation state system. Although this process is still only partially and imperfectly developed, it has been of decisive importance to the evolution of the post-war order and both its achievements and its limitations must be clearly understood if we are to grasp the true nature of its political economy.

If the above emphasis on the central role of the international firms and agencies is correct, then the whole theory of the capitalist state and of its relationship with the process of internal class struggle requires a substantial re-evaluation. The relative autonomy of the international sphere, and the corresponding freedom from the constraints imposed on domestic capital by interventionist and most especially reformist social democratic governments, has given the TNCs a decisive advantage in the competitive struggle. Their ability to evade these constraints, to move capital and commodities from place to place without let or hindrance, and to choose the locations that are to benefit from the productive capacity that they monopolise, makes it possible for them not only to maximise their overall rate of profit, but also to undermine the bargaining power of the individual governments with which they have to deal and to extract the optimum conditions out of each of them. The recent expansion of 'free zones' in a large number of third world countries[3] and the growth of subsidies to encourage investments in many industrialised countries is a clear indication of the present strength of their position *vis-à-vis* supposedly sovereign national governments. Further, when particular national states are unable to meet the foreign obligations which their integration into this open economic system imposes on them and suffer a corresponding balance of payments crisis, it is the IMF which is expected to intervene and to impose a policy package designed to keep the local economy within the limits of the liberal trading and monetary order. Hence the essentially directive and political nature of the internationalised intervention is clearly exposed, as is the control that it exercises over the notionally sovereign agencies of the nation state.

The establishment of this dual system in the post-war period appears to provide international monopoly capital with the best of all possible worlds. While it liberates them from many of the constraints imposed on domestic capital by the interventionist state, it nevertheless allows them to take full advantage of the social investments and regulatory controls which these states must now provide for all of their producers irrespective of origin.[4] And whereas the evolution of the inverventionist state in the 1930s and 1940s was usually associated with nationalist and protectionist policies which interfered with the free movement of capital and commodities, their present integration into the liberal international economic order created at Bretton Woods precludes any general return to these measures. The global agencies must, almost by definition, operate in accordance with the principles of *laissez-faire* and have thus established at the international level an incipient state system organised along the lines set out by the classicial political theorists and capable of exerting a decisive influence upon the freedom of action of nation states and their class actors. Thus a functionalist logic concerned to identify the dominant institutional structure of post-war capitalism as an 'instrument' of its leading class would see this process as no more than a direct response to the needs of capital and its outcome as the means of extending and deepening its domination.

Now it would be wrong to deny the link between monopoly capital and the evolution of the international monetary order, but a purely functionalist account would necessarily leave out the most crucial fact of all. The existing system, far from providing capital with a secure field for its operation is in deep crisis and this, while strengthening some fractions of capital, is destroying the viability of many of its weaker links and thereby inducing immense and potentially uncontrollable strains into its operation. Were capital able to order the world in accordance with its own requirements, it would have done a better job of it than this. Bourgeois theorists and their mentors observe this situation with desperation, not satisfaction, and privately concede that it stems from structural contradictions that they can neither understand nor bring under control.

While the fundamental source of this problem lies in the underlying tendencies of capitalist accumulation – to be considered in detail in

Chapters 3 and 4 – its superstructural complement manifests itself in the structural inadequacies of the system of dual power set out above. The modern capitalist state system has to provide for both the further extension of the essentially unified system of internationalised production, and for the maintenance of the provisions and social investments required to guarantee political stability and social reproduction at each particular point in it. While the former task falls to the international firms and agencies with their *laissez-faire* principles, the latter falls to the national state. This task has increasingly required higher levels of direct intervention into the production process to provide both a wide range of essential services to capital as well as provisions for labour of a redistributive kind designed to ensure both its effective physical reproduction and its political incorporation into the state system.[5] This process has required that the state exercise both the coercive capacity to tax productive capital to provide the resources required to perform these services, and the capacity to subordinate the interests of particular capitals in order to be able to guarantee the long-term requirements of capitalism as a whole.[6]

This structure can only exist effectively if all capitals are equally subordinated to its controls and levies. The existence of the essentially unregulated international sphere, however, makes it possible for the most powerful capitals to escape these limits and to minimise their contributions to social reproduction by setting up in the most advantageous locations and using a wide range of well documented mechanisms to reduce taxation and maximise global profits. This process intensifies the problem of uneven development internationally and undermines the economic and political viability of all of the states which cannot offer capital the most favourable conditions. These become 'weak links' in the capitalist chain and are then increasingly unable to make adequate provision for economic growth or for social reproduction. Their capacity to consume therefore declines as does their ability to contain social and political unrest. This both diminishes the markets for the output of the capitals located in the strong centres and therefore presents them with a realisation crisis, and also creates the basis for revolutionary politics which threatens the integrity of the system itself.

The solution to this problem clearly lies in the further development of the international system to the point where it would be able to exercise enough of the control and redistributive functions now monopolised by the local state to be able to offset this tendency towards uneven development and breakdown. Indeed, most of the politics of international monetary relations has always been concerned with the attempt to do exactly this. But the transfer of these powers as a way of creating an 'adequate' form of state at the global level has always been effectively precluded by the conflict between various fractions of capital which have never been willing to accept the limitations on their freedom of action which such a change would necessarily require. The resulting failure, although producing a system which gives signficant advantages to some sections of monopoly capital, notably at the moment the transnational banks and the oil cartels, nevertheless makes it impossible to deal coherently with the problems of integrating and legitimating the system as a whole. Its origins and implications are so crucial that they will be central to the theoretical concerns of the rest of this work.

While a great deal of work has been done on the national aspect of this problem, much less has been done on the international structures and linkages which are of such central importance, no doubt because they operate so much less directly and have thus far been largely insulated from mass political struggle.[7] The rest of this work must therefore be taken as an extremely tentative attempt to remedy this deficiency by trying to develop a theory about the structure of the international state system and of its evolution in the post-war period.

The international sphere exists mainly as a structure of regulation rather than intervention. The IMF and GATT mainly serve to enforce a set of national commitments to liberal monetary and trading practices which leave direct control in the hands of private producers regulated by market competition. This does not make their role any less 'political' or crucial to the trajectory of economic development, however, since it seriously limits the ability of nation states to use a wide range of policies to secure domestic economic objectives. Because of the signficance of these inhibitions, a good deal of attention will be devoted to a review of the theoretical assumptions on which they are based and of their effect on the actual evolution of the production process. But the international system has *had* to go beyond pure regulation in at least one crucial area. International trade requires international money, and the Bretton Woods system has been directly responsible for developing a monetary unit which could perform this role in a stable and expansionary way. Now control over money is both an essentially political function and a prerogative of national sovereignty. Thus it is in this area that the creation of the new system has required the greatest innovations and has impinged most directly on the prerogatives of the nation state system. Because most of the unresolvable conflicts that now confront it stem from the inadequacy of these arrangements, it is essential that we begin this study with an attempt to formulate an adequate theorisation of the problem of sustaining a feasible form of international credit money.

Money as Credit in Capitalism

Money is essentially a form of credit[8] which serves to separate the sale of any commodity from a subsequent purchase, thus eliminating the need for, and inefficiencies of, barter. Thus money is not obtained for its own sake, but as a receipt for the value[9] of the services delivered by the individual to the society and hence as a claim upon an equivalent value of commodities to be provided in exchange. Thus while most commodities enter the market as exchange values and are purchased because they constitute specific use values, money exists as pure exchange value and serves to represent not its own value but that of all of the other commodities in circulation. Thus Hegel argues:

> The value of a thing may be very heterogeneous; it depends on need. But if you want to express the value of the thing not in a specific case but in the abstract, then it is money which expresses this. Money represents any and every thing, though since it does not portray the need itself but is only a symbol of it, it is itself controlled by the specific value of the commodity.[0]

Now the use of money is a function of and prerequisite for the existence of an extended division of labour in which individuals perform highly specialised services for, and satisfy the bulk of their own needs by purchase from, a multitude of other individuals to whom they will be otherwise indifferent and with whom they may even be competing. Thus:

> A fairly developed division of labour presupposes that the needs of each person have become very many-sided and his product has become very one-sided.... Hence the necessity for a *general medium of exchange*, where the specific product and the specific labour must be exchanged for *exchangeability*.[11]

The more developed the division of labour the longer the possible time span between transactions and the more crucial the guarantee that the money form will not be devalued, in the interim especially as money can be used to buy labour power as well as goods and can therefore serve as the basis for the subsequent creation of *capital* by the individuals able to accumulate it. Thus money exists in capitalist society to perform a specifically *social* function, but one of a very particular type – that of linking the otherwise disconnected labours of the mass of individuals producers involved in a system of atomised and competitive market relations. Thus the money form provides the basis for the interaction between these producers, sustains the integrity of the system of exchanges in which they are involved, and guarantees the value of the social credit which particular individuals may have accumulated in the form of savings. Thus:

> The reciprocal and all-sided dependence of individuals who are indifferent to one another forms their social connection. This social bond is expressed in *exchange value*, or, by means of which alone each individual's own activity or his product become an activity and a product for him; he must produce a general product – *exchange value*, or, the latter isolated for itself and individualised, *money*. On the other side the power which each individual exercises over the activity of others or over social wealth exists in him as the owner of *exchange values*, of *money*. The individual carries his social power, as well as his bond with society, in his pocket.[12]

Thus the possession of money guarantees individuals the control not only of goods but also of the labour time of others and, in so doing, gives its owner the capacity to control their relationship to both consumption and the production process. Yet it is not generated and allocated through a socially planned process in which everyone takes part, but through an unmediated process of atomised market exchange. In this process of exchange money must exist as a stable measure and store of value insulated from manipulation by any of the protagonists in the competitive struggle. Thus it is essential that this long-term value be guaranteed by a social mechanism which puts it beyond the control of any particular individual or group of individuals directly involved in the social process that it serves to regulate. To provide an adequate form of credit for an extended capitalist division of labour, an adequate monetary unit cannot simply depend upon mutual trust (since the competitive nature of capitalist production precludes this) but must contain some intrinsic guarantee against the possibility of default or fraud. Establishing and sustaining this guarantee is the central *political* problem involved in the creation of a workable form of monetary organisation at both the domestic and international levels.

Historically, before the evolution of an adequate form of capitalist state and a developed system of banking and financial intermediaries, this problem was solved by using monetary units which directly embodied the values of the commodities which they served to exchange. As the political and financial superstructure evolved, however, it has been possible to move from units involving real values such as gold and silver, to those, such as paper tokens and credit cards, which rest upon guarantees which are purely social and political. Thus the evolution of the money form in late capitalism can best be understood by coming to terms with the political developments required to make the transition from the system in which gold played the dominant role to the present one in which its position is merely residual.[13] The history of this transition cannot concern us here, but it is important to establish some theoretical points about its nature and that of the role of the state in making it possible.

The social utility of gold derived from the fact that it could only be produced through the direct expenditure of labour and therefore could not be acquired by government or individual (legally at least) without the payment of an equivalent value for it. The price of gold could change in relation to changes in supply and demand, but it would be controlled at the margin by the costs of producing an increase in its output. Thus the value of the gold supply could not be manipulated by anyone, and it could not increase any faster than the increase in the productivity of the other economic activities required to sustain the gold producers themselves.[14] Thus the use of gold as money *did* depend upon the social agreement to use it as the money material, but required almost no other form of social organisation to ensure its value and acceptibility. It could therefore function effectively even in countries where law and order had broken down and, more significantly for our purposes, as the basis for trade between individuals in different and even hostile countries.

But it would be incorrect to assume that the use of gold excluded all forms of state intervention or manipulation. Gold could only be used in regular commerce when it had been minted into coin whose weight and fineness was guaranteed, and it was the state which soon provided this guarantee by acquiring a monopoly over their issue. By so doing, of course, the early states were able to manipulate the gold content of the coins which they issued and to use the debasement of the coinage as a means of financing their own activities – notably the waging of wars – for which regular means of raising taxes were inadequate.

While these kinds of activities made it possible for governments to appropriate resources from their populations and thereby depreciate the real value of the currency, it is almost certainly the case that most gold standard systems also incorporated some form of credit money because of the enormous savings in social costs which this necessarily involved. Once a reasonably secure system of property rights and economic exchange had been established, producers would be able to conduct more and more of their activities on the basis of credit rather than direct payments. Goldsmiths could begin to issue receipts for the metal stored in their vaults, receipts which could circulate as a surrogate for it; banks could operate a more advanced form of the same process. Both could effectively create credit money by issuing more tokens than they could cover with the gold they had actually received. As this process expanded the need for central control to protect against fraud or failure increased, and central banks were given monopoly powers of enforcement in relation to the issue of notes and reserve requirements. This process in effect signalled the transition from the direct use of gold as a medium of exchange to the use of gold as the standard measure supporting credit money as a means of exchange. Therefore Vilar is quite correct to argue that

> It would therefore be quite wrong to conterpose some imagined age of metallic currency, presumed to cover the whole of previous history, to a period of modern currency which began at some point in the 1920s.[15]

With the consolidation of the bourgeois state, and the corresponding ability to guarantee the stability of the credit system, it became possible to dispense almost entirely with gold even as a reserve asset and to give the central bank the monopoly of the issue of token money and to allow the private sector to provide various forms of near money under some degree of central control.

This transition from a gold to a credit system has been essential for the full development of capitalist production which would have 'encountered barriers in the volume of production of precious metals'[16] without it. Further, the resulting development of credit creation through the banking system has created the basis for the development of large-scale industry and therefore for the greater part of the increase in the social productivity of labour which capitalism has engendered. In Keynes's words it has performed the miracle 'of turning stone into bread'.[17]

These advantages, however, have not been secured without the creation of corresponding risks. Firstly, the power to issue an inconvertible paper currency makes it possible for the state to expand the supply of money almost without limit and thereby to undermine the integrity of all of the contracts entered into in the previous period. In John Stuart Mill's words the power to

> depreciate the currency without limit ... is an intolerable evil. All variations in the value of the circulating medium are mischievous: they disturb existing contracts and expectations, and the liability to such changes

renders every pecuniary engagement of long date entirely precarious....
Great as this evil would be if it depended only on accident, it is still greater
when placed at the arbitrary disposal of an individual or a body of individuals, who may have any kind or degree of interest to be served by an
artifical fluctuation in its fortunes... .[18]

Since World War II it has been widely assumed that the money supply
could be manipulated as a direct instrument of economic policy in
advanced industrial states, while its expansion has been used by a
variety of less developed governments as a means of attempting to
reconcile the interests of competing classes in situations where coherent growth strategies had failed. The lack of success of both of
these tendencies has now opened the way for a revival of the classical
orthodoxy in which it is argued that the 'monetary authority should
operate as a surrogate for the gold standard',[19] and that it should only
allow it to expand by something very close to the growth in real
productivity.[20] Although I would want to question the causal relationship between the money supply and the evolution of the real
economy asserted by the monetarist school, there can be little doubt
that the maintenance of a feasible economic system now depends
directly upon the willingness of the state to refrain from expanding
the money supply more rapidly than the expansion of the production
process. Secondly, the expansion of the credit system makes it possible for private capital to be extended on a massive scale and for a
complex network of interdependent contracts to be entered into. For
as long as production is expanding the bulk of these obligations can
be met and debts ultimately paid; once it begins to contract and
businesses to fail the network of credit will be disrupted and a general
collapse ensue. Thus the expansion of credit becomes 'the main lever
of over-production and over-speculation in commerce [forces] the
reproduction process ... to its extreme limits [and] accelerates the
material development of the productive forces and the establishment
of the world market'. But given the inability of capitalism to control
the relationship between supply and demand in this process, it also
'accelerates the violent eruptions of this contradiction – crises – and
thereby the elements of disintegration of the old mode of production'.[21] The outcome of this is likely to be 'a regression of the whole
capitalist financial organisation'[22] and a reversion to the use of gold
with a corresponding withdrawal of social resources from productive
use, a process which can clearly be seen at work in the unprecedented
increase in the gold price which has occurred in the second half of the
1970s.[23] The social costs of such a credit failure are now enormous,

most notably demonstrated in the consequences of the bank failures of the early 1930s which initiated the worst phase of the depression. These, too, have led to an expansion of the role and responsibilities of the state, which has taken on a more and more directive role in regulating the activities of the private credit system to prevent a recurrence of those events.

Thus it is clear that the maintenance of the benefits to be derived from the extension of the credit-money system depends more and more directly upon the capacity of the state both to sustain a workable relationship between its own activities and the evolution of the production process proper and to ensure that the latter can be insulated from major recessions which will induce a crisis in the credit system and thus in the operation of the economy as a whole. It is therefore no accident that the new neoclassical orthodoxy has singled out the relationship between money and the state as the central factor in its attempt to reassert capitalist discipline over levels of public spending and wages which have tended to expand beyond the levels of production and thereby induce more or less permanent inflation. Although they are almost certainly wrong in assuming that a reduction in the money supply through a reduction in spending and wages will necessarily eliminate inflation, they are almost certainly correct in believing that a continuous and uncontrolled expansion of it will lead to a collapse in the underlying system of social organisation which makes capitalist production possible. Although their diagnosis is inadequate, they are quite correct to emphasise the essentially *political* nature of the monetary problem.

If we now consider this line of argument in relation to the issues raised in the previous section, it immediately becomes evident that it raises some fundamental questions about the possibility of creating a feasible form of international credit money. We saw there that the level of social organisation at the international level, while crucial to the operation of the global economy, was nevertheless very inadequate compared with that attained at the national level. Yet we have now seen that no credit money can operate effectively without a unified system of control capable of sustaining a pattern of highly complex yet intrinsically atomised and competitive economic relations. Without an adequate form of state there can be no adequate form of credit money. Does this mean, then, that the attempt to organise a unified system of capitalist production on a global scale is intrinsically impossible?

The Politics of International Credit Money

Without some form of international political organisation, therefore, international capitalist exchange must ultimately depend upon a monetary unit containing real values. Thus Marx argued that a token money could only exist if it had 'its own objective social validity' acquired by 'its forced currency' guaranteed by 'the state's compulsion'.[24] He assumed that this could only provide for its function as means of circulation and not for its other functions, and would only hold 'within the inner sphere of circulation ... circumscribed by the boundaries of a given community'.[24] Outside that sphere he felt that it was 'always the genuine money commodity, gold and silver in their physical shape' which would be required as 'the universally recognised social materialisation of wealth' to transfer 'wealth from one country to another'.[25]

Although the recent increase in the gold price and strong tendencies towards a reaffirmation of its role in international monetary relations demonstrate the continuing strength of these arguments, there can be little doubt that late capitalism has been able to develop at least partially workable forms of international credit money from the latter part of the nineteenth century. While the pound sterling and the dollar acquired a part of their validity from their convertibility into gold, their role derived much more directly from their relationship to the dominant imperialist power of the day than from the value of the actual gold reserve which served as their theoretical backing. Thus between 1900 and 1913 the ratio of gold reserves to imports in Britain fell from 7 to 5 per cent and international trade was therefore being financed on the basis of 'reserves which seem to us now to have been astonishingly slender compared with the volume of trade and other transactions'.[26] And American gold reserves have covered less and less of the dollars held in foreign reserves since the early 1960s when the 'dollar overhang' first emerged. The failure of the French attempt to convert the bulk of their dollar assets into gold in the mid-1960s indicated clearly that convertibility was no longer a realistic political guarantee, while its unilateral termination in 1971 has left the world almost entirely dependent upon the credibility of the American monetary authorities and the functioning of the American economy for the long term stability of the currency in which it conducts the bulk of its trading and financial transactions.

This situation is now regarded as very unsatisfactory by most observers, but the dollar has nevertheless provided the basis for a massive expansion of international credit which has been essential for the growth of international productivity and trade. Given the obvious significance of this development and the increasing difficulties, which it is now confronting, it is essential that we attempt to understand the nature of the mechanisms which have made the transition from gold to credit money system possible. We can perhaps begin to do this by attempting to relate international trade and monetary theory to the problems of sustaining an adequate relationship between national and international state forms set out in the preceding section.

Within a single economy individuals use a single currency which must be accepted as legal tender. The state can manipulate the supply of money, thus altering the distribution of wealth, the accumulation of capital and ultimately the locus of social control itself, but all of the individuals affected by this are directly involved in the political process and can therefore attempt to correct policies which affect them adversely by altering the composition of the state apparatus. It is this power which ultimately legitimates the state's right to exercise the compulsion which it exerts through its right to issue a token money with a 'forced currency'. Internationally, however, exchanges occur between individuals in states using distinct monetary units. Without the use of gold to equate the exchange value of these currencies and to guarantee their long-term stability, very serious economic and political problems must arise. These can only be resolved if a very specific and problematic pattern of economic and political exchange can be sustained between all of the countries involved in the system. Sustaining an international credit money system depends directly upon the capacity to meet these requirements in a coherent and stable fashion.

Without gold, transactions have to be conducted between individuals holding paper currencies guaranteed only by the political and economic strength of their respective state systems. Settlements have now to be made by relating the respective exchange values of two token currencies by establishing a rate of exchange that must reflect the relative productivities of the two countries if each currency is to be equally acceptable to individuals in the other country. Because relative productivities vary constantly in relation to differences in rates of investment and growth, the stability of these rates of exchange must be problematic over the long term. The threat of a decline in the exchange value of any currency threatens the individual or central bank in another country holding it with a loss of the real values which they exported in order to obtain it. Thus the long-term viability of a system of international token money must depend upon the maintenance of conditions .which will guarantee a reasonable degree of stability in the relative rates of exchange of the various currencies in the system. An examination of what is required to sustain this guarantee should provide us with a theoretical starting point for an examination of the fundamentals of international monetary stability and disintegration.

Individuals and, at a higher level, the monetary authorities in one country will only be willing to accept a token payment for goods supplied to another if they can eventually realistically expect to be able to import goods of an equivalent value with that payment. This is obviously only possible where a balance of payments equilibrium can be maintained between the two over the long-term. For payments stability in a system of multilateral trade each country must sustain a stable overall balance with all of the rest over the long-term.

With gold it is possible to separate this mechanism from direct political intervention since a deficit will lead to an outflow of the metal and to a corresponding decline in the internal money supply. This will reduce internal demand and force deflation and a return to the external equilibrium. Without gold, however, policy choices become central as the state can respond to the deficit through policies which may or may not contribute to the maintenance of the integrity of the system. It is, of course, possible for them to follow Friedman's injunction set out earlier, and act as though the gold standard was still in operation. They would then adopt deflationary policies, reduce internal consumption and shift resources into the export sector in order to be able to correct the imbalance and pay off their debts in full. We might note, in passing, that this is exactly the policy enforced by the IMF when it is called on to provide balance of payments assistance to deficit countries, a clear recognition of the fact that it represents the most 'responsible' means of dealing with the problem from the point of view of the integrity of the monetary system as a whole. But at least two other options are open to deficit countries which would necessarily have much more destructive results. The authorities might simply continue to sustain expansionary policies by expanding the money supply, thus drawing in additional imports and failing to correct the weakness in productive capacity which created the problem in the first instance. This would rapidly lead to a devaluation of the currency and losses to all of the foreign exporters who were holding it. The surplus country would continually suffer losses in real value and would soon seek to limit its dealings with the country concerned by refusing to sustain the free convertibility of their currencies. Secondly, and even more disastrously, the deficit country could seek to correct its deficit by introducing direct controls on imports through tariff and currency controls, and thus destroy the equality of treatment between domestic and foreign producers which is the prerequisite for the maintenance of the legitimacy and efficiency of the market competition which is seen to be the only rational and neutral means of allocating productive resources between the two. This will attack the integrity of the monetary relations even more directly, especially where currency controls are used as the main form of intervention.

Because of these possibilities, it is evident that feasible monetary relationships can only be sustained where reasonable expectations can be established as to the willingness and more especially the ability of all the governments in the system to use policies that do not threaten the long-term competitiveness of their productive base and the integrity of their external monetary obligations when they have to deal with a substantial balance of payments deficit. This also demonstrates that the ability of any country to sustain liberal trading relations with others, and therefore the ability to maintain workable credit money relationships, depends upon a corresponding ability to sustain a long-term balance of payments equilibrium with them. And this, in turn depends upon two closely related factors – the ability to maintain the relative productivities of all of the countries in the system in some kind of balance and the willingness of the governments involved to adopt policies which deal with this problem without debasing the currency or restricting the flow of payments or trade.

Now liberal economic theory assumes that perfect competition and comparative advantage will tend to generate a long-term balance of payments equilibrium in the system as a whole. Thus a standard textbook asserts that 'the requirements for normal balance of payments adjustment are not very stringent and are almost certain to be satisfied in reality'.[27] This assumes that economic 'adjustments' required to keep particular economies in balance will not seriously disturb the normal process of policy-making or impose very serious constraints upon the autonomy of the national governments involved. Yet recent history demonstrates that competition has been far from perfect and the tendency has not been towards equilibrium, but towards a process of uneven development which has imposed increasingly severe pressures upon weaker centres attempting to sustain open trading relationships with stronger ones. In these circumstances the adoption of the 'responsible' option required to sustain the integrity of the overall system becomes increasingly difficult for the government concerned, since it forces it to impose increasingly restrictive policies on both capital and labour, policies which are likely to be resisted and to lead to the loss of political support and even power itself.

Thus, the maintenance of effective international monetary structures imposes very considerable external limits upon the autonomy of national governments, limits which are being clearly exposed through the increasingly problematic results of recent IMF interventions designed to impose policies on deficit countries aimed to meet this need. Governments operating in this sytem can no longer adopt deficit financing and import restriction policies which were once considered fundamental to successful economic intervention. Internal options are now decisively conditioned by the level of external competition which transfers its pressures to the domestic economy through the operation of the balance of payments. In marxist terms this is to say that the operation of the law of value has now to be seen as an essentially international phenomenon which imposes determinate solutions on national governments. Capital now exerts its pressures through the international economy and forces national agents to respond to its needs through its effect on the balance of payments.

What will concern us in the rest of this work is the assumptions which have induced virtually all of the states in the capitalist world to accept the undertakings required to maintain this system of exchange relations, and the extent to which its actual operation has actually provided them all with sufficient benefits to make it worth their while to continue with it. Before we can do this, however, it is necessary to look in general terms at the conditions which have had to prevail to enable that system of open exchange relations to sustain a universally valid token money by adopting the regulations required to allow first the dollar and then the special drawing right (SDR) to fulfil that role.

Now it is clear that the Bretton Woods settlement, with its commitment to a system of fixed parities, and of limited intervention by the IMF to assist and direct countries with balance of payments deficits, was predicated upon the need to guarantee the behaviour required to sustain the 'responsible' behaviour described above. The settlement, however, also attempted to establish an international currency which would serve the functions of money for all of the agents in the system, thus simplifying the transactions involved in making payments and providing the basis for a broad extension of credit on an international scale.

An international credit money must be accepted by country A as a payment from country B on the assumption that it can subsequently be used as legal tender to make equivalent purchases from countries B, C, D, etc. Its social validity *is* established through 'the state's compulsion', but only at the level of an international political structure created through an international treaty where all of the individual states have agreed to accept it as legal tender and hence to give up their own right to conduct their external payments on the basis of direct negotiations with specific countries in the system. They are now obliged to accept these tokens in payment for their own goods and will therefore accumulate them in their foreign exchange reserves as their primary form of national savings. The strength of their own economies will therefore now depend directly upon the ability of the international system to guarantee that the exchange value of the international currency will not be debased or manipulated to provide an unfair competitive advantage to any particular unit in the system. What are the economic and political implications of this requirement?

An international currency, like any other, can only be expanded as rapidly as the growth in the productive resources which it is to circulate if it is not to be debased and undermine the value of the existing stock of money. Since it is being used for international rather than domestic transactions, it should expand only as rapidly as the growth in international trade. The international currency will be accumulated by particular countries through the export of goods or services and will then give them, in the exchange value of their foreign exchange reserves, a claim upon goods produced anywhere else in the system at any point in the future. This means that the accumulation of stocks of international money must in the last analysis (that is to say leaving out of account flows of credit which will be considered elsewhere) be determined by the scale of the balance of payments surpluses being maintained in the system. These, representing the transfer of real resources which has taken place in the system, guarantee that the international stock of tokens reflect the real value of productive capacity involved in international trade. These tokens, in turn, can only be validated through the eventual purchase of an equivalent quantity of commodities from the deficit countries which absorbed the goods that created the original surpluses.

This implies that a feasible international credit money system requires two mechanisms. First, it must be able to issue enough tokens to cover all valid international transactions and to guarantee that the stock of money does not fall below or rise above this limit. Second, it must be able to ensure that the balance of payments requirement set out for a system of multilateral payments outlined above is also met. To sustain the system over the long-term the surplus countries must be able to validate their claims on external resources by being able to exchange their tokens for goods and services produced in deficit countries, thereby turning the latter into surplus countries and cancelling out all debts. They will only wish to make such external purchases if the prices in the deficit countries are competitive with their own domestic producers, so *the system can only operate effectively if it can sustain a process of even and balanced development between the productive capacities of all of the units in it.* If it fails to achieve this the value of the tokens held by the surplus countries will be depreciated and they will have incurred a loss of real values by holding them.

Thus the political legitimacy of an international credit money depends upon the ability of the international state system to sustain the balanced growth in international productive capacity required to maintain a long-term balance of payments equilibrium. We can now consider the theoretical problems posed by the emergence of the dollar and the SDR in relation to these considerations.

Marx argued the necessity for gold at the international level because capitalist development had not yet created the basis for the organisation of the world market which was only to be achieved in the latter part of the nineteenth century. This was a function of what Mandel calls the transition from 'freely competitive capitalism to classical imperialism',[28] based on the emergence of monopoly capitalism, and involving the division of the world into a series of empires controlled by the leading industrial powers. By the end of the nineteenth century the world was no longer a place where small capitals competed with each other in a relatively open international environment, but had become one where large joint stock companies, backed by enormous concentrations of finance capital, were able to exert a decisive influence over the growth of international production and over the political apparatuses of the national and international state systems. Neoclassical theory continued to discuss competitive exchange between equal individuals and countries, but the world was divided into empires with integrated monetary systems dominated by the political and economic power of the monopoly companies which at that stage tended to operate as national rather than transnational organisations, but nevertheless on an international scale.

In these circumstances some national currencies were more equal than others, and the pound sterling, backed by the productive capacity of the largest empire of them all, was the most equal of them all. Its value, notionally tied to gold, was in fact validated by the resources of an entire empire, all of which could be used to guarantee its ability to retain its real value. After World War II the US was in a comparable position. Its internal productive capacity was probably as great as that of the rest of the world combined; it appropriated a vast income in profits and interest payments on massive overseas investments; and its troops were stationed all over the world as the primary defence against communist expansion. The old European empires exerted less and less real influence; the new, less formal American empire provided the world with the material and military basis for a system of integrated political and economic control. The monetary correlate of this system of organisation was the universal acceptability of the US dollar as a form of international credit money. How can the considerations set out earlier in this chapter help us to understand both its initial ability to perform that role and its subsequent inability to sustain it? We can deal with this apparent paradox by looking at the problems first of issuing it internationally and then of sustaining its real value over the long term.[29]

The dollar, unlike a genuine international currency, is both domestically and internationally valid and issued by a national, not an international, monetary agency. Thus dollars can only be obtained in two ways: in payment for goods and services sold on the American market or as credit obtained from public or private American financial institutions. Thus dollars can only be built up abroad as a source of international liquidity by sustaining a balance of payments surplus with the US or by convincing its financial institutions of the need to provide foreign credit. In the context of a system of competitive capitalist exchange the former possibility cannot be planned, but must be the outcome of the greater efficiency of the producers in the exporting country than those in the US. Where this is not the case, notably so in the 1940s and 1950s, then the expansion of international liquidity requires that it issue loans or grants 'so that simultaneously there can be a balance of trade surplus and a balance of payments deficit'.[30]

Thus it might appear that the use of credit can resolve the problem of liquidity creation without requiring a fundamental decline in the relative competitiveness of the centre economy, but this cannot be anything more than temporary. No country can provide international liquidity on a grant basis without threatening its own productive capacity; it must extend the greater part of this as credit which will therefore have to be repaid with interest. This will only be possible if the debtor countries can achieve a positive balance of payments with it in the long-term which, again, will only be possible if they can raise their productive capacity above that of the centre country at some point in the future. This is only to say that the balance of payments equilibrium requirement for a system of multilateral payments set out above must also hold in the case of a centre currency, but in a very specific and, we will see, contradictory way. For international liquidity to be freely available, therefore, the centre country must allow the relative economic dominance which made it the leading imperial power to be reduced in order to enable the debtor countries to expand their productive capacity and pay off their international debts in a non-inflationary way.

On the other hand, the validation of the dollar depends upon an entirely opposite principle. Dollars are acceptable partly because they can be used to buy any goods, partly because they can be used to buy US goods. Many dollars can therefore circulate outside the US and be sustained by productivity gains made in these external economies. But their exchange value can never be separated from the activities of the US economy and monetary authorities since any expansion in the supply of dollars over and above the expansion in American productivity can be used by Americans to buy foreign goods and to pay for them with tokens. This expansion will then lead to a direct expansion in the money supply of the exporting countries which will have inflationary consequences if they cannot create an appropriate increase in output to absorb it, while American consumers will have secured a cost-free transfer of real resources from abroad. This process, accurately described by a West German banker as 'forcing monetary debauchery on surplus countries',[31] must destroy the workability of the system if it is not checked. Thus we can again see that the balance of payments equilibrium requirement must operate in the long term, this time forcing the centre country to increase its efficiency to create a surplus once the necessary deficits required to create a sufficiency of liquidity have begun to threaten the productive capacity required to guarantee the validity of the centre currency.

Thus the requirements for sustaining an international currency must impose an almost impossible set of demands on the authorities and producers in the centre country as the doleful recent history of the pound and the dollar demonstrate. But if we look more closely at the requirements set out earlier for the maintenance of a system of multilateral international payments, we can see that a more workable alternative system does exist. The prime requirement for the validation of a credit money is that it must represent exchange values based on real productive capacity which can be internationally realised. It must therefore exist either as actual savings of foreign exchange derived from past exports or as spare productive capacity which can be used to generate the real values represented by the additional credit money. It is a mere accident that makes it possible for one country to be able meet these demands and almost impossible for it to sustain that ability; it is almost certain that there will always be some countries in the system technically able to do so as a result of being successful exporters in the previous period. If they can be persuaded to put their resources at the disposal of the system as a whole by allowing them to be used to back the issue of an international credit money, then one could be created which could be both issued and validated in a politically and economically coherent way over the long-term. The creation of the SDR at the end of the 1960s was the first attempt to harness these potentialities in a planned and systematic way.

The introduction of the SDR was, indeed, a major innovation since it implied the possibility of separating the creation of international money from the activities of any particular economic system and organising it instead through a form of international political organisation. It can be seen as a necessary step in the attempt to rescue capitalism from the contradictions imposed by the dollar standard, and as the basis for a further extension of the role of internationalised institutions in the development of the international economy. Most importantly, by giving the IMF a direct role in the creation of a form of credit money, it indicated the extent to which it was coming to take on responsibilities usually considered to be the exclusive prerogative of national sovereignty. But while the SDR represented all of this in its potentiality, its actuality was hedged around with so many restrictions and limitations that its real contribution to the resolution of the crisis has been negligible. The reasons for this are to be sought in the contradictions of the Capitalist Mode of Production (CMP) which, while creating the need for a form of planned international monetary organisation, simultaneously operates through a system of unequal competition which makes its effective realisation an impossibility. The reasons for, and history of, this contradiction and for the decline of the dollar will be the subject of the theoretical and substantive sections of this book.

Thus far we have attempted to demonstrate that an incipient international state system has now come into *de facto* existence responsible both for sustaining the regulations required to enforce 'responsible' monetary behaviour on all of the member states and for creating the framework required to issue and validate the international token currency. Both of these requirements are of a directly political nature. The way they are performed determines the substantive nature of the organisation itself, and has also been the focus for all of the major political battles associated with international monetary reform since World War II. We can now turn to a general consideration of the institutional forms that evolved to deal with these problems.

Institutionalising International Control
The international financial system in operation prior to World War I was based upon a substantial degree of political and economic agreement and organisation but created no separate institutional structures of its own. It was mainly sustained by the hegemony of the British Empire, the degree of co-ordination which could be secured by agreement between the major powers, and the general acceptance 'of the gold standard system, and of stable exchange rates within it, as the only desirable monetary system'.[32] Institutionally its major innovation occured in the private sector in the form of the growth of international banking and more especially of the City of London which performed a wide range of crucial functions by providing:

> Widespread and effective facilities for granting credits ... to governments and other official agencies as well as to overseas banks and foreign traders. London was responsible for the greater part of this financing, which not only supplemented international liquidity in a very important way but also gave London large sight claims on firms and banks in other countries.[33]

Here private banks were mediating between private investors and governments to provide both the developmental and short-term financing required to sustain international exchange. During periods of expansionism few problems arose between debtors and creditors and the system could operate on the basis of purely commercial considerations and create the illusion of a complete separation between economics and politics. But in times of crisis governments were forced into default and the power of the British and other imperialist states had to be drawn in to ensure that the rules of the capitalist market system were observed, whatever the cost to the political sovereignty of the countries involved.[34]

This system depended upon British hegemony and economic expansion and collapsed when this hegemony was displaced and contraction set in in the early twentieth century. Its total bankruptcy was demonstrated in the 1930s with the depression and the corresponding reversion to autarchy based upon 'four major trends away from liberal trading principles', namely:

Special treatment of international trade in agricultural products, private regulation of international trade through cartel agreements, the subordination of foreign trade policies to the requirements of domestic employment and development policies, and the intensification of regional trading arrangements.[35]

In this context a unified international monetary order was impossible, and it was widely assumed that the inability to achieve this was a major obstacle to the restoration of economic prosperity. Thus the theorists concerned with the original formulations for the Bretton Woods conference, and the Americans in particular, set to work in a context in which their primary concern was to provide a basis for a return to a liberal trading and monetary system based upon non-intervention and multilateralism.

Neoclassical economic theory, the dominant ideology among the key decision-makers at this point, suggested that an open trading system would be bound to maximise benefits for all of the units involved in the international economy, but this, as we have already argued, depended upon the existence of a substantive degree of competitive equality between them. Had the world been made up of countries of roughly equal economic strength, the problem of devising an agency capable of supervising a set of regulations designed to preclude a return to the practices of the 1930s would have been a relatively easy one. But the autarchic policies of that period were a defensive response to the failure of the capitalist system operating without them to guarantee a process of even, crisis-free development to strong and weak countries alike. The end of the war would see an intensification of earlier inequalities with a growth in US dominance, the economic devastation of the strong industrial powers once able to compete on relatively equal terms with it, the continuation of colonial subordination for the bulk of the world's population and, perhaps most threatening of all, a continuous process of communist expansion in Europe and Asia. In these circumstances a simple reversion to free trade would merely intensify the inequalities between the strong producers and the weak and push the latter back into extreme forms of protectionism or, more likely, out of the capitalist system altogether. To succeed a new international monetary agency had therefore to be able to transcend the limits of pure *laissez-faire* and promise an effective solution to the problems facing the weaker countries of the West and the third world. This meant that the founding fathers of the IMF had to find an institutional solution that reconciled two potentially conflicting requirements – on the one hand to create the monetary framework for a system of unregulated trade, on the other to provide the resources needed by the weakest countries to finance the interventionist policies required if they were to be able to develop the economic strength sufficient to compete with the dominant industries of the USA. The first pointed towards free trade and *laissez-faire*, the second towards centralised intervention and economic planning. The debate over the structure of the Bretton Woods institutions can best be understood as a struggle to find some means of reconciling these two principles.

While it is possible to express these options in purely theoretical and academic terms, they were in fact the means of defining the competing interests in what was an essentially political struggle. For the strong producers in the new world economy – primarily those located in the US – the concern was to maximise their access to foreign markets in order to make use of the surplus capacity which they expected to emerge with the end of the war.[36] For the weak the problem was to gain access to the credit required to re-equip their war damaged factories before they had to face the full force of American competition which they could not hope to deal with on equal terms. If the strong producers had their way the result would be an intensification of the process of uneven development with disastrous results for the weak countries; if the weak were allowed to dominate the outcome might be a return to the autarchic policies of the 1930s and the destruction of the unity of the capitalist system. Some form of compromise was therefore required which could be institutionalised at the international level. The Bretton Woods system has to be seen as exactly this.

To say that an international monetary institution could only emerge on the basis of a compromise between liberal and interventionist positions, however, is not to say anything about the form which that compromise might take, nor the nature of the balance it would strike between the competing principles. What is important about the Bretton Woods settlement is the very heavy emphasis which it placed upon liberalisation, and the very limited mechanisms and resources it created for interventionism. In this respect it contrasts strongly with the subsequent proposals for the creation of the International Trade Organisation in the Havana Charter. These, decisively influenced by weaker countries insisting on the right to intervention in trade and domestic economic policies to secure full employment and growth, incorporated a wide range of rights and obligations that went well beyond the free enterprise principles being propounded by the leading factions of American capital.[37] As a result Congress failed to ratify the Charter despite the fact that the ITO initiative had originated in the US, and the organisation never came into existence.[38] No such problem arose in the case of the IMF. Here an important interventionist initiative was taken into account, but this, in the form of Keynes's proposal for an international bank, did not interfere directly with liberal trading principles and could, in any case, be so diluted that the new institution came into existence with very limited independent resources at its disposal and with US domination built deeply into its decision-making structure.

The details of the Bretton Woods negotiations and of the final settlement have been extensively dealt with in the literature, and cannot detain us here. More important is an evaluation of the balance struck between liberalisation and interventionism, and between the influence to be exerted over policy by strong countries in contrast to weaker ones. To do this we can look at the way in which the demands of both sides were formulated and reflected in the final agreement in relation to three key issues – the structure of the exchange rate and payments system, the resources to be offered to countries in weak balance of payments situations, and the pressures to be exerted on those whose strength had provided them with persistent balance of payments surpluses. Our problem can be greatly simplified, perhaps unduly so, by confining attention to the key official proposals debated at the Bretton Woods conference and in the negotiations which preceded it, especially the White and Keynes proposals which emanated from the US and UK respectively.

The key objective of American policy was to create a fund that would 'maintain international equilibrium at a high level of international trade', and therefore to secure from members 'commercial policies designed to reduce trade barriers and to terminate discriminatory practices'.[39] The US therefore proposed that the Fund aim to achieve exchange rate stabilisation, a reduction in balance of payments disequilibria, a fostering of trade and capital flows, the liberation of blocked foreign balances, and the reduction in all restrictive foreign exchange practices,[40] and it called for policies that would allow these objectives to be met, including a commitment to abandon all restrictions over foreign exchange transactions on current payments 'as soon as the member country decides that conditions permit'.[41] The proposals accepted the possibility of restrictions on capital movements, notably to control such movements from nationals of countries 'imposing restrictions on the export of capital'.[42] In the Keynes plan emphasis was wholly on the necessity of finding some means of financing the developmental needs of the deficit countries and little said about monetary regulations. Here it was assumed that if a mechanism of this kind could be found, then it would be relatively easy to move towards the removal of the most 'dislocating forms of protection and discrimination'.[43] The French, on the other hand, without the commitment to an extended financing mechanism put forward by the British, made it very clear that

> a return to a generalised system of multilateral international trade, excluding foreign trade control and foreign exchange control, cannot be expected for some time after the end of hostilities. For numerous countries a premature suppression of these controls would have ominous effects.[44]

Thus in their opinion the fundamental requirement of 'a practical system' was that it should be applicable both to countries practising trade and monetary controls and to those that did not, and, while taking account of these needs, to have some means of making itself 'a step toward ... a better system of international economic relations'.[45]

The emphasis in the struggle to eliminate trade barriers must necessarily be on the problems of deficit countries, as it is these that are normally going to introduce restrictions in order to defend their productive capacity from stronger competitors. Looked at from the deficit country point of view, however, the trade problem is in fact created by the 'mercantilist' orientation of surplus countries unwilling to accept the neoclassical assertion that there is 'little basis for regarding a permanent current surplus as a rational objective'.[46] Hence Keynes in an early draft of his proposals, argued that the maintenance of a continued creditor position meant that resources were being 'voluntarily left idle', and that, as a result, the country concerned was 'exerting a deflationary and contractionist pressure on the whole world including the creditor country itself'.[47] The objective of his proposal to create a 'Clearing Union' which was to be an international bank which would receive surpluses from creditor countries and lend them to deficit ones for development financing was essentially oriented towards a solution to the problem by institutionalising at the international level the process of using credit to offset trade inequalities and thereby to avoid the problems of overproduction and underconsumption developing at the international level which his domestic policies were concerned with at the national. Thus his proposal allowed the surplus countries to deal with the pressures they were imposing on the world economy by making a forward commitment to provide effective amounts of credit to offset them; and also involved the pressure to change the policies which had produced the surplus.[48] Other proposals, notably the Canadian, included more stringent measures, including the right to impose 'restrictions ... on the importation of goods' from such countries without this constituting 'an infraction of the most-favoured nation obligations of commercial treaties'.[49] The US proposals, on the other hand, merely incorporated an obligation on the Fund to discuss proposals relating to improvement of the situation to which members would be expected to 'give immediate and careful attention'.[40]

But for all of the deficit countries the key problem was seen to lie in the quantity of direct assistance they might receive for the financing of the reconstruction process. Given the strength of American productive capacity, they could not hope to earn the dollars required to finance the capital goods imports needed for industrial re-equipment, and expected instead a more or less permanent 'dollar shortage' when the war ended. This would both inhibit European development and restrict foreign markets for US exports, thus leading to a return of the recessionary conditions which had followed World War I. In the previous section we noted that the prerequisite for the successful operation of a centre currency was that it be supported by credit and trading arrangements that produced a balance in international payments at a high level of economic activity. The strength of Keynes's proposals lay in the fact that they recognised this problem and incorporated a means of resolving it without recourse to the protectionist policies which Keynes himself had supported during the pre-war period.[51]

The Keynes plan attempted to resolve the contradiction between surplus and deficit countries, and the corresponding tendency towards recessionary conditions, by creating a central institution which would automatically recycle savings from the former to the latter. Starting from the assumption that the surpluses and deficits in the whole world economy must balance each other out by definition, he argued that any tendency for a particular unit to move into chronic surplus (as the US had in the inter-war period) must lead to hoarding, a break in the link between demand and supply, and the imposition of deflationary pressures on the system as a whole. Keynes made no attempt to explain why such a situation might arise – to do so would undoubtedly have required a fundamental re-evaluation of his whole theoretical position – but he did accept it as a real possibility. This meant that the market mechanism could not be relied on to generate balanced international growth, and would have to be supplemented by an interventionist agency designed to offset its shortcomings.

He saw this institution as a bank which would centralise all of the surpluses being generated in the system and lend them to deficit countries for 'prudent' investment. These transactions would be conducted through the development of a new international money which would be able to meet the conditions required for a centre currency because it would automatically draw upon the surpluses of *all* the countries in the system and therefore would not be tied to the fate of any particular national economy. Here he was consciously drawing his analogy from the historical experience of the development of the credit money system at the national level where private and subsequently national central banks had eliminated hoarding by centralising savings and recycling them to investors with positive results for all. Thus he wrote:

> Just as the development of national banking systems served to offset a deflationary pressure which would have prevented otherwise the development of modern industry, so by extending the same principle to the international field we may hope to offset the contractist pressure which might otherwise overwhelm in social disorder and disappointment the good hopes of our modern world. The substitution of a credit mechanism for hoarding would have repeated in the international field the same miracle already performed in the domestic field of turning stone into bread.[51]

While he accepted that such a mechansim might generate inflationary pressures if improperly used, he felt that this could be avoided by following the same principles as are generally followed in domestic banking so that there could be

> no more reason for refusing the advantages of international banking than the similar risk in the domestic field is a reason to return to the practices of the seventeenth century goldsmiths (which we are still following in the international field) and to forego the vast expansion of production which banking principles have made possible.[53]

This conception therefore appeared to overcome the contradiction between deficit and surplus countries at the economic level; it also appeared to resolve the political difficulties associated with the need to create an agency for international interventionism in a world of national sovereignties outlined in the first section. Operating as a bank it would make its allocations on an entirely 'impersonal' basis and thereby become an institution 'of a purely technical and non-political character'.[54] Because of the obvious advantages that it appeared to offer to surplus and deficit countries alike membership could be entirely voluntary and need impose no serious limits upon the right to adopt particular domestic policies. (p. 20) Yet at the same time he was aware of its larger political implications. In the early draft he noted that it might involve 'a greater surrender of ... sovereign rights' from member countries 'than they will readily concede', but argued that this would be no greater than that required in any treaty, and that in any event 'a greater readiness to accept super-national arrangements must be required in the post-war world than hitherto'.[55] Further, he noted that the existence of the fund, however voluntary the membership, might 'become the pivot of the future economic government of the world', and that its economic power could be used in the services of 'any super-national policing body which may be charged with the duty of preserving the peace and maintaining international order' by providing the 'machinery for enforcing a financial blockade'.[56] Here there is a clear recognition of the political implications of the unification of an international monetary order without the willingness to integrate them fully into the theory itself.

There can be no doubt that the implementation of this proposal would have represented a major advance in the level of social organisation of capitalism at the international level by offsetting its tendency towards uneven development through the creation of an effective credit money system. It represents, perhaps, the highest aspirations of that system, and contains within itself the formulations required for all of the subsequent attempts to reform the system which was actually created and which will be dealt with in the substantive section of this book. But, like many other aspirations of capitalist theory, it failed to acknowledge that the reality of capitalist competition at the economic and political levels precluded the automatic transfer of surpluses from creditor states (where they could be directly used to advance national interests) to an impersonal national bank concerned only with the development of the system as a whole. Thus the Americans, who at this stage could be expected to provide any such agency with virtually all of its resources, brought forward a much more modest proposal. They reduced the deficit financing recommendations to the suggestion that the Fund be able to raise gold and foreign exchange resources from its members of 'at least $5 billion',[57] to be drawn on to meet 'an adverse balance of payments'.[58] And while Keynes had accepted that drawings on the fund would have to be associated with 'some rules and some machinery' to ensure that an eventual equilibrium was restored (p. 28), the Americans insisted that it be given the right to 'place such conditions' on lending where a country is 'exhausting its permissible quota more rapidly than is warranted, or is using its permissible quota in a manner that clearly has the effect of preventing or unduly delaying the establishment of a sound balance in its international accounts'.[59] The latter formulation, clearly indicates the origin of the now notorious IMF conditionality which has the effect of imposing liberal policies directly on deficit countries as the price of any substantial access to Fund resources, with deflationary effects quite opposite to those which Keynes intended.

In the event the US view obviously dominated because no organisation could come into existence without the resources which it could provide. Thus the main goals of liberalisation were more or less those set out by the Americans. A 'scarce currency clause' was introduced after great pressure from deficit countries which incorporate the right for members to limit 'the freedom of exchange operations' in it (Article VII 3b). But this article, however, was harldy relevant until convertibility was established at the end of the 1950s, and thereafter became 'a dead letter' through 'the conclusion of the General Arrangements to Borrow in 1961'.[60] But most important of all, the quota set for the US was only $2750 million, providing the new Fund with a very limited basis for positive intervention. This money, again, was only to be made available on the basis of conditions determined by the agency, and the US, on the basis of the weighted voting system which it insisted on, together with its overwhelming economic and political strength, ensured that these conditions would incorporate the liberal principles central to US policy.

Thus, at the expense of a very small contribution to be made use of for deficit financing on conditions over which it had decisive influence, the USA obtained an international agency fully committed to creating a liberal international monetary order which would provide the dominant fractions of capital with an ideal environment for their operations. At the Bretton Woods conference the complementary establishment of the World Bank as an agency for long-term development financing was seen as a move in the direction of positive intervention, but it was expected to raise its resources on the private money market and was therefore precluded from being used as a conscious instrument of counter-cyclical intervention. It was only in 1960 that it established the International Development Association (IDA) as its 'soft loan window' to provide concessional finance to the poorest countries derived from government contributions.[61]

Nothing has been said here about the adequacy of the exchange rate regime, the technical mechanisms established to deal with tendencies towards balance of payments disequilibria or the mechanisms developed to organise IMF interventions through stand-by arrangements. These problems have generated a large literature and will be dealt with subsequently. What has been our major concern is to demonstrate how the actual structure of the Bretton Woods system fell far short of the requirements set out in the first part of this chapter for the maintenance of a stable, fully internationalised credit money system. The new system did create an international institution with the power to limit national economic policy choices, particularly for deficit countries looking for official sources of credit. However damaging the limitations so imposed upon their economic autonomy, virtually no countries have as yet been willing to break decisively with their commitments to the organisation and adopt a set of policies which it would find totally unacceptable.[62] The system has also taken on some of the qualities of a supranational state – however reluctantly – and a distinctive ideological position has evolved to serve as the basis for its increasingly direct interventions in national and international policy-making as the crisis has intensified.

These are very considerable achievements, and account for the massive increase in political and academic attention being devoted to its activities and its shortcomings.[63] For there can be little doubt that the latter impose decisive limits upon its capacity to intervene effectively to deal with the problems of competitive inequality and structural balance of payments crisis now afflicting most of the countries in the system, even the most powerful. It does not have the resources to provide them with anything like the credits envisaged by Keynes for deficit financing and, given the commitments to liberal trading policies built into its structure by the dominant American interests that presided over its creation, is forced to impose deflationary solutions of a highly conservative kind on weak countries. In so doing it intensifies the problems of structural weakness which it is supposed to be alleviating and accelerates the tendency to uneven development which, as we have shown, must, in the long term, destroy the possibility of economic co-operation and force a return to the autarchic policies of the 1930s. This latter tendency is clearly visible with the growth of protectionism on all sides. Thus we have here a potential 'organ of truly international government', but one whose activities are becoming increasingly paralysed by the limitations imposed by its own constitution and its uneasy location in the overall system of capitalist power relationships.

The US Congress's treatment of the Havana Charter which attempted to provide the International Trade Organisation with far more interventionist obligations, illustrates how the constitution of the IMF represented the most that dominant capitalist interests were prepared to concede by way of an extension of the powers of international economic managment. Their subsequent resistance to attempts at reform designed to widen these powers suggests that this was not an accident of immediate post-war history, but originates in the underlying structure of the relationship between classes in the capitalist system itself.

Notes

1. K. Marx, 'Manifesto of the Communist Party', in K. Marx and F. Engels, *Selected works*, London, Lawrence & Wishart, 1968, p. 39.
2. For an excellent account of the nature of this process of internationalisation, see N. Poulantzas, *Classes in contemporary capitalism*, London, New Left Books, 1975, Part 1.
3. In most of these zones the attempt is made to create perfect conditions for international capital by eliminating all duties on inputs and outputs, cutting taxes to the minimum and prohibiting all forms of labour organisation.
4. For excellent accounts of the relationship between nation state and transnational corporations see Poulantzas, op. cit., Chapter 2; R. Murray, 'The internationalisation of capital and the nation state', *New Left Review*, Vol. 67, 1971.
5. See in particular E. Altvater, 'Some problems of state intervention', in J. Holloway and S. Picciotto, *State and capital*, London, Edward Arnold, 1978.
6. The best account of the demands which these requirements place upon the capitalist state is probably still to be found in N. Poulantzas, *Political power and social classes*, London, New Left Books, 1973, notably on pp. 284–5.
7. Significantly enough a local newspaper newly revealed that the IMF intervention in Jamaica in the late 1970s created a situation which made 91 per cent of the population aware of its existence there. Personal communication, Norman Girvan, formerly Director of National Planning.
8. A useful account of the nature of Marx's view of the relation between money and credit is to be found in S. de Brunhoff, *Marx on money*, New York, Urizen, 1973. I

am attempting to avoid entanglement in these complexities, by treating literally Marx's assertion that 'In developed capitalist production, the money economy appears only as the basis of the credit economy'. (*Capital*, Vol. II, London, Lawrence & Wishart, 1970, p. 119).

9. Complex problems about terminology clearly arise here. I have attempted to sustain consistency – using 'value' when referring to the quantity of socially necessary labour time embodied in any commodity determined by the outcome of capitalist competition; 'exchange value' when dealing with problems arising specifically in the field of circulation. I am therefore short-circuiting a series of important issues that arise out of Marx's formulation of the transformation problem in Volume III of *Capital*, (London, Lawrence & Wishart, 1972) for lack of space, but hope that this does not undermine the main thrust of the argument.

10. G.F. Hegel, *Hegel's philosophy of right*, London, Oxford University Press, 1967, p. 240.

11. K. Marx, *Grundrisse*, Harmondsworth, Penguin, 1973, p. 199.

12. Ibid., pp. 156–7.

13. I am heavily indebted to Mike Hall, a graduate student at Sussex University for help in my formulation of this problem.

14. According to Mill the value of gold and silver 'depends, like that of other things, on their cost of production'; (*Principles of political economy*, London, Longmans, 1900, p. 305). While Marx also accepts that their value is 'like other forms of wealth … determined by the quantity of labour embodied in them', *Capital* Vol. III, op. cit., p. 573. For his discussion of the relation between changes in the prices of commodities and the value of money see *Capital*, Vol. I, Harmondsworth, Penguin, 1976, p. 193.

15. P. Vilar, *A history of gold and money*, London, New Left Books, 1976, p. 344.

16. Marx, *Capital*, Vol. II, op. cit., p. 351.

17. J.M. Keynes, 'Proposals for an international currency union', 11 February 1942, in J.K. Horsefield, *The International Monetary Fund, 1945–1965*, Vol. III, *Documents*, Washington, IMF, 1969, p. 5.

18. Mill, op. cit., p. 330.

19. M. Friedman, cited in I.H. Rima, *Development of economic analysis*, 3rd edn., Homewood, Ill. Richard Irwin, 1978, p. 445.

20. M. Friedman, 'The role of monetary policy', in *The optimum quantity of money and other essays*, London, Macmillan, 1969, p. 109, where he puts the optimum rate of growth at '3 to 5%'.

21. Marx, *Capital*, Vol. III, op. cit., p. 441.

22. de Brunhoff's phrase; see op. cit., p. 115.

23. For a useful assessment of the role of gold since the end of the 1960s, see Financial Times survey, *Gold*, 12 February 1979.

24. Marx, *Capital* Vol. I, op. cit., p. 226.

25. Ibid., p. 243.

26. IMF, 'International reserves and liquidity', in Horsefield, op. cit., pp. 351 and 352.

27. L.B. Yeager, *International monetary relations*, 2nd edn., New York, Harper & Row, 1976, p. 69.

28. E. Mandel, *The second slump*, London, New Left Books, 1978, p. 56; note here

also Lenin's assertion that 'imperialism is the monopoly stage of capitalism', (*Imperialism*, Moscow, Progress Publishers, 1970, p. 85). The implications of his analysis to the general problem of crisis considered in this book will be explored in the final chapter.

29. Here see M. Hall, 'The decline of the dollar', in E.A. Brett, *International money, the IMF and deflation in the periphery*, Geneva, International Foundation for Development Alternatives, 1979.

30. David Evans, Fellow, Institute of Development Studies, Sussex University, personal communication in written comments on an earlier draft of this book.

31. O. Emminger, *Inflation and the international monetary system*, Basle, Per Jacobssen Foundation, 1973, p. 40.

32. IMF, op. cit., p. 351.

33. Ibid.

34. See in particular H. Feis's account of the political subordination of Egypt and Morocco by Britain and France in order to secure the effective repayment of their international debts. (*Europe the world's banker, 1870–1914*, New York, Kelley, 1971).

35. W.A. Brown, *The United States and the restoration of world trade*, Washington, Brookings Institution, 1950, p. 45.

36. For the relation between surplus capacity in American industry and US aid policy see 'Marshall aid and US interests', in D. Burch, *Overseas aid and the transfer of technology*, Sussex University PhD., 1979, pp. 115–22.

37. The American Chamber of Commerce argued in 1948 that a Charter for an International Trade Organisation 'must provide positive declarations in behalf of the maintenance of private initiative and enterprise in world commerce', and that the Havana Charter 'was not consistent with these principles' and should therefore be renegotiated by the US. See W.A. Brown, op. cit., pp. 370–71. See also note 6, Chapter 2.

38. For a good account see K. Kock, *International trade policy and the GATT, 1947–1967*, Stockholm, Almqvist & Wiksell, 1969.

39. Quoted from Henry Morgenthau's foreword to the White Plan written as Secretary of the Treasury. ('Preliminary draft outline of a proposal for an Inernational Stabilisation Fund of the United and Associated Nations', 10 July 1943, Horsefield, op. cit., p. 85).

40. Ibid., p. 86.

41. Ibid., p. 95.

42. Ibid., p. 96.

43. Keynes plan, April 1943, pp. 32–3.

44. French plan, 'Suggestions regarding international monetary relations', May 1943, p. 97.

45. Ibid., p. 98.

46. The phrase is taken from J. Williamson's liberal interpretations of *The failure of international monetary reform, 1971–74*, London, Nelson, p. 169.

47. Keynes plan, February 1942, in Horsefield, op. cit., p. 4.

48. Keynes plan, April 1943, Ibid., p. 24.

49. 'Tentative draft proposals of Canadian experts for an International Exchange Union', 12 July 1943, Ibid., pp. 114–5.

50. White plan in Ibid., p. 90.
51. On the development of Keynes's international economic theories see S.E. Harris, 'International economics: introduction', and R. Nurske, 'Domestic and international equilibrium', in S.E. Harris, *The new economics*, London, Dobson, 1960.
52. Keynes plan in Horsefield, op. cit., p. 27.
53. Ibid., pp. 34–5.
54. Ibid., p. 21.
55. Keynes plan, February 1942, Ibid., pp. 13–14.
56. Keynes plan, April 1943, Ibid., p. 33.
57. White plan, Ibid.,p. 86.
58. Ibid., p. 89.
59. p. 90. White demonstrated a clear awareness of the extent to which countries might wish to avoid the external constraints which membership might impose on them, and the necessity for the 'suspension of certain elements of national sovereignity in favour of international collaboration'. (p. 62).
60. Wiliamson, op. cit., p. 14.
61. For the semi-official account of the evolution of the World Bank see E.S. Mason, and R.E. Asher, *The World Bank since Bretton Woods*, Washington, Brookings Institution, 1963; and for a critical appraisal see T. Hayter, *Aid as imperialism*, Harmondsworth, Penguin, 1971.
62. Here we should make exceptions of the communist countries that withdrew or were excluded from membership – Poland in 1950, Czechoslovakia in 1954 and Cuba in 1964.
63. Keynes's phrase; see Horsefield, op. cit., p. 35.

2 International Economic Theory and Policy

> To understand and evaluate realistically one's adversary's position and his reasons (and sometime one's adversary is the whole of past thought) means precisely to be liberated from the prison of ideologies in the bad sense of the word – that of blind ideological fanaticism. ...
>
> On the ideological front...the defeat of the auxiliaries and the minor hangers-on is of all but negligible importance. Here it is necessary to engage in battles with the most eminent of one's adversaries.
>
> (A Gramsci, *Selection from the prison notebooks*)

Chapter 2 will attempt to set out in some detail the elements of what was described in Chapter 1 as the 'neoclassical ideology' which has dominated the thinking of those who designed and have subsequently run the Bretton Woods system. It is not intended as a critique of this body of thought, but as an attempt to present a systematic and coherent view of the orientations and analytical tools which it provides these practitioners with for the resolution of the problems they deal with in the fields of trade and monetary policy.

Looking seriously at liberal and more especially at monetarist thinking rather than dismissing it out of hand is not a fashionable occupation on the left, but is nevertheless an essential preparation for the rest of this study. The rest of this book will, indeed, attempt a serious critique of both the liberal theory and practice of those responsible for international monetary management. It can therefore only be taken seriously if it is directed against the strongest case which they can make and not against some simplistic straw man. Again, the actions of those who control these organisations cannot be fully understood without reference to the theoretical formulations which provide them with their rationale. These men are for the most part both serious and competent and neither their work nor their achievements are to be underestimated. Finally, given the almost total absence of any developed Marxist theory of international economic relations, we must concede that we are, indeed, dealing here with something that does constitute virtually 'the whole of past thought' and should therefore treat it with the respect it deserves.

Given our primary concern with a concrete political problem, the intention here cannot be the presentation of a survey of academic ideas, but a delineation of the conceptual apparatus of those who make policy decisions at the highest level. While this apparatus is seen as constituting a political ideology (in the best sense of that word), it has to be examined as an integrated sysem of propositions setting out technically workable lines of action for the resolution of practical problems. These ideas will therefore be developed here in an intellectual framework which treats the relationship between science on the one hand and ideology and politics on the other as necessarily integrated rather than exclusive categories. [1] This suggests that we locate our source material first by identifying the key problems which have had to be resolved at the political level, then show how they have been resolved in the work of the relevant theorists.

Chapter 1 treated the Bretton Woods system as the outcome of a compromise between the desire for an open trading system on the part of the strong capitalist sectors, and that for centralised intervention and planning on the part of the weaker ones. The former produced a system of regulations based upon the assumption that, given the appropriate conditions, free trade would produce 'the maximisation of world income'; [2] the latter a system of international intervention involving the provision of credit and a domestic policy package to deficit countries confronting a 'fundamental' balance of payments problem. Chapter 2 therefore will proceed by looking at these two areas in that order. Before doing so, however, it is necessary to look more closely at the nature of the tension between the two principles and at the way it manifests itself in the theoretical literature and policy debate.

While it is certainly true that a real tension must exist between a commitment to pure market allocation as against one to some form of centralised manipulation, its nature and extent must depend directly upon the nature of the interventions that are being considered. Interventions, as the excellent analysis presented by Wiles points out, [3] can vary from those designed primarily to make the market function better to those designed to replace its effects altogether. It is impossible to separate entirely these two meanings, since market oriented interventions shade into market correcting interventions at the margin, but we can see that a system emphasising the former most is entirely compatible with – indeed depends directly upon – liberal theory, while one emphasising the latter must involve some displacement of it.

Now the final section of Chapter 1 argued that the Bretton Woods compromise was so heavily weighted in the liberal direction that its interventionist orientations were almost entirely of the former kind. Hence it placed a very heavy emphasis on the pure theory of trade which assumes a tendency for what Corden calls 'automatic processes'[4] to equate supply and demand and produce a welfare optimum. It does not, on the other hand, assume that the conditions for the effective operations of these processes can be separated from state policy nor, indeed, from the need for extensive interventions to enable them to be created. In this respect it shares the policy-oriented stance of contemporary monetarism which seeks to capture the state in order to liberate the individual entrepreneur. Hence we can see that the theory of 'automatic processes' must be complemented by what Corden sees as the key modern development in international trade theory since World War II – the creation of a basis for the 'determination of [the] optimum policies' required to sustain the basic objectives of 'internal and external balance'.[5] The first part of this chapter will therefore attempt to set out the fundamentals of both the pure and the policy-oriented theories dealing first with the equilibrium assumptions of the neoclassical resource allocation model, secondly with what can be called the 'monetary theory of the balance of payments', with its emphasis on the identification of the appropriate policy instruments required to achieve the full employment equilibrium.

Against this view of intervention we can set the other, more far reaching view of it which looks to central planning to produce better results than the market mechanism itself. While the Bretton Woods system was able largely to efface this orientation and treat it as somehow technically and morally inadmissable in the monetary field, it was not able to eliminate it as a potential focus for resistance to the outcome of the resulting policies. We have already noted that the inability to exclude them from the proposed structure of the International Trade Organisation led to its rejection by the dominant factions of American capital and the US Congress.[6] During the 1930s international economic relations were mainly conducted according to protectionist and interventionist principles which owed little to liberal thinking; in the post-war period the bulk of third world countries have continued to implement these policies and have been allowed to do so through the existence of escape clauses in the IMF's articles of agreement and as a result of its limited ability to force its opinions on countries not in direct receipt of conditional credit. During the expansionary period of international growth from the late 1940s to the early 1970s, boom conditions made it possible to secure relatively full employment without very extensive recourse to these measures, and concealed the constraints which the liberal nature of the IMF imposed upon its capacity to offer effective assistance to countries whose balance of payments weakness was of a structural kind. The depressed conditions which have existed since 1974 have again brought these issues to the surface and produced a phase of fundamental criticism of its operations which stems essentially from its market oriented emphasis and its corresponding inability to provide weak countries with the resources or policies required to achieve full employment and growth.[7]

The theoretical underpinnings of the various forms of state intervention under capitalism are by no means as extensive nor clearly delineated as those which sustain the liberal position. We can, however, identify two broad tendencies which have sought to question the necessary optimality of market allocation and to provide the basis for interventions of varying degrees of intensity. On the one hand we have a long-standing critique of free trade theory rooted deeply in the nineteenth century and, indeed, in the mainstream of the classical tradition itself. Starting from the 'infant industry argument' a long line of writers have argued the necessity for protection in the case of economies which have not yet achieved the level of development required to enable them to compete on equal terms with industries in already developed centres. These arguments have more recently been taken over and extended by what has been called the 'structuralist' school of development economists who have used it, in combination with Keynesian arguments, to justify a generalised process of intervention in third world countries which will include trade and monetary controls as necessary components. Secondly, we have the body of Keynesian theory, until recently regarded as the dominant tendency in economic theory itself, which emerged in response to the 'unemployment equilibrium' of the 1930s and served as the intellectual foundation for the interventionist policies which have dominated the western industrialised countries since World War II. This dominance has now been offset by that of the monetarists to the extent that a leading scholar of Keynes's work could claim that it was now only of 'historical interest'.[8] Yet we have already seen that Keynes himself was responsible for a very significant contribution to the Bretton Woods discussions, his theoretical position has served as the basis for some important components of the modern monetarist tendency which has displaced it. And his formulation of the international liquidity problem for Bretton Woods has yet to be transcended in any of the literature concerned with solving either the problem of the dollar deficit, the dollar glut or the developmental deficits confronted by third world countries.[9]

Although both protectionist and Keynesian arguments do not seek to transcend the fundamental assumptions of the capitalist system, they do argue the necessity for various forms of centralised intervention designed at least partially to displace market allocation because of its alleged irrationalities. Their orientation is therefore qualitatively different (at the margin at least) from that of the policy science of contemporary monetarism. Because of their historic significance, their direct relevance to the problems of the weaker countries and their likely revival in the face of the depression of the 1980s, it is important that their fundamental assumptions be given serious consideration here. Thus the second part of this chapter will deal in turn with the protectionist and Keynesian modifications of the classical and neoclassical traditions.

The Pure Theory of Exchange, Trade and Money
Although our main concern is with the international dimension, it is well known that any IMF intervention involves the imposition of a series of policies, to be considered in detail below, which impinge upon the whole range of what are usually considered to be purely domestic matters. Their orientation in this regard is clearly 'monetarist' and to be understood only in the light of the body of domestic theory which now goes by that name. Secondly, as we have already seen, the orientation to international trade depends upon neoclassical trade theory which as Haberler points out, cannot be sharply distinguished from theory concerned with the domestic economy and for the most part represents developments or extensions of it.[10] Thus both to understand the presuppositions of the IMF's domestic interventions, and to provide the basis for a consideration of trade theory proper, it is necessary to begin this section with a brief account of their view of money and exchange in a single economy.

Money and exchange in a closed system
The neoclassical world is made up of 'individual wealth owning units or individuals'[11] concerned to maximise their utilities by rationally

exchanging their products for those of others in a market place where prices are determined at the margin by the law of supply and demand. Individual decisions produce socially useful outcomes without coercive centralised state intervention as a result of the operation of free competition which will automatically tend to produce capitalist man as 'that manner of man, who, in spontaneously fulfilling his own nature, incidentally performs the functions of a social unit: and yet is only enabled so to fulfil his own nature by all others doing the like'.[12] Economic theory then becomes the study of the regularities arising out of this automatic tendency for individual decisions to be aggregated in determinate ways, with the role of the state confined to that of neutral arbiter in the competitive struggle able to use a monopoly of coercion to guarantee that everyone will accept its outcome whether they have gained or lost in the process. Here we can locate the basis of the distinction between economics and politics. The former is the arena in which power is exercised individually and outcomes determined by free competition, the latter that in which it is centralised and decisions enforced collectively. Should the state intervene to assist one or more producers in their struggle with others the 'natural' tendency for the market to produce coherent results will disappear in the face of what will then be called 'rigidities or imperfections'.[13]

Given its individualistic starting point, this body of theory cannot look seriously at the organisation of production itself, but only at the outcome of the exchange of already produced commodities between a series of notionally equal individuals. What we have, therefore, is a 'general equilibrium model of an exchange economy' in which 'the central emphasis of the analysis' must thus be 'on the scarcity of the goods in *given* supply'.[14] This must also exclude any examination of the processes leading to or of the effects on exchange of the existence of inequalities in the productive power of the various private agents operating in the market. Thus *monopoly* is seen as another form of imperfection to be offset by state action where possible,[15] while exchange is generally assumed to take place in the 'ideal conditions ... which usually underlie general equilibrium theory: free competition in all commodity and product markets as well as the absence of so-called 'external economies'.[16] The latter assumption, to be given a central place in the critique to follow, is central to both the inability to deal with the structure of production and the emergence of 'imperfect competition' because it is scale economies which decisively influence the uneven growth between both individual producers and sectors and which *must* eventually lead to monopoly and the destruction of the equilibrium.[17]

While the theory does not consider production directly, however, it does assert two tendencies which are of fundamental importance in supporting the belief that it will be maximised where the 'ideal conditions' for competitive exchange described above can be sustained. Firstly, it assumes that competition must maximise efficiency by forcing individuals to maximise their output and solving in the process 'the problems of the optimal allocation of labour, capital and natural resources' in an almost 'miraculous' way.[18] Secondly, in the form of Say's law, it asserts that a balance must always exist between supply and demand: full employment is hence the natural state of affairs and long-term unemployment necessarily the outcome of some form of exogenous interference or rigidity.[19] In Say's view supply must generate its own demand as the payments made in generating any output must necessarily reappear on the other side of the production/consumption equation in the form of an equivalent demand for a corresponding output of goods. And given perfect competition, the existence of underemployed resources, including labour, must push down their price, create a corresponding demand and lead to economic expansion until the full-employment equilibrium reappears.

If these two assumptions are accepted, the necessity for any close examination, let alone intervention in the process of production disappears since competition *must* produce a better outcome than any form of conscious intervention could hope to do. This statement implies that neoclassical theory is a necessarily normative science which is concerned to both describe *and* promote the mechanisms that it treats as its subject matter. This view, which I certainly share, is contested by many of its practitioners who make a distinction between economics as a positivist and hence value-free description of the necessary relationship between variables and welfare economics ultimately concerned to relate this exercise to 'political evaluation'.[20] Here I find it difficult to present an entirely impartial account of the positivist position because of my own view that any theoretical or political position must involve an inseparable mix of evaluation and analysis. In this respect I will merely point to Haberler's own demonstration of the inconsistencies of the positivist position and accept for present purposes his assertion that:

> the right attitude ... is that one need not shy away from the application of theory to problems of economic policy as long as one recognises the nature of the value judgements implied. This is the point of view which emerges with increasing clarity in modern welfare economics.[21]

Thus far we have considered what can be called the pure theory of exchange using categories which had been fully developed by the end of the nineteenth century. Monetarism, as the leading edge of contemporary neoclassical theory, has extended this analysis through a close examination of the significance of monetary relationships in a closed economy. This analysis is of critical importance to current forms of both domestic and international intervention and requires close examination; on the face of it its overt policy-relatedness would suggest that it be incorporated in the section dealing with 'applied' rather than 'pure' issues. Yet we have already seen that the objective of the monetarist analysis is to re-assert the necessary *neutrality* of money in order to re-establish the dominance of *automatic* adjustments in the resource allocation process. To understand their policy-orientations which will be considered in the next section, we have therefore to understand their attitude to what we may call the pure theory of monetary interactions.

Monetarist theory sees money as a quantity determined by the *demand* for it 'on the part of the ultimate wealth-owning units in the society' where it represents 'the demand for a consumption service',[22] and by 'business enterprises' who hold it 'as a productive resource'.[23] In the classical analysis broadly considered in Chapter 1, it was assumed that the supply of money would be adjusted automatically as a function of the relationship between the supply and demand for gold. In these circumstances money would be neutral with respect to both the distribution of income and the accumulation of capital. It could therefore be seen as no more than:

> a machine for doing quickly and commodiously, what would be done, though less quickly and commodiously, without it: and like many other kinds of machinery, it only exerts a distinct and independent influence of its own when it gets out of order.[24]

And in this analysis any attempt to tamper with this mechanism must necessarily fail since in any 'attempt to regulate the value of money artificially by means of the supply, governments have never succeeded in the degree, or even in the manner, in which they intended'.[25]

The transition from a gold to a credit money system necessarily politicises money in the manner described in Chapter 1 and allows the state the option of attempting to use money as an instrument of conscious economic manipulation. The displacement of the neoclassical and classical traditions by Keynesianism at the end of the 1930s then provided governments with a rationale justifying such policies; monetary expansion took its place alongside fiscal measures as a legitimate tool of demand management. Modern monetarism must therefore be seen as an attempt to re-establish the neutrality of the gold-standard mechanism by demonstrating the inconsistencies of the Keynesian analysis and hence persuading governments to act as if it still existed.[26]

Keynes's critique of neoclassical theory depended upon a rejection of Say's law on the assumption that individuals were likely to hoard a portion of their income and therefore destroy the necessary balance between supply and demand. Governments would then be justified in using monetary policy to expand effective demand in order to eliminate the resulting unemployment. The monetarists, however, revert to Say's law by asserting that the operation of the credit mechanism will eliminate hoarding, and denying the existence of the so-called 'liquidity trap'. Thus Friedman describes the effect of an expansion in 'the stock of money' as follows:

> From a longer-term view, the new balance sheet is out of equilibrium, with cash being temporarily high relative to other assets. Holders of cash will seek to purchase assets to achieve a desired structure. This will bid up the price of assets. If the extra demand is initially directed at a particular class of assets, say government securities, or commercial paper, or the like, the result will be to pull the prices of such assets out of line with other assets and thus to widen the area into which the extra cash spills. The increased demand will spread, sooner or later affecting equities, houses, durable producer goods, durable consumer goods, and so on, though not necessarily in this order.[27]

Implicit in this statement is the assumption that savings will be invested rather than hoarded. This denies the Keynesian conception of the 'liquidity trap' which assumes that an increase in income will lead to no more than an increase in savings and hence to a growth in liquidity rather than demand. The monetarist analysis, however, follows Patinkin and Pigou's critique of this position by arguing that the increase in income will not lead to an increase in savings but to an adjustment in the real as opposed to the nominal value of 'money balance and wealth'. Thus

> Patinkin argued that, in principle, flexible prices and wage rates can restore commodity, money and labour markets to equilibria which are consistent with full employment.[28]

The general implication of this argument that money is not going to be hoarded is therefore that 'if indeed there is short-run disequilibrium on this particular market there will be adjustments elsewhere in other markets which are also out of equilibrium until an equilibrium is restored through time'.[29]

Following from this it can be asserted that not only is intervention unnecessary to eliminate unemployment but, in an extreme formulation, that the authorities can exert no 'real' influences of a positive kind on the economy since all that they will be able to do is to alter the *nominal* as opposed to the *real* quantity of money in circulation. Here we have as the starting point Friedman's assertion that there is no 'flaw in the price system that makes unemployment the natural outcome of a fully operative market mechanism'.[30] And further, given conditions of full employment which are taken to be the norm, any increase in the money supply will manifest itself only in an increase in prices and not in a growth in real income. Thus Friedman argued:

> [The monetary authority] cannot use its control over nominal quantities to peg a real quantity – the real rate of interest, the rate of unemployment, the level of real national income, the real quantity of money, the rate of growth of real national income, or the rate of growth of the real quantity of income.[31]

If this line of argument holds then both the source and the remedy for unemployment must be sought, not in government action, but in the *inflexibility* in prices and wages which have produced the flaw in the system which can otherwise be relied on to eliminate it.

It is the elimination of these inflexibilities, therefore, which must become the prime object of policy. Government itself, of course, can become the biggest source of such inflexibilities if it continues to follow incorrect interventionist policies; 'political' pressures from special interests or the growth of monopoly power can generate another. Crucially here there is a close identification of the level of unemployment with the rate of wages which is seen to be the outcome of a 'voluntary' choice on the part of the working class. Thus, following the analysis which produced the Phillips curve relating levels of wages and employment, it can be argued that the workers themselves have to determine how much unemployment they are prepared to accept as the necessary result of pushing wages beyond the full employment level.[32]

The general implications of these arguments, therefore, is that where more or less full employment prevails, (and they were produced specifically to deal with the change from what Johnson called the 'Keynesian conditions of general unemployment' to the 'post-war situation of general inflation and overfull employment'[33]) the objective of policy must be to stop it from becoming 'a major source of economic disturbance' to allow it to provide 'a stable background for the economy', and to use it to offset 'major disturbances in the economic system arising from other sources'.[34] The main goal must therefore be to maintain a stable price structure which adjusts to allow for 'dynamic changes in tastes and technology'.[35] Hence the need to equate the growth in the money supply with the natural growth rate in production, or 'something like a 3 to 5 per cent rate of growth'.[36]

We can now turn to a consideration of trade and balance of payments theory which as we have already noted, must be seen as an extension of exchange and monetary theory from a single economy to one containing a number of autonomous national units. A good deal was said about the monetary aspects of this problem in Chapter 1; here we will begin with a consideration of the 'pure' theory of trade and conclude with a consideration of the 'monetary approach to the balance of payments'.

Pure trade theory
The main difference between trade and ordinary exchange theory is the existence of national frontiers which alter the nature and status of the interactions between individuals separated by them. Trade therefore involves exchanges mediated by the existence of political sovereignty which

> entails both a special concern for nationals, as distinct from foreigners, ... the existence of policies of intervention in economic relations with other nations ... [and] a distinctive national currency whose quantity and value in terms of other national currencies are subject to national control.[37]

Further, and arising out of possible limitations imposed by these considerations or of other factors such as distance or language, trade theory tends to assume the immobility of factors of production which means that the normal adjustment mechanisms assumed to operate domestically to correct imbalances cannot necessarily be expected to hold in exchanges between national units. Trade theory is then concerned to examine the equilibrium conditions for exchanges between national units with immobile factors with otherwise perfect competition. Steedman provides a highly condensed description of the 'pure exchange model' of the dominant Heckscher–Ohlin–Samuelson (H–O–S) theory where each of two countries:

> receives, as manna from heaven, a given endowment of ... two consumption goods, where the two goods enter in different proportions into the endowments of the two countries. Given the assumption of identical, homophetic preferences, it follows that the autarchy equilibrium price ratio would differ as between the two countries. If trade is possible within each 'period', then it is clear that it will actually take place, that the trade equilibrium price ratio will lie between the two autarchy price ratios and

that consumers in both countries will obtain an 'exchange gain' from trade.[38]

The H–O–S model goes back directly to Mill and more especially to Ricardo's still standard analysis of the principle of comparative advantage through his famous example of the exchange of wine and corn between England and Portugal which will be examined in detail in Chapter 3. The Heckscher–Ohlin theory then goes beyond the pure exchange model and comparative advantage by explaining 'a country's trade in terms of its factor endowments; a country will have a comparative advantage in those products which use more intensively the country's more plentiful factors'.[39] Samuelson subsequently refined this position by demonstrating that 'subject to certain assumptions, free trade would equalise factor prices [throughout the world] completely'.[40] Thus the H–O–S model suggests a necessary tendency towards equilibrium and mutual benefit from trade[41] provided that a set of necessary assumptions can be sustained. These assumptions include the standard exchange theory requirements of full employment, perfect competition, constant or diminishing returns to scale as well as immobility of factors and a series of more specific items which are summarised by Haberler.[42] If taken literally

> they are so restrictive and so unrepresentative of actual reality that the theory can be said to prove the opposite of what it seems to purport to say – namely, that there is no chance whatsoever that factor prices will ever be equalised by free commodity trade.[43]

Yet the theory continues to serve as the technical basis for the commitment to free trade and for the belief in an inherent tendency towards equilibrium stemming from it.

While the 'pure' theory set out above implies the optimality of free trade, it would be wrong to argue that its practitioners are unable to evolve justifications for interventions of a protectionist nature. Thus Haberler concedes that 'deviations from the competitive ideal, or the existence of external economies' might create conditions 'justifying certain departures from a free trade policy'.[44]

Corden, author of perhaps the standard work on the theory of protection, discusses three arguments put forward in its support in his survey, all of them mainly relating to conditions in underdeveloped countries. These justify it where the existence of a dual economy produces 'departures from Paretian optimum conditions' which will require special treatment of the industrial sector (the Manoilesco argument);[45] the 'terms of trade argument' which assumes that the elasticity of demand for the exports of developing countries is less than that for their imports; and the 'infant industry argument' where protection is required to enable local industry to reach the minimum level of scale required to enable them to compete with established foreign producers.[45] For what may be termed protectionist and more especially structuralist theorists the combination of these arguments leads to a position which must be held to be qualitatively distinct from the liberal position as we will attempt to show in the following section. For those who remain in the liberal tradition, as Corden perhaps still does, the optimality of free trade is generally asserted as the 'first-best' device, the arguments for protection a second-best solution to be adopted in response to 'some kind of externality or "distortion" ... or ... failure'.[46] In a world containing a sufficiency of distortions and failures, of course, the arguments for freedom tend to recede and the discussion centres entirely on the nature and extent of the protective measures required to deal with them. But it is nevertheless important to make the distinction between those who nevertheless consider the free trade equilibrium the appropriate theoretical starting point, and those who consider the possibility of achieving it so remote as to require an analysis which *begins* with the necessity to displace market theory.

The monetary theory of the balance of payments
As monetary theory has come to supplement pure exchange theory in the closed economy, so the monetary theory of the balance of payments has come to supplement it at the international level. Because of the growing significance of financial flows and especially of international credit, any discussion of international economic policy must take off from a concern with the balance of payments broadly construed rather than that of trade. This, therefore, leads us to 'a concern about the composition of a country's international accounts or the structure of its economic relations with the rest of the world',[47] which must place a strong emphasis on the significance of monetary flows and credit. We noted in Chapter 1 that it was the existence of the credit-money system which generated the problem of balance of payments theory in the first place by making it possible for disequilibria to emerge which would not be immediately removed through the automatic processes operating under any system of barter or the gold standard. The existence of credit money separates purchase from payment much more effectively than even the gold standard and creates the possibility – perhaps even the inevitability – of official

intervention to regulate the resulting exchanges. Thus we are again in a situation where 'pure' theory confronts the possibility of interventions designed to alter the outcomes which would otherwise emerge out of the operation of automatic market processes, and with their corresponding need to evolve a demonstration of the optimality of these processes as the basis for their policy prescriptions. We will therefore again deal with the 'pure'model in this section and with the policy results in the next section.

Balance of payments theory assumes the existence of a multi-currency world with convertibility established through a system of exchange rates with potentially adjustible parities organised by official authorities responsible for the supervision of the national reserves of foreign currencies. In Johnson's words:

> balance-of-payments problems presuppose the presence of an official foreign exchange authority which is prepared to operate in the foreign exchange market by the use of official reserves so as to influence the exchange rate; and 'disequilibrium' is defined by changes in the official reserves, associated with imbalances between the foreign receipts and foreign payments of residents of the country, where 'resident' is defined to include all economic units domiciled in the country *except* the foreign exchange authority.[48]

The correction of 'imbalances' then becomes the object of theory and policy; the starting point, however, is the assumption that free mobility of credit and trade must tend towards creating a long-term equilibrium between countries which Chapter 1 demonstrated to be the necessary basis for international monetary stability.

This belief is based upon two assumptions – that the existence of a long-term balance of payments surplus in any country will eventually lead to a self-correcting rise in its costs of production and that such a surplus must constitute an irrational act of international charity and will therefore have to be corrected in the national interest. The first of these arguments finds its classical expression in the quantity theory put forward by Hume in the eighteenth century. This asserted that the level of monetary reserves could not increase beyond the point where they balanced the amount of money demanded by domestic residents 'as determined by real income and the price level'.[49] This, as Hume demonstrates, is because the increase in the money supply resulting from the inflow of foreign currency must increase local costs while reducing foreign prices, thus leading to a deterioration in the terms of trade of the surplus country. The result must therefore be an outflow of money which will continue 'till we fall to the level with foreigners, and lose that great superiority of riches, which had lain us under such disadvantages'.[50]

This argument was used to dispose of the mercantilist belief that a country enriched itself by accumulating gold through foreign trade. We can see that it depends upon the Say's law assumption that money will not be hoarded, and, perhaps more importantly, upon that of constant or diminishing returns to scale as we will demonstrate in Chapter 3. By these assumptions the accumulation of pieces of gold or, even worse, of intrinsically valueless foreign paper tokens in exchange for real goods must be seen to be an irrational occupation equivalent to 'shipping goods to mid-ocean and dumping them there'.[51] Given that 'orthodox neoclassical theory [therefore] provides little basis for regarding a permanent current account surplus as a rational objective',[52] it can be argued that no fundamental conflicts of interest exist between countries of the kind which would emerge if the maintenance of long-term surpluses was in the national interest and that a basis therefore exsits for the creation of international regulation designed to achieve an open monetary and trading system.[53]

We have here, of course, the key theoretical postulate which underpins the belief in the workability of the Bretton Woods system. It does not, however, exclude the possibility that short-term 'dysfunctions' or the willingness of particular states to respond to pressures from vested interests with a commitment to protection might lead them to adopt such measures and destroy the equilibrium. Further, following the 'valid' arguments for protection outlined at the end of the last section, it may even accept the use of such measures in specific situations as a legitimate medium-term response. But the fundamental commitment to the equilibrium analysis remains with critical implications for policy as the next section will attempt to show.

Within the framework of balance of payments theory three potential areas for adjustment exist – in the level of foreign reserves, in the exchange rate and in the balance of activity in the domestic economy between imports, exports and production for local consumption. In the pure equilibrium model, the last of these problems can be seen to be disposed of through the restatement of Hume's description of the quantity theory and the corresponding balance of payments adjustment mechanism outlined above. Because of an absence of mercantilist interferences and the internal 'flexibilities' required by monetarist analysis in prices and wages a generalised tendency towards factor-price equalisation and payments equilibrium must emerge.

This, in turn, requires a particular orientation to the related problem of reserve holdings and exchange rates.

In the context of a 'neutral' payments situation official reserves can simply be seen as a stock of foreign exchange held by the authorities to settle claims against foreigners. Given the corresponding equilibrium conditions these would only have to be sufficient to finance short-term excesses of imports over exports because all other exchanges would be self-cancelling or add to the existing stock. Since foreign exchange reserves constitute underemployed resources, the concern of the authorities should be to retain supplies sufficient only to meet possible contingencies and not to accumulate them for their own sake. Indeed, the Humean mechanism implies that it will in any case be impossible to do so because of the difficulties involved in sustaining the long-term surplus which is the only way of accumulating *owned* as opposed to *borrowed* resources. There has been a good deal of discussion about how this minimum level is to be determined, but it is of a technical nature and need not concern us here.

Where the possibility of a medium-term deficit arises for whatever reason, however, adjustments in internal resource allocation will be required from local to export production. While these will occur automatically if the appropriate flexibilities exist, the long-term nature of modern investment and production processes will lead to a *lag* between the point at which the changes are initiated and that at which they generate the necessary switch in output and prices. If the balance of payments constraint is imposed immediately, however, the necessary *time* will not be available and the authorities might be forced to adopt direct controls which will undermine the integrity of the open exchange system. Hence a need exists either for some accumulation of reserves over and above the minimum specified in the previous paragraph, or for some form of international credit. James Meade concludes his classical formulation of the argument as follows:

> In such a case it would be essential that the authorities in the deficit country should possess an adequate reserve of gold, or the currency of the surplus country, or of some other acceptable international means of payment to tide over the period during which the price adjustment is working out its effect. There would be some period during which the mechanism of price adjustment alone could not prove effective.[54]

More recently this argument has been strengthened by the need for central banks to be provided with adequate reserves to defend parities against the effects of large-scale speculative movements. Thus we are already in the realm of policy-application concerned with the 'financing' of balance of payments deficits. The importance of including the analysis here is to stress how strongly it still depends upon the neoclassical view of automatic adjustments and how small a concession it makes to interventionism.

In the 'neutral' payments situation, again, the problem of exchange rate relativities also disappears for no country would need to alter parities in order to correct a 'fundamental disequilibrium'. This would eliminate the possibility of unfair manipulation as well as that of speculation against probable future parity changes and create the ideal conditions for trade and credit flows. In a world in which the relative productivities of different economies is changing, however, it cannot be assumed that an equilibrium level reached with a particular parity structure will necessarily be sustained indefinitely so that theory has to identify some mechanism for bringing such changes about. Despite the fact that a system of fixed exchange rates operated for the greater part of the post-war period there can be no doubt that the 'orthodox' position in this regard has been a commitment to a flexible exchange rate system. The argument has probably been most effectively stated by Friedman who claimed that fixed rates would be incompatible 'with unrestricted multilateral trade':

> With rigid exchange rates, any change in conditions of trade can be met only by changes in reserves, internal prices and monetary conditions, or direct controls over imports, exports, and other exchange transactions... the use of reserves is a feasible device only for mild and temporary movements. Primary reliance on changes in the internal price level is undesirable, and [most countries] ... would almost certainly be completely unwilling to allow the level of prices and employment at home to be determined primarily by the vagaries of foreign trade.
>
> The only other alternative to movements in exchange rates is direct control of foreign trade.[55]

Against this he could argue that flexible rates would produce an automatic adjustment to changes between domestic and foreign productivity levels and simultaneously allow domestic policy-makers to insulate their actions from external pressures. The effect of flexibility is seen to be the automatic adjustment of domestic to foreign price levels and this, in turn, is seen to exclude even the possibility of a long-term deficit. Thus Polak wrote:

> ... any regime under which the balance of payments adjusts itself automatically through changes in the rate [of exchange] excludes the possibility of a balance of payments deficit by assumption.[56]

This commitment to exchange rate flexibility does not, of course, imply any assumptions about the likelihood of exchange rate instability. The equilibrium assumptions from which it starts imply that changes will be relatively infrequent and small. Indeed Friedman argues that it is only through flexibility that long-term stability can be sustained. In his view the post-war commitment to fixed rates translated the belief in the need for stability into an attempt to enforce it through central intervention for reasons which will be considered in the next section. Its proponents backed it with additional arguments, most of them deriving from the political requirements for the creation of a unified international monetary order set out in the third section of Chapter 1. From the orthodox standpoint the enforced return to floating rates after 1973 can therefore be seen as a vindication of the orthodox position. However, given the operation of the credit money system and especially the separation of the dollar from gold in 1971, it is also the case that they have to accept the fact that parities cannot be entirely separated from policy because of the inevitability of central bank interventions in foreign exchange markets. But here, as with domestic monetary policy, the logic of the case is that the pure theory points towards the minimisation of these actions and the development of a strategy designed to ensure that the international value of the currency corresponded to its 'real' value as determined by the operation of the international market in both trade and financial transactions.

The Orthodox Policy Model
The preceding discussion identified three key areas for potential intervention to deal with disequilibria in international economic relations – domestic economic policy, credit creation and in the exchange rate regime. Direct interventions, notably through protection and direct transfers of productive assets are a fourth possible area on which leading liberal theorists – for example Corden, Johnson and Grubel[57] – have all taken positions derived directly from their orthodox paradigms, and which have necessarily to be incorporated in policy packages for all but tiny handful of countries that impose no limits upon imports at all. For reasons of space and because of the belief that these arguments fall outside the main tradition we will not consider them here, but postpone them to the following section where they will be considered in the broad context of the protectionist critique of the liberal position. This clearly over-simplifies and distorts the position of theorists like Corden, but it can be defended on the grounds that the main line of argument will be considered in due

course. Attention in this section will therefore be focused exclusively on the first three problem areas.

The protagonists in the political debate that surrounds policy decisions in these three areas operate at both the national and international level. Any government, whether in surplus or deficit, must take account of the economic implications of its external transactions and adjust policies in these three areas to secure optimum adjustments in relation to the demands being imposed upon it by the imperatives of domestic capital accumulation and the competing class interests operating at the political level. Thus even neoclassical theory has to recognise the existence of what they tend to call 'special interests' whose needs deviate from those of society in general and which can therefore be expected to attempt to 'reproduce their power in the long run and thus violate the neutrality assumptions of orthodox theory'.[58] Their response to it is to identify these pressures as 'political' and to put forward their own response as 'economic and technical'; to deal with the full implications of this argument we would have to move more directly into their theory of the state than is possible here. But we also argued in Chapter 1 that the IMF must also intervene in these areas as a particular kind of at least incipient state – one expected to take positions determined by the needs of the *world* economy, and hence on the basis of theoretical positions which treat the maximisation of global as opposed to any particular national interests as paramount. We have already argued that orthodox free trade theory, correctly described by List as *cosmopolitan theory*,[59] is to be seen as a theory which operates at the global level and which serves as the basis for their *modus operandi*. This analysis will therefore focus exclusively upon their orientation to the policy debate and thereby bypass the issues which must arise when it is considered more directly from the perspective of any particular nation state. In the post-war debate a separation has tended to exist between problems arising out of the exchange rate mechanism which has tended to be considered as a general problem (mainly, in fact, because it became a problem for the *whole* system as a result of the weakness of the dollar from the 1960s onwards), and those arising out of the credit and domestic policy mechanisms. These, treated as a choice between 'financing' as against 'adjustment', have tended to be closely linked. This section will therefore begin with an examination of the exchange rate issue and then deal with the nature of the choices involved in the choice between credit and domestic reallocations.

Exchange rate adjustments

During the inter-war period curriencies tended to be inconvertible
and were exchanged at rates which derived directly from attempts by
governments to maintain preferential trading areas and to obtain
competitive balance of payments advantages. These policies are
incompatible with the maintenance of an integrated monetary order,
so the founding fathers of the IMF were convinced that a secure basis
for such an order could only be obtained through a strong commitment to an almost absolute degree of exchange rate stability. They
assumed, for the reasons set out in the previous section, that such
stability would not be difficult to sustain provided that effective credit
and domestic policy programmes were created and therefore set up
the so-called 'adjustable peg system'. This required that countries
should 'not propose a change in the par value of its currency except to
correct a fundamental disequilibrium', and then only 'after consultation with the Fund'.[60] What constituted a 'fundamental' as opposed
to some other form of disequilibrium was not made clear, but what
the proviso did do was to impose the obligation on countries to
exhaust every possible domestic policy instrument before they had
recourse to a devaluation.

Between 1949 and 1971 it seemed that the equilibrium assumptions
actually held in reality as few changes took place in the developed
countries at least. But in fact the stability was little more than an
appearance since substantial changes in the underlying economic
conditions were taking place which finally culminated in the devaluation of sterling in 1967[61] and the much more fundamental change in
the status of the dollar which produced a devaluation in 1971 and the
transition to 'managed floating' in 1973. For the Americans the final
acceptance of devaluation, which, of course, had devastating efects
upon the monetary system because of the reserve role of the dollar,
occurred in their own view because they were no longer willing 'to
sacrifice jobs and output to the requirements of fixed exchange
rates'.[62] The change occurred without prior reference to the IMF and
initiated a period of theoretical debate designed to provide a feasible
alternative to the adjustable peg system which had collapsed so
ignominiously.

The underlying factors leading to this collapse will be dealt with in
the rest of this study; here it is only necessary to consider some of the
theoretical and policy issues which it raised. The primary obstacle to
the acceptance of the case for flexible exchange rates was the belief
that no national governments would be willing to give up their right to

intervene in setting it and that, where they did, they would be able to use devaluation as a means of transferring their economic difficulties to their neighbours. Thus orthodox theory demonstrated that 'under conditions of unemployment, devaluation may be expected to exert a favourable effect on production and employment', but only at the cost of increasing pressures on other countries:

> to the extent that the additional exports of the devaluing country displace those of its competitors, the levels of production and income in the competitor countries will be adversely affected.[63]

For the IMF officials, sitting at the centre of the system, the crucial political problem was to create a situation in which recourse to this mechanism, with its inevitably divisive effects, would be rendered impossible. They had therefore to push for one in which the bulk of the pressure on deficit countries would take the form of domestic policy interventions designed to shift resources out of consumption into exports. An important Fund report of 1970 made this political imperative abundantly clear:

> the need to defend a fixed exchange rate against depreciation may promote political willingness to impose unpopular domestic restraints; and where the attempt to defend the parity is ultimately unsuccessful, the psychological shock of devaluation may promote broad support for the adoption of the necessary associated measures to curtail domestic demand.[64]

Equally important, of course, was the threat to the creditworthiness of the centre currency. Fixed rates (rather than the notional link to gold) were the major guarantee of the long-term value of the dollar which made up the greater part of international reserves. Once the dollar was free to fall in response to American domestic policy imperatives, and a *de facto* 'dollar standard' system created, the whole basis of trust in the international currency collapsed. It made it possible for the US to deal with its internal problems by:

> pumping out an excessive quantity of dollars secure in the knowledge that this would depreciate the dollar while the rest of the world countered by a proliferation of exchange controls designed to repel the unwanted influx...[65]

Not only would this involve enormous losses in real purchasing power to all of the countries which had accumulated dollar reserves by exporting real goods and services to the US in the past, it would also create a situation of real political dependence:

> A situation of monetary dependence, such as was implied by a dollar standard, was unacceptable for broad political reasons of national self-

respect because of the resulting inequality of power.[66]

Thus the major international commission on the monetary system, the Committee of Twenty, could still recommend in 1974 that:

> Competitive depreciation and undervaluation will be avoided. The exchange rate mechanism will remain based on stable but adjustable par values, and countries should not make inappropriate par value changes.[67]

Yet they had to concede that devaluations might be inevitable in order to avoid recourse to direct controls over trade or payments, so the 1970 report accepted the necessity for 'moderate adjustments in exchange rates',[68] while IMF policies for third world countries maintaining fixed rate systems has always been to encourage devaluations rather any increase in direct controls to deal with the external imbalance.

Whatever the political importance of the committment to the adjustable peg system, the conditions of the 1970s made it impossible to sustain. With the weakness of the US economy now fully exposed, and 'fundamental' disequilibria emerging all over the rest of the system, it was no longer possible to believe that countries would fight for very long to maintain a particular par value. This made speculation in foreign exchange an almost risk-free form of self-enrichment and, with huge sources of short-term finance available in the international banking system, massive short-term flows occurred as soon as a change became apparent. Thus Williamson notes that:

> By the time that the adjustable peg was abandoned, capital mobility had developed to the point where the Bundesbank could take in well over $1 billion in an hour when the market had come to expect that another parity change was impending.[69]

Thus the old system could neither provide governments with the direct control over their exchange-rates which they needed to deal with the growing balance of payments disequilibria of the 1970s, nor with 'a viable crisis-free method of changing exchange rates in an era of capital mobility'.[70]

After an extended period of negotiations the *de facto* breach of the IMF Articles of Agreement which managed floating involved was retrospectively legalised with the introduction of a revised Article IV in 1976. This in effect attempted to impose on the IMF the obligation of ensuring that governments followed the Friedmanite requirement of automaticity in exchange rate adjustment. It gave the Fund the obligation of exercising 'firm surveillance' over the conduct of national policy in this area and an obligation to intervene by initiating a 'discussion with a member' in response to, among other things, 'behaviour of the exchange rate that appears to be unrelated to underlying economic and financial factors affecting competitiveness and long-term capital movements'.[71] It is, of course, evident that the IMF has no more power to enforce this obligation than it had to control the actions of the US government in 1971 because of the intrinsic weaknesses in its political position set out in Chapter 1. On the face of it, however, the present system of 'managed floating' conforms more directly to neoclassical orthodoxy than did the previous more rigid system. It is clear, however, that it emerged accidentally and in response to a breakdown in the conditions which made relative stability in exchange rates a real possibility in the 1950s and 1960s and not in response to the superior force of academic argument. The implications of this change will be considered later, here we must now look at the other side of intervention, that concerned with financial flows and domestic policy adjustment.

Financial flows and policy adjustments
The IMF becomes directly involved in domestic policy issues when it is called on to intervene by countries that have exhausted their reserves and see no prospect of an immediate return to balance of payments surplus. It has then to design a 'stabilisation' programme designed to restore external balance through the provision of short-term credit, combined with a policy package designed to switch resources from the domestic to the export sector. The nature and more especially the stringency of these packages must be decisively influenced by the relative emphasis placed on the credit provided as against the policy adjustments required.[72] The former, if invested in export production, could be a means of providing an expansionary route out of the problem by increasing output without cutting domestic consumption significantly; the latter, without any significant increase in investment, must almost certainly involve a deflationary solution since the short-term reduction in domestic consumption required to reduce the deficit is very unlikely to be associated with an equally immediate increase in export sales. We saw in Chapter 1 that the balance between these two mechanisms was a crucial problem in the Bretton Woods negotiations, separating the deficit from the surplus countries with the former supporting the Keynes' proposal for large-scale recycling and the latter placing most of the emphasis on domestic adjustments. In the event, as we have seen, the conflict was resolved through a compromise which placed almost all of the weight

upon the latter mechanism turning the Fund as a result into an institution concerned almost exclusively with short-term 'monetary' problems as opposed to one able to involve itself in the sort of developmental interventions that would have emerged out of a full acceptance of the Keynes proposals.

This emphasis, built into the constitution of the Fund itself, means that an IMF team has relatively little scope for positive investment proposals oriented towards providing the funds required to enable countries to resolve their difficulties by creating new resources in export-promoting industries. Their credits are therefore intended almost exclusively to provide the limited function of giving the government concerned the *time* required to make the necessary policy adjustments in the manner specified by Meade above (see note 54). Some might even argue that in these circumstances the role of credit provision is merely to draw the country directly under the control of the Fund in order to impose these controls upon it,[73] others that they are no more than an 'inducement' to forestall the adoption of more direct and more effective forms of direct controls. At the other end of the political spectrum, orthodox theorists have argued that the availability of concessional credits of this kind (and IMF lending is provided at short-term but nevertheless at concessionary rates of interest) merely allows countries to postpone essential policy adjustments and make the underlying situation worse, leading to 'not only international financial crises, but also the encouragement of the use of ... direct controls'.[74] Few would be prepared to criticise the Fund for implementing its policies in an excessively soft way, however, since, once we examine their domestic strategy, we can see that this is where the major emphasis always lies.

A balance of payments disequilibrium represents a gap between domestic production and consumption which is being closed through an external flow. A surplus involves the acquisition of foreign claims, and can continue for as long as any country is willing to go on accumulating them, a deficit involves foreign borrowing which must end once the creditors refuse to continue to pay. Further, a period of borrowing must ultimately be followed by a repayment which will only be possible if the deficit is reduced, thus, however great the access to credit for the debtor, the need to work for a long-term balance remains. Here we have, on the grand scale the problem of the free meal – however extensive the credit facilities, payment must eventually be made. For the former Managing Director of the Fund, J. Witteveen, the matter could be expressed very simply. A deficit involved 'national overspending' which could only continue for as long as 'the international community' was 'ready to finance that country's BOP deficits'; once that readiness disappeared 'the country has to adjust'.[75] The appropriate response must then be, in Friedman's words:

> domestic monetary and fiscal policy directed towards holding down or reducing domestic prices relative to foreign prices when the country is experiencing a deficit, or towards permitting domestic prices to rise relative to foreign prices when the country is experiencing a surplus.[76]

A good deal of technical debate has surrounded the question of the appropriate policy instruments to be chosen which cannot be considered here.[77] Mundell's work has been especially influential in this area with a demonstration that, in a world where capital is becoming increasingly mobile, monetary policy (control over the interest rate through open market purchase of securities) will always be effective in adjusting the balance of payments under fixed exchange rates, whereas fiscal policy (a change in government spending) can be used to maintain the internal balance necessary for full employment, but not to maintain the external balance.[78] Under flexible rates, on the other hand, fiscal policy will still mainly affect internal stability, but will also be 'more effective in improving employment' because of the tendency for exchange rate changes to offset the resulting changes in the balance of payments.[79] Whether this distinction is a valid one in practice, depending as it does upon a rigid separation between activities of central bank in controlling the money supply, and treasury in controlling government spending, is open to question.[80] In real world situations, with a virtually bankrupt government confronting an IMF team representing its international creditors all the emphasis tends to be upon the use of *both* monetary and fiscal policy as a means of reducing domestic consumption in order to re-establish international solvency.

The starting point of any IMF package is the necessity for domestic deflation to reduce the external deficit and rate of inflation:

> in order to lower inflationary expectations, reverse the wage/price spiral, and thus ease pressures on their exchange rates, [deficit] countries have decided to emphasise demand restraint to achieve the desired balance of payments adjustments and, ... their growth will remain below that of potential output.[81]

Much emphasis is placed on credit constraints with increases in interest rates and severe limitations on 'fiscal deficits financed by banking system credit'.[82] With credit restrictions in force social services have to be cut to avoid an 'increase in effective tax rates [that] may have adverse effects on economic performance'.[83] In this situation the need for increased output oriented towards exports requires a substantial increase in the rate of profit, especially given an infla-tionary situation and the high interest rates imposed to reduce con-sumption where 'it is likely that firms would look for a higher rate of return on investments than in the past'.[84] Hence the policy accepts the necessity for a fundamental realignment in the relationship be-tween consumption and productivity:

> This can be ensured if the incomes of the saving and investing classes (including government enterprises) increases at a rate higher than overall labour productivity. As a corollary to this, the incomes of the classes with low saving propensity (which includes landless labourers, domestic ser-vants, and industrial labour) should increase correspondingly slower than overall labour productivity.[85]

The overall implications of this message are clear and consistent – where the 'automatic' mechanisms have failed to produce the ap-propriate flexibility in prices and wages, presumably because of monopolistic rigidities arising out of 'political' variables, policy should be designed to replicate them by transferring resources from both wages and social expenditure to profits. The whole process is accompanied by a call for a return to market competition as the primary source of establishing the rationality of resource allocations and away from the planning and import substitution orientation dominant in the 1960s with their Keynesian and protectionist orient-ation.[86] The rejection of protectionism is especially marked, with strong pressures being applied to countries with exports likely to be price responsive to use devaluations (accompanied by the elimination of all forms of dual exchange rates) as the primary source of external balance.[87] As against this 'the Fund considers that restrictions on trade are not an acceptable means of tackling balance of payments pressures',[88] since the 'disadvantage of protectionist policies for the growth of world trade are self-evident'.[89]

The potential political difficulties arising out of the implementation of policies requiring so clear a redistribution of resources from labour to capital are self-evident, and attested to by the frequency of severe political crises following their visitations.[90] But the Fund officials continue to argue the purely technocratic nature of their diagnosis and proposals and the correspondingly apolitical nature of their intellectual position and interventions. Thus their former managing director could argue that they avoided 'taking a view on the ap-propriate distribution of the burden of adjustment as between various sections of society'. However, he did concede that inflation and payments deficits 'reflect efforts on the part of society, seen as a whole, to avail itself of more resources than it can currently generate';

that the reductions in consumption involved in dealing with them might lead to 'fears on the part of each section of society that it may have to assume a disproportionate share of the burden', and hence to 'strong resistance' and politicisation of 'such matters'.[91] Yet given the overall equilibrium assumptions of the monetarist position, the IMF theorists assume that the underlying problems are less serious than they seem since their policies 'need not be detrimental to growth and employment but ... can provide in many cases an essential basis for a healthier and more sustained economic development'.[92] Thus, given the essentially technocratic assumption that they are doing no more than ensuring that 'aggregate demand for goods and services is brought into line with output',[93] they attempt to disregard the fact that their interventions do involve questions involving serious matters of domestic policy choice.

Thus far we have been concerned exclusively with the problem presented by deficit countries. Equilibrium analysis suggests that it is as – perhaps more – important for surplus countries to adjust, though no equivalent package exists to guide them through the process since the pressure on them to do so is in fact very small. Briefly, theory assumes that they should adopt policies opposite from those required for deficit countries – an appreciated exchange rate, external lending, reduced tariffs, and an expansion in domestic demand. Considerable moral pressure has been placed upon such countries to adopt liberalised policies of this kind recently,[94] on the assumption that they would increase domestic consumption and lead to an increase in imports which would stimulate activity and offset the deflationary policies being adopted by the deficit areas.

The limitations involved in these arguments will be examined in some detail in the following chapters. Before doing so, however, it is necessary to look more closely at the variants of neoclassical theory which have questioned the optimality of market assumptions in all situations and provided a rationale for systematic processes of intervention to offset certain negative consequences arising from it. The most influential of these arguments have certainly been Keynesian theory most recently, and protectionism historically with its recent conversion into 'structuralism' through an integration of Keynesian assumptions into the original, more liberal version.

Keynesian Demand Management

The *General Theory*, usually seen as Keynes's major contribution, was mainly concerned with potential failures of demand in the closed economy and with the corresponding need for state intervention to offset the corresponding disappearance of investment opportunity. In his preparatory work for Bretton Woods, examined in Chapter 1, he attempted to extend this analysis to the international level, thereby demonstrating the conditions which would have to hold if domestic governments were to be able to implement his policies without having to resort to the protectionism which he had supported during the 1930s.[95] To understand the implications of this work, and therefore of many of the reform proposals being put forward for the IMF, we must demonstrate the close links between his analysis of the demand and investment problems at both domestic and international levels.

Keynes, as Leontief correctly argues, 'did not attack the internal consistency of [orthodox theory's] logical structure; he rather attempted to demonstrate the unreality of its fundamental empirical assumptions'.[96] In particular he challenged the Say's law assumption that supply must generate its own demand by identifying the possibility of *hoarding*, which he saw as the outcome of an excessive propensity to save on the part of individuals and public and private enterprises. In this situation a portion of the money generated in production would not return to the market as effective demand, a corresponding portion of the goods produced would remain unsold, and production, and hence employment, would have to be cut. The multitude of entrepreneurs making future investment decisions would thus have no reason to expect that demand would increase in the future, they would fail to invest an adequate proportion of their profits, even with falling wages, the 'liquidity trap' noted in the previous section would be created and an *unemployment* equilibrium would result.

The effect of the liquidity trap will be to create a situation in which unemployed capital and labour coexist, leading to massive social waste; the solution must be to eliminate hoarding by an increase in *investment* which will involve a period of consumption (during the creation of the productive asset) which will not be matched by an equivalent increase in output and which will therefore absorb the excess of current output over current consumption created by the propensity to save. Thus Keynes's full employment equilibrium can only be secured with a very specific balance between investment and savings, that is 'an amount of current investment sufficient to absorb the excess of total output over what the community chooses to consume when employment is at a given level'.[97] Because of the voluntary nature of the propensity to save there is no guarantee that automatic processes will in fact produce this level, especially given the atomised nature of the capitalist class, where competition prevails, and their corresponding tendency to pessimism about future prospects when demand is declining. In this situation the only recourse must be to the state with its capacity to represent the collective interest which, by increasing the level of demand (and he was relatively imprecise about how this should be done), could compensate for the excess of savings by creating safe investment opportunities of the appropriate size. Once capitalist expectations about the future improved, their 'animal spirits' could be expected to revive, and the generation of new investment would become a mutually reinforcing process multiplying the effect of the original state input to the point where full employment was reached.

A crucial element in this argument is its dependence on the existence of unemployed resources in the first instance since it is only then that the increase in demand could be expected to have its effect on income rather than prices, since it is only then that output will be able to expand to increase the supply of money.[98] With unemployment 'an increase in the quantity of money will have no effect whatever on prices ... and ... employment will increase in exact proportion to any increase in effective demand brought about by the increase in the quantity of money', but once full employment is reached it will be wages and prices which will rise in exactly the same way as they will in the orthodox analysis.[99] Hence we can see that the possibility of positive employment effects through direct interventions exist only where unemployed resources are available.[100] Once full employment has been reached it ceases to be possible or necessary and the orthodox relationships come back into play. Further, the Keynesian critique operates almost exclusively at the level of the macro economy where he assumes that *voluntary* choices may lead to a failure to produce the optimum relationships. He explicity repudiates any criticism of the role of competition in producing optimum allocations at the micro level and accepts all of the orthodox assumptions about its superiority to centralised planning for this level. Thus, however important its role in legitimating post-war interventionism, we can see that the main thrust of Keynes's attack was focused on a narrow area of the orthodox case and seen to be relevant only in very specific circumstances.

When we look at the transposition of this argument to the international level embodied in the proposals for the International Clearing Union examined in Chapter 1, the parallels are very clear.

At this level the equivalent of the individual with an excessive propensity to save is the country with an excessive propensity to maintain balance of payments surpluses. Where the surplus country then refuses to release the resulting savings for investment abroad Say's law ceases to operate, a failure in demand emerges and this exerts 'a deflationary and contractionist pressure on the whole world including the creditor country itself'.[101] His solution, as we have already seen, was the creation of a central bank which would in effect serve as a substitute for the domestic banking system and the national state by collecting these otherwise under-utilised surpluses and lending them to governments of deficit countries to serve as the basis for an expanionist rather than a deflationary solution to their external imbalance. In these circumstances external weakness would cease to be a constraint on domestic reflation and the rigidities and tensions resulting from the otherwise inevitable tendency towards protectionism could be done away with. All of the policies designed to bring 'aggregate demand into line with output' by reducing activity along the lines set out at the end of the previous section would therefore become unnecessary and countries could thereafter 'abjure the instruments of bank rate and credit contraction operating through the increase of unemployment as a means of forcing [their] domestic economy into line with external factors'.[102]

Keynes was obviously premature in arguing in 1944 that domestic deflation and unemployment would no longer be used to deal with an external imbalance, but then he was also mistaken in his belief that the surplus countries could be persuaded to agree to give up a substantial portion of their surpluses to an autonomous international agency.[103] The relevance of his analysis has remained, however, with the demand for an agency to develop an effective international money form based upon the surpluses of the strong countries emerging again with Triffin's seminal critique at the end of the 1950s of the role of the dollar[104] and the eventual creation of the special drawing right at the end of the 1960s. Equally important has been the integration of Keynesian thinking into development theory to provide a basis for an interventionist strategy which calls for substantial supplies of foreign aid designed to offset the 'external bottleneck' which must otherwise arise as a result of the 'increase in imports that the rapid growth in the product may involve'.[105] At the monetary level this has consistently manifested itself in the demand for the creation of a 'link' between developmental credit and the creation of SDRs by a range of authoritative groups which have looked at the monetary problem from the third world point of view.[106] At this point the Keynesian proposals become inextricably mixed with the other main line of criticism of orthodox theory, the protectionist and structuralist arguments.

Protectionism and Structuralism

The theoretical positions we are to consider now find their origin in a strange paradox where, as Emmanuel notes, 'the normal practice of the world ... has been and still remains protectionism' while 'imperturbably and tirelessly the post-mercantilist economists, from François Quesnay and Adam Smith onward, went on demonstrating the errors of protectionism and the advantages of free trade'.[107] We have already noted that orthodoxy has attempted to respond to this paradox by dealing with protection as a 'theory of the second-best' and then demonstrating how various protective regimes can be devised to optimise the resulting relationship between internal and external activities (see note 57). What we are concerned with here, however, are the more thorough-going critiques which have argued that the special circumstances of particular kinds of situation make free trade a necessarily incorrect choice and protection essential if a particular pattern of growth is to be achieved. Historically we can perhaps point to three situations of this kind and to specific bodies of theory which have emerged to deal with them – the problem of unequal competition between the rising capitalist interests of Europe and the USA and established British capital in the nineteenth century, that of the post-colonial attempts to industrialise the periphery since independence, and that of the marginalisation of established industry in the advanced countries as a result of the intensified competition following the recessions of the 1930s and 1970s. Let us now consider the theoretical response to these situations.

While free trade arguments dominated Britain in the nineteenth century a variety of continental and American writers produced the arguments required to justify the protectionist policies adopted everywhere else to offset the competitive strength of British exports. List, a German who spend a considerable period as a political exile in America, produced what has probably been the most influential account which places primary emphasis on the infant industry argument and on the central importance of the state as a directly productive social agency. He argues that orthodox theory is essentially a 'cosmopolitan' theory of exchange which pays no attention to the conditions which make production possible. In fact, once these have been developed in any country, industry will be more efficient there and will be able to appropriate an ever-increasing share of markets in less developed countries. Thus if the most advanced country is not to appropriate 'all the wealth and all the power of the globe', and so that 'free trade may operate naturally, it is necessary that the nations less advanced than England should be raised by aritificial means to the same degree of development at which England has arrived artificially'.[108] While the infant industry argument (subsequently taken up and legitimised by Mill) is clearly evident here, this case goes beyond the mere consideration of the 'size of firm' to one which incorporates a broad notion of 'external economies' arising from the provision of social infrastructure by the state. Hence the 'individual' ceases to be the only or even the most important agent in the theory and the 'nation' emerges as a major focus:

> However industrious, thrifty, enterprising, moral and intelligent the individuals may be, without national unity, national division of labour, and national co-operation of productive powers the nation will never reach a high level of prosperity and power, or ensure to itself the lasting possession of its intellectual, social and material goods.[109]

In this context the state becomes a crucial *productive* force in society responsible for excluding foreign competition and creating the conditions which will eventually make equal trade possible, and nationalism rather than individualism becomes the crucial motivating force in economic life.

These all represent fundamental divergences from orthodox positions, but equally fundamental assumptions remain. Crucially, market competition of the classical kind continues to guarantee efficiency and equity internally, while protection is only justified externally for as long as the fundamental inequalities in productive powers remain. As the leading European and American producers had achieved parity with the British by the end of the nineteenth century, and most of the rest of the world was subordinated by colonialism, the relevance of these arguments therefore appeared to have disappeared.

If the process of capitalist development was an even and linear progression towards an increasing degree of integration at high levels of development then nothing more need have been heard of protectionism for the industrialised world at least. But not even the most advanced countries are altogether sheltered from the uneven nature of the capitalist development process which, after the devastation of World War I, led to a major dislocation and to a crisis for most of them and a resurgence of protectionist thinking. Here we find two new kinds of argument emerging. In Britain the outcome of a process of relative decline was a demand for Imperial Preference which emerged before the war under the leadership of Joseph Chamberlain and reached fruition in 1932 in the form of the Ottawa Agreements which established the basis for turning the Commonwealth into a sheltered trading and monetary area.[110] Here the starting-point could perhaps best be described as the 'geriatric industry argument' where protection was required to sustain mature industries with high wage costs against competition from newer areas with more modern equipment and lower wages. A second and more powerful argument which rejected the perfect competition assumptions of orthodox theory on the grounds that scale economies were characteristic and necessarily destroyed the advantages of free trade to the weaker country emerged at the same time. This argument, which will be followed through in detail in Chapter 3, produced an extensive literature on 'imperfect competition' in the 1920s and 1930s,[111] and a coherent exposition about the effects on trade in an article by Frank Graham in the *Quarterly Journal of Economics* in 1923.[112] These imperfect competition arguments were then used in Germany in the 1930s,[113] to justify the establishment of a corporatist state designed to correct the resulting imperfections in resource allocation which also included a move to extreme autarchy in external economic relations.[114]

The force of these arguments was dissipated during the expansionist phase which followed the consolidation of the monetary arrangements at the end of the 1940s. However uneven the subsequent pattern of international growth, its scale was such that even weak centres could benefit and therefore be drawn into the liberal consensus. While the problems of the third world continued to be looked at as 'structural' and distinct, rapid progress was made in the developed economies in reducing monetary and tariff obstacles to trade through the activities of the IMF and GATT. The degree of academic support for this process has probably never been greater than it has during the 1970s, and has even extended to the field of development theory which was previously insulated from it.

Yet it is equally evident that the re-emergence of the crisis tendencies in capitalism have recreated the conditions for protectionist thinking and policy, particularly in the weaker industrial centres. Thus we find a return to the geriatric industry argument in Britain, where the process of relative decline has continued unabated. This has been put forward with greatest force by the Applied Economics Group at Cambridge. Identifying Britain as a relatively unsuccessful

(RU) country, it argues that a long period of relatively low industrial investment has produced 'serious weaknesses on the supply side ... which makes it increasingly difficult for it to meet competition in either home or overseas markets', leading to a dangerous process of 'de-industrialisation'. This, then, has created structural deficiencies 'which pertain to dynamic factors in the production system' which must 'continue to deteriorate' if left to themselves. The result must be 'growing inroads by competitive imports', and a 'vicious circle' of 'poor export performances and hence balance of payments difficulties and low growth.[115] The outcome must be a deflationary syndrome which will not be corrected through any 'automatic market mechanism',[116] but 'may well require, perhaps for a considerable period, an abandonment of the regime of free trade and free convertibility of currency'.[117]

In a subsequent Cambridge article, Francis Cripps and Wynne Godley spell out the macro-justification for the adoption of protection in RU countries that reject entirely the 'fiscal and monetary' policies described in the previous section, and reproduce arguments remarkably similar to List's.

> Our central hypothesis is that trends of both price and quality factors are sufficiently unequal and inflexible to generate dynamic processes in international trade such that if (*per impossible*) there were no constraints at all imposed by balance of payments deficits in relatively unsuccessful (RU) industrialised countries, and that if all of them chose fiscal and monetary policies to maintain full employment with stable real exchange rates and without control of imports, then the production of tradable manufactured goods would tend to become very predominantly located in the relatively successful (RS) countries.[118]

They do not consider the relationships in production which lead to this inequality, but reject orthodox trade theory because of its full employment assumption and corresponding exclusion of a concern with policies designed 'to arrange trade so as to change [upwards] the level of employment'.[119] They reject the Humean assumption that costs must rise in surplus and decline in deficit countries, and argue that inflation in the latter will continue under unemployment and only be worsened by devaluation for this raises 'import and export prices relative to home costs and prices', thereby 'cuts real wages and raises export profits', and involves 'a highly inflationary transfer of income ... before there is any significant gain to real national income'.[120] Against this they argue that it is 'unrealistic' to assume that RS countries can 'be made to reflate most in order to overcome their tendency to trade surpluses' because they must be choosing 'the level of demand they desire' and do not wish to reflate further for fear of running into 'severe problems of "overheating" long before relatively unsuccessful countries were able to achieve full employment'.[121] Given protection, however, generalised reflation again becomes possible since the growth in employment in the RU countries will lead to increased demand which will also lead to an increase in imports. To the extent that this occurs, and, more especially, these are drawn from other RU and less developed countries, there will be an overall *increase* in trade and a reduction in the structural disequilibrium stemming from the failure of the surplus countries to adjust. A little optimistically, perhaps, they feel that all of this will occur '*without* loss of trade and employment in RS countries as a group'.[122]

Finally we can consider the theoretical problem defined by the situation confronted by third world countries which, for the most part, had been kept in a state of structural dependence and underdevelopment through their relationship with the colonial power until the period following World War II. A group of intellectuals mainly associated with the Economic Commission for Latin America responded to this situation by appropriating most of the arguments outlined above and integrating them into what came to be called 'structuralism', concerned to create a system of centrally planned import-substituting industrialisation with a heavy emphasis on the need for direct external controls over money and trade. Relatively uncontroversial in this context was a reassertion of the infant industry argument, which figured prominently in even Lewis's very orthodox work on development economics.[123] We have also already noted the use made of the 'dual economy' model in the Manoilescu argument (see note 45) to justify trade interventions to give special protection to local industry. These views were then appropriated by more radical theorists such as Myrdal and Balogh[124] to argue the necessity for a substantial displacement of the market mechanism because of its tendency to produce a cumulative tendency towards inequality and industrial stagnation. Perhaps the most influential of these theorists, however, was Prebisch whose position at the UN Economic Commission for Latin America enabled him to exert a powerful influence at the policy level.

While accepting the preceding arguments, Prebisch placed most stress on the 'terms of trade' problem, arguing that the much lower growth in demand for primary products meant that third world export prices must expand less rapidly than those of the imported capital equipment which they would need for industrialisation, thus creating a 'development deficit'.[125] This then served as a basis for a call for a substantial flow of credit on concessional terms, as we have seen (see note 105), an argument directly complementary to the Keynesian emphasis on the use of monetary mechanisms for development financing and the subsequent calls for a link between aid and the SDR (see note 106). Because of this tendency for primary prices to be inelastic it is crucial that primary production be improved through technical progress which requires the development of local industry since

> Industry and technical advance in primary production are ... complementary aspects of the same process. And in this process industry plays a dynamic role, not only in inducing technical progress in primary and other activities, but in the new attitudes fostered by industrial development.[126]

When the Manoilescu argument is added to this one we find that the displacement of labour from the primary sector resulting from technical progress will be especially large because of 'disguised unemployment of a pre-capitalist character',[127] and the increase in output stemming from their employment in industry correspondingly great. Hence the full advantages of new industry to a country are not calculable through a straight comparison between internal costs and external prices, but by

> comparing the increment of income obtained in the expansion of industry with that which could have been obtained in export activities had the same productive resources been employed there.[127]

Hence optimal results cannot be obtained 'if market forces are left unrestricted',[127] devaluation will not have strong enough effects on 'structural changes in the economy', and a 'selective protection policy' must be adopted, 'notwithstanding the obstacles that have to be overcome in practice'.[128] And in the same context, Kaldor produced a case for dual exchange rates as the optimum means of securing the advantages to industry required by the Prebisch argument.[129]

Given the need for official capital inflows to offset the development induced trade gap and for selective protection to induce a transfer of resources from primary production to industry, it becomes evident that the state must play a major role in the development process for as long as the structural inequality with developed economies remains. Once this is overcome, again, these arguments fall away since at that point equal competition is thought to provide a superior method of resource allocation than direct controls. Prebisch was later willing to concede that 'overprotection' would discourage 'efficiency in production ... when prolonged unduly'.[130] But during the necessarily extended transitional period planning was to be the dominant mechanism, and trade planning through direct controls a crucial aspect of it.

This body of theory was dominant in the periphery until the end of the 1960s when it came to be subjected to the critique referred to in the earlier section of this work (see note 86). While its intellectual dominance was substantially reduced, however, it has continued to exercise a strong influence on policy in the weaker countries and in the critique of the nature of IMF interventions, and must be taken very seriously as a result.

Notes

1. This sentence of course by-passes a multitude of very critical problems which cannot be considered here. It should perhaps be said that my own position in this area has been most influenced by the work of Lukacs and Gramsci.
2. H.G. Johnson, 'International trade: theory', *International encyclopedia of the social sciences*, Vol. 8, p. 88.
3. See the opening chapters of P. Wiles, *The political economy of communism*, Oxford, Blackwell, 1962.
4. W.M. Corden, *Recent developments in the theory of international trade*, Princeton, Princeton University Press, 1965, p. 9.
5. Ibid., pp. 9, 10.
6. See Chapter 1, note 37. To supplement that note consider the following comment by the US Council of the International Chamber of Commerce of May 1950: '[The Havana Charter] is a dangerous document because it accepts practically all of the policies of economic nationalism; because it jeopardises the free enterprise system by giving priority to centralised national governmental planning of foreign trade; because it leaves a wide scope to discrimination; accepts the principle of economic insulation and in effect commits all members of the ITO to state planning for full employment' cited in K. Kock, *International trade policy and the GATT, 1947_67*, Stockholm, Almquist and Wiksell, 1969, p. 59.
7. See in particular the material contained in *Development Dialogue* 1980, no. 2, 'The international monetary system and the new international order'.
8. Donald Winch, Professor of Economics, Internal Memorandum, Sussex University, 27 November 1977.
9. On the concept of 'development deficits' see J.F. Rweyemamu's contribution to *Development Dialogue*, op. cit., pp. 85–7.
10. G. Haberler, *A survey of international trade theory*, Princeton, Princeton University Press, 1961, Section 1.

11. M. Friedman's description in 'The quantity theory of-money: a restatement', in *The optimum quantity of money and other essays*, London, Macmillan, 1969, p. 60.
12. H. Spencer, 'Social statics', in A. Arlbaster and S. Lukes, *The good society*, London, Methuen, 1971, p. 194.
13. Friedman's phrase used in a slightly narrower context. ('The role of monetary policy', in *The optimum quantity of money*, op. cit., p. 97).
14. I. Steedman, ed., *Fundamental issues in trade theory*, London, Macmillan, 1979, p. 1.
15. See for example, M. Oakeshott's now classic essay, 'The political economy of freedom', in *Rationalism in politics*, London, Methuen, 1962.
16. Haberler, op. cit., p. 13.
17. Here see F. Knight, 'Some fallacies in the interpretation of social cost', *Quarterly Journal of Economics*, Vol. 38, 1924, p. 597; and P. Sraffa, 'The laws of return under competitive conditions', in P.C. Newman et al., *Source readings in economic thought*, New York, Norton, 1954.
18. W. Leontief here describes the system of 'perfect competition' as 'an impersonal automatic' and, later, 'miraculous computer'. ('Modern techniques for economic planning and projection', *Essays in economics*, New York, Oxford University Press, 1966, pp. 237–8.) The overall effect of these processes is to demonstrate in Bhagwati's phrase, that 'laissez-faire is Pareto optimal for a perfectly competitive system with no monopoly power in trade'. ('General theory of distortions and trade', *Trade, balance of payments and growth*, Amsterdam, North Holland, 1971, p. 22).
19. For the classic formulations of this proposition by J.N. Say and J.S. Mill see H. Hazlitt, ed., *The critics of Keynesian economics*, Princeton, van Nostrand, 1960.
20. Haberler's phrase op. cit., p. 3.
21. Ibid., p. 3.
22. Friedman, 'The quantity theory', op. cit., p. 52.
23. Ibid., p. 58.
24. J.S. Mill, *Principles of political economy*, London, Longman, 1900, p. 296. This quotation is used as a starting-point by Friedman in 'the role of monetary policy', in *The optimum quantity of money*, op. cit., p. 105.
25. Ibid., p. 303.
26. See Chapter 1, notes 18–20. While the main political thrust of monetarism is critical of Keynesianism as manifested in the *General Theory*, its main proponents have also fully acknowledged their positive debt to his work on monetary theory.
27. M. Friedman, 'The lag in effect of monetary policy', in *The optimum quantity of money*, op. cit., p. 255; for a description of the mechanism that would operate to secure full employment where a disturbance produced a 'decline in aggregate monetary demand' see his 'Monetary and fiscal framework for economic stability', *Essays in positive economics*, Chicago, Chicago University Press, 1953, pp. 149–50.
28. I.H. Rima, *Development of economic analysis*, 3rd edn., Homewood, Ill., Richard D. Irwin, 1978, p. 433.
29. David Evans, Fellow, Institute of Development Studies, Sussex University, personal communication in a written comment on an earlier draft of this book.
30. M. Friedman, 'A theoretical framework for monetary analysis', in R.J. Gorden, ed., *Milton Friedman's monetary framework*, Chicago, University of Chicago Press, 1974, p. 18.

31. Friedman, 'The role of monetary policy...' in *The optimum quantity of money*, op. cit., p. 105.
32. Ibid., pp. 101–5. The 'Phillips curve' is described in A. W. Phillips, 'The relation between unemployment and the rate of change of money wage rates in the United Kingdom', *Economica*, November 1958.
33. Johnson, op. cit., p. 93.
34. Friedman, 'The role of monetary policy' in *The optimum quantity of money*, op. cit., pp. 106–7.
35. Ibid., p. 106.
36. Ibid., p. 109. The emphasis in the above description has been on the negative prescripticns of monetarist thinking. We should note, however, that Friedman does accept that where unemployment exists the authority should increase the money supply to restore expansion. Thus he attributes the depression of the 1930s to the failure of the Federal Reserve System to intervene to keep 'the stock of money from falling'. ('The monetary theory and policy of Henry Simons', *The optimum quantity of money*, p. 91). He also argues in the rest of the long passage cited in the text (note 27) that the increase in the prices of assets resulting from the increase in the money supply will encourage 'the production of .... sources of both producer and consumer services'. How far is this from Keynes's own position?
37. Johnson, op. cit., p. 83. See also Haberler, op. cit., pp. 1–3.
38. Steedman, op. cit., p. 2. See also Haberler, op. cit., pp. 16–7 and Corden, op. cit., pp. 24ff.
39. Corden, op. cit., p. 24.
40. Ibid., p. 25.
41. Note here Johnson's assertion that trade will 'maximise world income' cited above (note 2), and the textbook descriptions of its benefits, for example L.B. Yeager, *International monetary relations*, 2nd edn., New York, Harper and Row, 1976, p. 11 and Mill, op. cit., Book III, Chapter XVII.
42. See Haberler, op. cit., p. 18 and Corden, op. cit., pp. 25–6.
43. Haberler, op. cit., p. 18.
44. Ibid., p. 14.
45. Corden, op. cit., pp. 60–4.
46. M. Corden, *The theory of protection*, Oxford, Oxford University Press, 1971, p. 2.
47. H.G. Johnson, 'The monetary theory of balance of payments problems', in J.A. Frenkel and H.G. Johnson, *The monetary approach to the balance of payments*, London, Allen and Unwin, 1976, p. 263.
48. H.G. Johnson, 'Towards a general theory of the balance of payments' in Frenkel and Johnson, op. cit., p. 48.
49. Johnson, 'The monetary theory', op. cit., p. 273.
50. D. Hume, 'On the balance of trade', in *Writings in economics*, London, Nelson, 1955, p. 63. See also Joan Robinson's account of how competition serves, in this argument 'to correct discrepancies between costs in one capitalist country and another', and therefore to restore trade balance. (*Reflection on the theory of international trade*, Manchester, Manchester University Press, 1974, p. 2).
51. J. Williamson, *The failure of international monetary reform*, London, Nelson, 1977, p. 170.
52. Ibid., p. 169.

53. Ibid., p. 172.
54. J.E. Meade, *The balance of payments*, London, Oxford University Press, 1951, pp. 209–10.
55. M. Friedman, 'The case for flexible exchange rates', in *Essays in positive economics*, op. cit., p. 196–7.
56. J.J. Polak, 'Monetary analysis of income formation and payments problems,' in IMF, *The monetary approach to the balance of payments*, Washington, IMF, 1977, p. 45, fn. 26.
57. Corden, *The theory of protection*, op. cit.; H.G. Johnson, *Aspects of the theory of tariffs*, London, Allen & Unwin, 1971; H. G. Grubel and Johnson, eds., *Effective tariff protection*, Geneva, GATT, 1971.
58. David Evans, personal communication.
59. F. List, *The national system of political economy*, London, Longmans, 1904.
60. IMF, 'Articles of Agreement', IV (5), [1944].
61. For a banker's account of the background to and significance of the British devaluation see R. Solomon, *The international monetary system, 1945_76*, New York, Harper & Row, 1976.
62. US Senate, Committee on foreign relations sub-committee on banking, currency and housing, *Briefing on the IMF*, Washington, Government Printing Office, 1976, p. 24.
63. S.S. Alexander, 'Effects of a devaluation on the trade balance', in American Economics Association, *Readings in international economics*, London, Allen & Unwin, 1968, p. 363.
64. IMF. 'The role of exchange rates in the adjustment of international payments, 'in M. de Vries, *The International Monetary Fund, 1966–71*, Vol. III, *Documents*, Washington, IMF, 1976, p. 299.
65. Williamson, op. cit., p. 54.
66. Ibid., p. 83.
67. IMF, Committee on reform of the International monetary system, *International monetary reform*, Washington, IMF, 1974, p. 11
68. IMF, 'Role of exchange rates', op. cit., p. 300.
69. Williamson, op. cit., p. 50.
70. Ibid., p. 51.
71. IMF, 'Surveillance over exchange rates', *Finance and development*, Vol. 14, no. 2, 1977, p. 5.
72. For a more extensive discussion of the 'financing' vs. 'adjustments' issue see E.A. Brett, 'The IMF, the international monetary system and the periphery', International Foundation for Development Alternatives, *IFDA Dossier*, Vol. 5, 1979.
73. In this regard note the following comments by the deputy manager of the Fund: 'Programmes of the type normally supported by Fund resources are badly needed because of the contribution that the conditionality attached to such resources makes to the adjustment process'. (W.B. Dale, 'The relationship between adjustment and economic growth' – see *Finance and Development*, Vol. 14, no. 3, 1977, p. 9).
74. M. Friedman, 'Post-war trends in monetary theory and policy', *The optimum quantity of money*, op. cit., p. 78.
75 J. Witteveen, 'A conversation with Mr Witteveen', *Finance and Development*,

Vol. 15, no. 3, 1978, p. 9.

76. Friedman, 'Post-war trends', op. cit., p. 78.

77. Some of the issues are covered in Corden, *The theory of protection*, op. cit., Chapter 1.

78. See in particular R.A. Mundell, 'The appropriate use of monetary and fiscal policy', in his *International economics*, New York, Macmillan, 1968, p. 239.

79. Mundell, 'Flexible exchange rates and employment policy', Ibid., pp. 244–5.

80. I owe this point to Rob Eastwood, Lecturer in Economics, University of Sussex.

81. J. Witteveen, Speech in Brazil, *IMF Survey*, 1 August 1977, p. 248.

82. D.E. Johnson, 'Use of Fund resources and stand-by arrangements', *Finance and development*, Vol. 14, no. 1, 1977, p. 21.

83. Witteveen, Speech in Brazil, op. cit., p. 250.

84. Ibid., p. 249.

85. V.V. Bhatt, 'Incomes policies and development planning', *Finance and development*, Vol. 13, no. 4, 1976, p. 40.

86. For an excellent review article dealing with the emergence of the new liberalism and its critique of the structuralist case see D.T. Healey, 'Development policy: new thinking about an interpretation', *Journal of Economic Literature*, Vol. X, no. 3, 1972.

87. See A.D. Crockett and S.M. Nsouli, 'Exchange rate policies for developing countries', *Journal of Development Studies*, Vol. 13, no. 2, 1977 (the authors are Fund staff members); and note the rejection of the multiple rate system in Jamaica and insistence on a large devaluation closely linked to wage controls. See N. Girvan et al., 'The IMF and the Third World: the case of Jamaica', *Development dialogue*, op. cit., 1980, pp. 123ff.

88. UNDP/UNCTAD *The balance of payments adjustment process in developing countries: report to the group of twenty-four*, New York, UNDP, 1979, (the 'Dell' Report), p. III–36.

89. Witteveen, Speech in Brazil, op. cit., p. 251.

90. See for example N. Girvan, 'Swallowing the IMF medicine in the seventies', *Development Dialogue*, op. cit., 1980. (This deals with Jamaica, Peru and Portugal.)

91. J. Witteveen, 'World economic outlook and working of the adjustment process', *IMF Survey*, 22 May 1978, pp. 146–7.

92. W.B. Dale, (Deputy General Manager, IMF), Speech in Geneva, *IMF Survey*, 18 July 1977, p. 230.

93. Witteveen, op. cit.

94. Note for example the request by the 'Committee of Twenty' that surplus countries increase aid and market access to developing countries (IMF, Committee of reform of the international monetary system, op. cit., pp. 8–9); and the request by the IMF's Interim Committee that they 'make every effort to ensure adequate growth in domestic demand compatible with containing inflation' to increase the growth of world trade. (Cited in *IMF Survey*, 10 October 1977, p. 306).

95. See S.E. Harris, 'International economics: introduction', R. Hinshaw, 'Keynesian commercial policy', and R. Nurske, 'Domestic and international equilibrium', in S.E. Harris, *The new economics*, London, Dobson, 1960; J.M. Keynes, 'National self-sufficiency', *New Statesman & Nation*, 1933.

96. W. Leontief, 'Postulates: Keynes's *General Theory* and the classicists', in *Essays in economics*, New York, Oxford University Press, 1966, p. 93. I have not followed the rest of his analysis of Keynes since I feel that he places an undue emphasis on the 'wage rigidity' as opposed to the 'Say's law' assumption.

97. J.M. Keynes, *The general theory of employment interest and money*, London, Macmillan, 1973, p. 27.

98. I am indebted to Michael Lipton here, Fellow, Institute of Development Studies, Sussex University.

99. Keynes, op. cit., p. 259.

100. This point is clearly demonstrated in P. Mattick, *Marx and Keynes*, London, Merlin, 1974, Chapter XIV.

101. J.M. Keynes, 'Proposals for an International Clearing Union', in J.K. Horsefield, *The International Monetary Fund, 1945–1965*, Vol. III, *Documents*, Washington IMF, 1969, p. 4.

102. J.M. Keynes, 'Speech to the House of Lords', 23 May 1944, 'The International Monetary Fund', reprinted in Harris, op. cit., p. 374.

103. For a critical contemporary account of Keynes's role in the negotiations see T. Balogh, *Unequal partners*, Oxford, Blackwell, 1963; for the 'official' view see R. Harrod, *The Life of John Maynard Keynes*, London, Macmillan, 1951.

104. R. Triffin, *Gold and the dollar crisis*, New Haven, Yale University Press, 1960.

105. R. Prebisch, *Change and develolpment – Latin America's great task*, New York, Praeger, 1971, p. 135.

106. See in particular UNCTAD, *International monetary issues and the developing countries*, New York, UN, 1965 (TD/B/32); *IMF Survey*, 15 October 1979, for the proposals of the semi-official 'Group of 24'; and most recently, the 'Arusha Initiative', *Development Dialogue*, 1980. no. 2, p. 20.

107. A. Emmanuel, *Unequal exchange*, London, New Left Books, 1972, p. XIV.

108. F. List, op. cit., cited in S.H. Patterson, *Readings in the history of economic thought*, New York, McGraw Hill, 1932, p. 389.

109. Ibid., cited in P.C. Newman et al., *Source readings in economic thought*, New York, Norton, 1951, p. 301.

110. For a description see E.A. Brett *Colonialism and under-development in East Africa*, London, Heinemann Educational Books, 1973.

111. Notably in Sraffa, op. cit.; J. Robinson, *The economics of imperfect competition*, London, Macmillan, 1933; E. Chamberlain, *The theory of monopolistic competition*, Cambridge, Harvard University Press, 1933; A. Berle and G. Means, *The modern corporation and private property*, New York, Macmillan, 1932; and J. Schumpeter, *Capitalism, socialism and democracy*, London, Unwin, 1952.

112. F.D. Graham, 'Some aspects of protection further considered', *American Journal of Economics*, Vol. XXX, 1923.

113. Notably in H. von Stackelberg, *Theory of the market economy*, New York, Oxford University Press, 1952.

114. Dislike of the system was 'part of the common ground on which the US and the UK stood in their subsequent approach to international economic relations'. (Horsefield, op. cit., Vol.1, *Chronicle*, p. 5).

115. A. Singh, 'UK industry and the world economy: a case of de-industrialisation', *Cambridge Journal of Economics*, Vol. 1; no. 2, 1977, p. 132.

116. Ibid., p. 135.
117. Ibid., p. 134; for a general survey of the 'de-industrialisation' problem, see F. Blackaby, *De-industrialisation*, London, Heinemann, 1978.
118. T.F. Cripps and W.F. Godley, 'Control of imports as a means to full employment and the expansion of world trade: the UK case', *Cambridge Journal of Economics*, Vol. 2, no. 3, 1978, p. 328.
119. Ibid.
120. Ibid., p. 331
121. Ibid., pp. 331–2; note, in this regard, the view of the West German Banking Federation, that 'One cannot hitch the German economy before world business as a locomotive and at the same time worsen the [German] competitive position.' (*The Guardian*, 14 Febraury 1978).
122. Ibid., p. 332. Here we should perhaps add the beginnings of a 'neo-Ricardian' critique of orthodox theory to this catalogue which, while accepting many of the standard assumptions, attempts to relate domestic growth theory to the external constraint and concludes that 'except by fluke, full employment growth is inconsistent with balanced trade' but 'requires that capital funds be exported or imported according to circumstances'. (J.S. Metcalf and I. Steedman, 'Growth and distribution in an open economy', in Steedman, op. cit., p. 225). The relevance of this argument to the Keynesian position set out above and the structuralist case developed below is clear. A very recent and undoubtedly important addition to the argument is R.R. Neild, 'Managed trade between industrial countries', in R. Major, *Britain's trade and exchange rate policy*, London, Heinemann Educational Books, 1979.
123. W.A. Lewis, *The theory of economic growth*, London, Allen & Unwin, 1955, pp. 348ff.
124. T. Balogh, *The economics of poverty*, London, Weidenfeld and Nicolson, 1955, esp. Chapter 1; G. Myrdal, *Development and underdevelopment*, National Bank of Egypt, 50th Anniversary Commemoration Lectures, Cairo, 1956.
125. For a general outline of the argument see R. Prebisch, 'Commercial policy in the underdeveloped countries', *American Economic Review*, Vol. 49, no. 2, 1959; for a powerful critique of the empirical basis of the assertion see P. Bauer, *Dissent on development*, London, Weidenfeld, 1971.
126. Prebisch, op. cit., p. 252.
127. Ibid., p. 255.
128. Ibid., p. 257.
129. N. Kaldor, 'Dual exchange rates and economic development', in *Essays in economic policy*, Vol. II, London, Duckworth, 1964, Chapter 19.
130. Prebisch, *Change and development*, p. 182.

Part II
The Roots of Uneven Development and Structural Disintegration

3 The Dynamics of Uneven Development

The normal case of modern industry [involves] an increasing productivity of labour and the operation of a larger quantity of means of production by fewer labourers.

(K. Marx, *Capital*, Vol. III, p. 58)

Chapters 1 and 2 attempted to set out the theoretical and institutional requirements for the evolution of an integrated and stable international monetary and trading system based upon competitive capitalist market relations. They attempted to demonstrate the correspondence between the analysis and prescriptions provided by neoclassical theory and the political structures and practices developed at the international level to manage the economic exchanges between nations. They also attempted to demonstrate the intellectual coherence and power of this construct without reference to the fact that the degree of unity and stability in international economic relations that it assumes no longer exists, and that its proponents show less and less confidence in their ability to restore them. Given this failure however, we must now question the ability of the existing international economic order and its theoretical correlate to survive in a world in which governments are being increasingly driven towards the adoption of the policies of ultra-nationalism which destroyed the unity of the capitalist order in the 1930s and led directly towards world war. These conditions create an obvious opening for the evolution of a radical critique of a structure of theory and practice which, whatever its rigour and past success, is so evidently unable to cope with the present crisis.

Bourgeois theories are concerned to demonstrate how a system moves from one equilibrium position to the next and are therefore concerned to identify the conditions required to sustain the stability of economic, political and social systems. Given crisis conditions, however, the problem must become the explanation of disequilibrium – the evident inability to sustain reciprocal relations within a system and its corresponding tendency towards dislocation and the intensification of conflict. To do this we must identify the factors operating in the real world that contradict the equilibrium assumptions of bourgeois theory and produce the inequalities and disproportionalities which now undermine the unity and integrity of the system, and provide the basis for a more adequate understanding than can be derived from the orthodox analysis.

Marx's analysis of the nature of the crisis tendencies in capitalism is the obvious starting-point for this task, but it must be complemented by a consideration of trade theory (which hardly appears in *Capital* at all) and of the implications of the transition from competitive to monopoly capitalism which has taken place since his work was completed. With these additions it should be possible to demonstrate both the direct relevance of classical Marxism to the issues raised in bourgeois trade and monetary theory and its much greater capacity to come to terms with the reality which now confronts us. What we are concerned with is two very different views of the functioning of capitalist society and of how it is to be understood; what we have now to consider is how exactly they can be differentiated.

Some Theoretical Presuppositions
Bourgeois theory is, as we have seen, primarily a way of understanding capitalism as a process of *exchange* between a series of individuals (persons, firms or countries) which relate to each other as autonomous and formally equal agents. Indeed, the arguments outlined in Chapter 2 suggest that it goes further than this in that it asserts that where these exchanges are allowed to take the optimum form (that characterised as 'perfect competition'), they will tend to generate an *even* distribution of activity and resources world-wide. The implications of Hume's examination of the balance of payments, of Ricardo's demonstration of the tendency towards comparative advantage in trade

and of the Heckscher–Ohlin–Samuelson (H–O–S) argument that free trade must equalise factor prices world-wide all point in this direction. At the most general level we can read the same implications into Say's law, the basis of neoclassical theory, which necessarily involves a tendency towards full employment equilibrium where the 'natural' tendency for supply to create its own demand is allowed to operate. This theory has been rigorously tested for more than a century and survived so there is little point in attempting to 'attack the internal consistency of its logical structure'; instead we must 'demonstrate the unreality of its fundamental empirical assumptions',[1] and show how the introduction of new ones produces results that do provide us with a more adequate insight into what is happening. If we are not to open 'a non-discriminating sniping at the orthodox adversary all along the line of the argument'[1] we must begin by identifying the points at which the argument is most vulnerable.

Now many Marxist critics commonly argue the irrelevance of bourgeois theory because of its static nature and its emphasis on relations of exchange rather than production. There is some truth in these assertions, but they are usually pressed to the point where they genuinely falsify and underestimate the strength of the bourgeois argument which can be shown to have fundamental implications for the nature of the process of capitalist development. Thus while the central emphasis of the H–O–S analysis may well be 'on the scarcity of the goods in *given* supply' so that it 'has said rather little about the continuous expansion of output',[2] it nevertheless *implies* a great deal about the dynamic consequences for production of the processes set in motion by trade, including, most fundamentally the assertion that 'subject to certain assumptions, free trade would equalise factor prices completely',[3] itself. The method being used is in fact comparative statics which *does* make predictions about the dynamic consequences of policy choices as is perfectly clear both in the policy model described in Chapter 2 and more especially in its use by the IMF and governments in dealing with balance of payments crises. The fact that the implicit arguments about growth and production are not clearly developed does not mean that they do not exist and are not taken into account when practical problems have to be confronted. The real problem with the theory is not that these elements are absent, but that, because of the unreality of the fundamental assumptions, they cannot be dealt with adequately and are never effectively confronted. The critical difference between Marxist and bourgeois theory is not that the former is concerned with dynamic production relations and the latter not, but that it brings more realistic assumptions to bear on the problem.

The fundamental weakness of bourgeois theory is not that it ignores dynamic changes in production relations, but that it assumes that capitalist development will take a particular form – one characterised by *even* development throughout the system, *reciprocal* benefits to all of those engaged in its exchange relationships, and *equilibrium* solutions to the input–output equations generated by the evolution of the international division of labour. This theory of *even development* emerges logically and consistently from an examination of the interactions generated by a situation of perfect competition. If we wish to produce an alternative theory of *uneven development* we must identify and consider the dynamic implications of the key factor which introduces imperfections into competition by leading to the processes of unequal accumulation which make it possible for some producers and centres of economic activity to grow more rapidly than others. Now there can be little doubt that the key weakness of bourgeois theorists lies in their inability to incorporate the existence of *scale economies* (otherwise expressed as increasing returns or diminishing costs) into their argument since, by so doing, they necessarily ignore the fundamental dynamic element in the nature of the capitalist growth process. Once this problem is incorporated into the argument we can demonstrate both the relationship between Marx's analysis of the rising organic composition of capital and trade theory, and produce the basis for a more adequate theory of *combined and uneven development* and of the corresponding tendency of the system to move towards disequilibrium and crises unless some form of external political force is available to offset these tendencies. This should enable us to provide a more adequate understanding of the reasons for both *the relative success of the Bretton Woods system during the period that the imperial power of the USA was able to provide this external support, and of its subsequent failure once that ability had disappeared*, the focus of the substantive section of this work.

The rest of this chapter will therefore attempt to provide a theoretical basis for an understanding of the relationship between free trade and uneven development which underlies the collapse of the Bretton Woods compromise and the failures of the various attempts to reform it from within. It will begin with an examination of the way in which scale economies manifest themselves at the international level, consider the historical evidence for the claim that the tendency towards agglomeration rather than equalisation has been predominant in the overall trajectory of capitalist development, and finally show how the introduction of this more realistic assumption into the argument undermines the neoclassical trade equations, and creates the possibility of losses from trade, the likelihood of a disjunction between supply and demand, and the necessity for social intervention to plan trade in weaker centres to offset these negative tendencies. Chapter 4 will then consider in more detail the implications of the resulting growth of monopoly power for the ability of TNCs to manipulate international costs and prices, and in relation to the evident inability of monetarist solutions to come to terms with the present crisis.

The Nature of Scale Economies
Increasing returns can be said to prevail where average costs are a decreasing function of output. Before we can relate this apparently simple proposition to trade theory, however, we must look in some detail at the nature of the entity undergoing the cost reductions and at the way in which they are generated, focusing on dynamic processes rather than the static ones which generally characterise neoclassical analysis in this field. For orthodox exchange theory the protagonists are formally equal individual and firms at the national, and nation states at the international level. With significant scale economies, however, formal equality must disappear because some competitors must then become significantly more powerful than others for reasons which will be considered in Chapter 4. To understand the resulting tendency towards agglomeration we must therefore consider how this process affects the productive capacity of the various actors involved in the economic process.

International trade involves three levels of activity, those at the plant, the firm, and the nation. Different factors can be seen to operate at each of these levels with varying implications for the nature of the international growth process. *Internal* economies at the level of the plant will derive from the exploitation of mass production techniques involving the specialisation of labour, machinery and management,[4] and the accumulation of knowledge as to the optimal operation of the plant acquired through experience. *External* economies, on the other hand, will result from access to credit and to cheap inputs of wage goods and capital equipment resulting from easy access to other suppliers, and from the availability of social infrastructure (communications, education, research, law and order, etc.) which will reduce the cost and increase the efficiency of their general operation. Internal *firm* economies on the other hand will relate to the scale of management, distribution, the acquisition of inputs,[5] and the organisation of research and development facilities.[6] External firm economies will be mainly located in the access to professional and other services required at the managerial level, access to large scale credit facilities, and to the communications and social and educational services required to maintain a high level manpower division able to sustain a span of control of international dimensions.

The distinction between firm and plant is of particular importance at the international level because different effects will be experienced when the tendencies to concentration operate at one level rather than the other. Where the greatest economies result from an increase in *plant* size the tendency towards uneven development is likely to be at its strongest. Here countries first in the field will find themselves with plants which, by exploiting their ability constantly to reduce costs, will be able systematically to eliminate the possibility of setting up new plants in other countries unless these can be given protection and access to a sufficiently large market to enable them to achieve the minimum scale required to begin. The tendency is likely to be less severe when the main economies lie at the level of the firm, while the structure of technology makes it possible to operate relatively small plants profitably. Here one would expect the head office to be located in a city providing the external economies outlined above, but with actual productive activity widely distributed in small plants located in a number of countries. Here the parent country will clearly benefit from the spending generated by the activities directly associated with the firm's headquarters, but these effects will be considerably offset if the pressure to decentralise actual production is strong.

Scale economies of these kinds can therefore have real effects on the evolution of production relations at different points on the globe and thus on the trade relations between them. Yet it is also clear that this does not yet demonstrate the necessity for the emergence of uneven development defined as a tendency for the productivity of certain regions or countries to grow more rapidly than others. If one assumes that the existence of increasing returns does not upset the Say's law assumption and that a 'balance' or 'proportionality' can be sustained between the various activities concerned as, for example, Young does in a classic article, then there is no reason why 'an increase in the supply of one commodity' will not become 'an increase in the demand for other commodities',[7] and that a generalised process of very rapid expansion will not be induced world-wide. Where plant economies are strong this will lead to a tendency towards regional specialisation for the reasons set out above, but, given free trade, new plants relating to new activities will be attracted to underdeveloped regions because of the existence of underutilised resources there and the possibility of exporting their output to the whole world. Where firm economies are dominant and plant size can be kept down the situation is likely to be even more favourable for the reasons set out in the preceding paragraph. To take the problem a step further we have therefore to devise some means of giving it a *spatial* and *political* dimension by identifying the variables which given particular locations, and most especially those characterised as *nations* in the sense defined by Johnson in the previous Chapter 2 (note 37), a cumulative advantage in the competitive struggle to attract and sustain productive activities. Why should any region become a 'centre for accumulation',[8] able to attract an exceptional number both of the large firms capable of generating scale economies and usually of small ones as well? To answer this question we must look more closely at the way in which such economies are generated.

Here it is critical that we distinguish between the effects of internal as opposed to external economies. All scale economies are in the last analysis *time* economies in that they enable the producer to reduce the socially necessary labour time (whether embedded in existing capital goods or labour) involved in the creation of the product, thereby reducing unit costs.[9] Internal economies are specific to the individual firm and allow it to reduce costs by expanding output, thereby reducing prices and increasing market penetration. These economies will not lead to agglomeration by themselves, but will only do so where they can be shown to be associated with *location specific* external economies which reduce the costs of inputs or increase the demand for the output of the firms occupying a particular space. Where these exist a tendency towards uneven development and unequal trade *must* emerge.

External economies derive from the social effects of the internal economies secured by particular firms, and from the social capital and organisational economies generated by the state. In considering the first of these, we can see that the outputs of any one firm constitute the inputs of the others, whether in the form of capital equipment or wage goods. Thus its ability to reduce costs and prices becomes an external economy for its neighbour which will enable it to produce more cheaply even at the same level of output. Thus the existence of a particularly efficient producer or group of producers at a particular location will attract others to the area in order to secure the advantage of immediate access to cheap inputs. Unless locational diseconomies emerge (for example those of 'rent and congestion'[10]) or there are immobile factors or resources involved, this tendency will therefore become cumulative as more and more economies in the production of inputs will be generated there. Secondly, this process will automatically increase market size in the region and thereby guarantee the existence of the minimum level of demand required to justify the very large investments required to exploit the full effects of scale, thereby reducing costs of circulation as well as the uncertainty involved in the investment decision. To be effective, these tendencies must also be complemented through the intervention of a state capable of creating and maintaining the 'social capital' necessary to sustain this growth of activity in the private sector. Health, education, primary research, communications, law and order, foreign affairs, and much else has to be provided collectively and to operate at a certain level before a large and technologically sophisticated industrial base can be created. Here again the minimum costs of providing these facilities at an adequate level are very high so that they cannot be infinitely disaggregated. Further, their provision must be financed through taxes on the productive activities located in the area subjected to the state's jurisdiction, so that the ability to extend them depends upon the scale of operation which has already been achieved. The income of many African states would not be sufficient to finance the operation of a single large American university. It is therefore inconceivable that any of them could create the infrastructure required to sustain anything like a modern industrial structure. Further, once we move outside the free trade framework into a more realistic world where states are actively involved in managing trade through overt and covert protectionism and the provision of more or less direct subsidies to domestic producers, we can see that all of the advantages lie with those that command the greatest taxable resources and whose producers have unrestricted access to the largest home markets. Had the developed world been willing to allow free access to industrial imports from third world countries the international division of labour would have developed very differently. For as long as state intervention can have decisive effects both on the cost of domestic production and on the terms of access to the largest concentrations of purchasing power, however, all of the advantages remain with the established centres of accumulation.

The uninterrupted operation of these forces must produce a

tendency towards the intensification of international concentration, but it is important to note that this has to be seen as a *tendency* rather than an inescapable law of motion. If economies always outweighed diseconomies the whole productive capacity of the world that did not require access to immobile factors would be concentrated in a single firm in a single country. If, however, we are to be able to understand the circumstances that give rise to the emergence of new centres (for example the Newly Industrialising Countries (NICs)), or to the relative decline of old ones (for example Great Britain and the USA), we have to be able to develop an effective theory of the 'counter-tendencies' to the concentration process.[11] Having done this it will be possible to evaluate the relative strength of each and establish the reasons for the predominance of one or the other at particular points in time. To do this adequately would be a very substantial under-taking, here we can merely point to what seem to be the key variables involved and the nature of the broad tendencies which have emerged at the international level in the immediate past. We can again begin by looking at the issues involved at the level of plant, firm and region/nation.

Neoclassical theory attempts to evade the problem of scale econ-omies by assuming the existence of an optimum size of plant and firm beyond which diseconomies will emerge, and that the effect of ex-ternal economies will be spatially diffuse rather than specific. While neither of these assertions are adequate, they do suggest considera-tions that will have significant effects in the real world. With a given range of technological options, an optimum size of plant will exist for each.[12] Further, with the emergence of capital saving technology (in Marx's terms the 'cheapening of the elements of constant capital'[13]), it may be possible for a new plant to come into existence requiring a smaller investment and a lower output than existing plants to secure a particular level of costs. Thus where optimum size has been achieved in any area, increased output will generate diminishing returns and require the introduction of an additional one and thus create the possibility of de-concentration. Where new low cost options emerge the possibility will be even greater, especially where the small unit can be more competitive than the large one.

Some empirical substantiation of the operation of this tendency can be derived from Blair's major study of economic concentration in the USA. Here he argues that the technological impetus toward plant growth was dominant from the late nineteenth century until the end of the 1930s, but that this was followed by the introduction of 'new technologies' which made possible 'economic production with smaller capital outlays, thereby reducing barriers to entry, stimulating the entrance of newcomers, and lending a strong impetus to the restoration of competition'.[14] It is also possible that the emergence of microchip technology may operate in the same way, thereby reducing the minimum size of market required to justify a new unit in a particular sector, thus allowing the establishment of facilities in small countries which would previously have been impossible. While it will be possible to demonstrate that the claims made for these processes have been greatly exaggerated, it is nevertheless true that they lie behind the success of much of the import substitution, and export promotion activity which has created some important centres of accumulation in a limited number of relatively successful third world countries since World War II.

Secondly, it is true that some external economies will be spatially diffuse, so that the economies generated in centres of accumulation will be passed on to producers elsewhere, thus enabling them to cheapen their costs and compete more effectively. Thus Marshall, for example, argued that external economies would be 'accessible to any branch of production',[15] and would therefore have no effect upon the relative competitive advantages which any group of producers enjoyed. As a general statement Marshall's proposition is clearly untenable, but it is nevertheless important that we identify the factors which do operate in this direction. Thus the economies associated with a reduction in the cost of inputs through the increased efficiency of the private sector in a particular locality will be diffused more generally to the extent that the costs of communication and obstacles to circulation have been minimised, thus also minimising the advantages to be derived from spatial proximity. Major improvements have taken place since World War II, and these have allowed new producers in underdeveloped countries to acquire new technology in the form of advanced capital goods and managerial inputs at a cost very much less than that which would have been involved in developing them for themselves. Complementary to these advantages on the supply side are those derived from access to the large markets of the developed centres which enable some new producers to initiate activities in small countries on a scale far larger than would have been possible in relation to the home market alone, with corresponding reductions in cost of production and increases in competitiveness.

Economies derived from the provision of public investment are perhaps less likely to be externalised as most of them are very consciously directed at the improvement in the relative efficiency of a particular national and therefore spatial unit. Yet even here diffusion does take place. Thus the access of third world students to universities in the advanced countries, and the availability of their technical personnel at much less than the full cost of their production, can transfer productive capacity to new centres at less than full cost, provided the skills involved are relevant to the conditions prevailing in the new environment. Again, an improvement in communications in the developed centre cheapens the cost of delivering imports to it, while the wide publication of the results of fundamental research can also initiate improvements elsewhere. Further, this process can be directly extended where governments in developed regions are willing to transfer productive capacity directly through the operation of aid programmes, or where they are prepared to improve the access to their markets by reducing the tariff and monetary obstacles previously blocking the access of producers in less developed regions. While aid expenditure has been relatively stagnant over the past few years it has certainly been greater since World War II than at any previous period in history, while it is also true that third world exporters have gained directly, though probably not as much as those in developed regions, from the process of liberalisation of monetary and trade restrictions which has been such a marked feature of the 1960s and 1970s.

Given these factors it is therefore perfectly possible to imagine a process of 'catching up' in less developed regions with the emergence of new centres of accumulation potentially able to displace some of the existing industries of those already established. Bourgeois theorists place virtually all of the emphasis on this side of the argument, and, for example, now use the relative success of the NICs (Brazil, Taiwan, Korea, etc.) as evidence for the assertion that open trade can promote development everywhere provided only that the monetarist prescriptions set out in Chapter 2 are adhered to.[16] Given the critical political importance of this analysis which dominates both international agencies and the thinking of most of the governments in the capitalist system, it is essential that realistic balance be struck between these tendencies towards diffusion, and those producing concentration examined earlier.

The Tendency towards Agglomeration

The historical evidence in this field points decisively in one direction. Kuznets notes a general tendency over 'the last century to century and a half' for per capita product to grow 'much more rapidly' in developed than in less developed countries, despite the fact that the former took off from a higher initial level.[17] His figures gave the underdeveloped world 67.6 per cent of world population and 16.9 per cent of world income in 1949,[18] those of the Club of Rome 71.4 per cent of population as against 19.3 per cent of income in 1973, though now with Japan excluded.[19] The differences between the performances of the small number of NICs and the rest of the third world within these figures are also very large, so that the disparities between the developed world and the great mass of the underdeveloped are even more dramatic than these figures suggest. An overall view of the evolution of the international division of labour therefore suggests that the operation of the tendencies to decentralisation is much weaker than those towards concentration. We can identify some of the reasons for this by looking more closely at the operation of the former, mainly in relation to the recent development of the third world where growth would have had to be most rapid to generate a movement towards the kind of 'even development' pre-supposed by bourgeois theory.

There can be no doubt that the emergence of capital-saving technology and improvements in communication have created the possibility of effective import substitution and export promotion strategies in a few centres in the NICs in the immediate past and in previous 'newcomers' such as the former British Dominions in an earlier phase. Yet the assumption that this process can be universalised leaves out of account a number of critical variables. Increasing scale economies arise in Marxist terms from a rising organic composition of capital (ROC) involving an increase in the ratio of capital assets to living labour in the production process,[20] and producing a transition from small-scale 'manufacturing' industry to large-scale 'machinofacture' involving a total transformation of both the organisation of the workforce and of its relationship to its raw materials.[21] During the early phase of capitalist industrialisation when, according to Blair, plant size was constantly expanding, the bulk of the third world was colonised and local manufacturing of any kind strongly discouraged. The new capital-saving technologies emerged during the transition to independence after World War II and made it possible for many nationalist governments to acquire a range of production facilities for simple consumer goods. Here 'machinofacture' was being used in small units in terms of actual plant size as measured by the number of workers involved, but the productivity of the processes involved was such that the *scale of output* was very large, especially when compared to that of the craft or 'manufacturing' processes employing similar numbers of workers in the same sectors and countries which these new activities tended to displace. The more recent transition from 'machinofacture' to automation must simply extend this process since, as Barratt Brown notes:

> The introduction of numerical control machine tools had increased productivity per machine by as much as 600 to 700 per cent and have often permitted each man to operate two or even three machines where one was operated before, or permitted semi-skilled labour to operate where skilled men were needed before.[22]

The introduction into any third world country of even the smallest viable plant utilising modern methods must therefore have a dramatic effect upon the position of existing producers employing earlier methods. Thus de Coninck shows how the establishment of a modern shoe plant undermined existing craft producers in Uganda, and Langdon how the introduction of a foreign controlled soap plant undermined existing local manufacturers in Kenya.[23] This tendency must lead to a process of regional concentration where the country is large enough to sustain at least one viable unit, to a process of international concentration where it is not. Further, the members of the 'small is beautiful' school rarely take into account the actual range of activities in which production has still to be organised on a massive scale even by the standards of the already developed regions where no underdeveloped country can hope to compete where open competition is allowed. Thus Nurske points out that few LDCs can

> capture through domestic production the tremendous economies of scale that arise from the mass production of steel, machinery and transport equipment in the advanced developed countries. Over 90 per cent of the total investment going on in the world (outside the Soviet Union area) now takes place in the industrial countries.[24]

No doubt the proportion has improved somewhat during the 1960s and 1970s, but the dominance of the established western centres continues to intensify.

This argument clearly demonstrates the inadequacy of the neoclassical equilibrium assumption of optimum firm size and corresponding tendency for diseconomies to set in. It may be true that an individual firm making a specific investment choice is confronted with an array of production possibilities, each of them implying an optimum scale of output with corresponding diseconomies setting in once that level has been reached. But this ignores the fact that the plant will be competing with other plants potentially able to take advantage of locational factors to choose an existing technology guaranteeing lower costs with a higher output: this would lead to dynamic consequences in the form of the growth of a competing centre able to undercut and destroy it. Equally important, it leaves out of consideration the fact that new technologies are always emerging that are capable of extending 'the range over which economies of scale apply',[25] which can then be adopted where locational factors are most favourable, and disrupt all of the equilibrium conditions which made for the feasibility of a production structure based upon an optimum size derived from an earlier technological phase. The destructive implications of these changes for the operation of Say's law will be considered in a later section, here it is simply important to note that they point towards the correctness of Schumpeter's analysis of capitalism as a dynamic process of 'creative destruction' with an intrinsic tendency towards concentration and disequilibrium.[26]

This line of argument is further consolidated if we consider further the relationship between firm and plant size which was excluded from our examination of the centrifugal tendencies because almost all of the variables at the higher level point in the other direction. Because of important economies in the fields of marketing, technology control, management, and access to capital Blair concedes that the tendency towards declining plant size 'has *not* been accompanied by any similar tendency on the part of the largest companies'.[27] Thus he notes that the 'share of value added accounted for by the 200 largest companies' in the USA increased from 30 to 40 per cent between 1947 and 1966,[28] while Holland notes an increase in the share of the top hundred from a fifth to 'some half of net manufacturing output' between 1950 and the early 1970s in Britain.[29] It is well known that these firms are becoming increasingly multinational in their sphere of operation, and that an increasing proportion of industry in the third world is coming to be 'controlled by the subsidiaries of foreign corporations whose local sales in many cases increase faster than those of nationally owned firms ... or than the country's overall economic activity', with the result that foreign control 'of the more dynamic Latin American sectors', for example, is 'somewhere between 50 and 75 per cent.[30] Thus the form taken by the decentralising process based upon declining plant size is one which involves a greatly intensified centralisation of the control of economic activities with decisions concentrated in the hands of a tiny group of executives mainly located in the dominant industrial centres.

Neoclassical theorists characteristically discount the negative effects of foreign control over domestic resources because the individualistic nature of their theory makes them treat any producer as directly equivalent to any other. Yet there can be no doubt that the tendency towards transnationalisation and monopoly involved in the evolution of late capitalism must have dramatic effects upon both the tendencies towards uneven development and dislocation. A voluminous literature now demonstrates its damaging consequences for the possibilities of an autonomous industrialisation process in the third world.[31] Here Sunkel, for example notes its tendency to create an increase in internal polarisation between 'modern dominant advanced economic activities, social groups and regions on the one hand, and backward, marginal and dependent activities, groups and regions on the other', and an intensification of external dependence and weakness characterised by:

(a) a persistence and even worsening of the primary exporting character of the economy; (b) exogenous source of the economy's dynamism; (c) exogenous character of most of the fundamental centres of decision in finance, economic policy, science and technology, access to foreign markets, etc.; (d) acute and persistent tendency to foreign indebtedness, denationalisation and subsidisation; (e) a great danger of Latin American integration efforts ending up in favour of transnational conglomerates: a definitive liquidation of the remaining local enterprise; (f) a growing income gap between developed and underdeveloped countries.[32]

Small national firms cannot secure the cost and marketing economies available to equivalent sized subsidiaries of TNCs, nor can they match their ability to adopt larger-scale technologies when either an expansion in the scale of the market or a change in the technological possibilities requires the movement upward to a qualitatively higher scale of operation. Most important, they cannot match the resources required to generate a global production process capable of centralising huge quantities of resources, taking full advantage of what Adam calls 'international sourcing' with respect to the supply of their inputs,[33] using their international linkages to evade the controls imposed on them by nation-states attempting to limit the external leakages which they generate,[34] and exerting considerable controls over total output in their field thus enabling them to act to some degree as price makers rather than price takers. This later point is of crucial importance in undermining the Say's law assumptions of neoclassical theory and its implications for dislocation will be developed in Chapter 4.

When we then come to consider the relative effects of public investment on the rate of accumulation, in strong as opposed to weak centres, we can also see that the balance of advantage is even more uneven. It would be impossible to quantify the relative benefits accruing to local as opposed to foreign producers from the provision of local infrastructure, but it is clear that the vast bulk of this investment goes directly into the strengthening of local productive capacity, and the external benefits are little more than the crumbs fallen almost inadvertently from the master's table. The provision of aid is little more, is declining, and is characteristically used to resolve the problems of the donor country by funding the export of inappropriate technology which is usually highly inefficient and serves to sustain local inequalities and the power relations which maintain them. The net flow of capital since World War II has been *from* the less *to* the more developed world from the beginning of the colonial experience, since direct plunder and more recently the payment of dividends, royalties and interest have always outweighed the flows moving in the other direction.[36] Again, the willingness of strong countries to reduce the obstacles to circulation which increase access to their markets and their control over credit, gives them immense leverage in international trade and monetary negotiations. For reasons that will become clear in the next section, the overall tendency towards concentration is such that it is the strong which benefit from free trade more than the weak. Small countries in fact *need* trade more than strong ones. Indeed, Kuznets argues, they 'can attain economic growth *only* through heavy reliance on foreign trade'.[37] Yet if they allow free access to their markets, established foreign producers will wipe out their infant industries so that they can only develop effectively if they are given preferential access to foreign markets and can establish an effective range of the *controls* over their own imports which will enable them to *plan* non-contradictory expansion in both imports and domestic output. Yet the strong countries have used their political leverage to push the international agencies, and indeed the mass of the economics profession, towards the free trade policies which must have disastrous effects on industrial activities in weak centres and have even insisted on controls on imports from low wage countries when these threaten vulnerable sectors in their own economies.

None of the above precludes the possibility of the emergence of new centres of accumulation, nor of the relative decline of old ones. Capitalism involves an inherently 'discontinuous development of the division of labour and of the instruments of labour'[38] which must have dynamic spatial effects. Where a national economy is able to expand, through whatever mechanisms (and these will characteristically require the ability to sustain a more effective process of super-exploitation of its work- force than that of its neighbours), then it may be the case that 'if they can produce at a sufficiently high level of capacity utilisation they can produce unit costs so low that the consequent adjustment problems will fall on the shoulders of their competitors'.[39] The latter, and more especially those who have been unable to sustain a sufficiently high level of surplus extraction and reinvestment, will then move into a period of relative decline so that the overall structure of the international division of labour will be altered. But this process, viewed by liberals as the validation of their assumption that the system will always tend to move back into equilibrium, in fact merely involves violent alteration in its topography, which must impose a heavy burden of adjustment on the shoulders of strong and weak but more so on the latter.

All of this evidence therefore strongly supports Murray's assertion that the nature of capitalist development must lead to concentration not merely at the level of plant and firm but also at that of region and state, and that the strength of the dominant 'agglomerative tendencies' derives mainly from the existence of the 'agglomerations themselves'.[40] Technically, we can therefore see that developing the notion of scale economies in this way, and relating it to the necessity to create an integrated production structure of private and public enterprise in a particular locality of international competitiveness is to be sustained, gives us a far more powerful insight into the operation of unequal trade and the emergene of uneven development than do bourgeois conceptions which leave these considerations entirely out of account, and even Marxist analyses which attribute the inequalities to unequal wages between countries.[41] This, too, enables us to give a substantive content to Balogh's notion of 'infant countries and regions'[42] which is in fact clearly spelled out technically by Leontief and historically by Kuznets. Thus Leontief argues:

> The larger and more advanced an economy is, the more complete and articulated is its structure. The US and western Europe respectively produce about a third and a quarter of the world's total output of goods and services. It is not surprising, therefore, that their input–output tables yield the same triangulation [structure of input–output relationships].[43]

It is this input–output structure which constitutes that of 'a fully developed economy,' whereas 'an underdeveloped economy can now be defined as underdeveloped to the extent that it lacks the working parts of this system'.[43] Kuznets then arrives at a formulation very similar to this, attributing historical differences in performance between countries to a shift in activity from agriculture to industry where

> the increasing use of mechanised power, the greater control over materials, and the greater articulation of the underlying basic knowledge, made for greater economies of scale, and for an optimum size of industrial plants far larger than that of pre-modern times .... And the economic requirement of such large-scale industrial production – for labour force and capital, not only for itself but for the necessary 'infrastructure' (the supplementary complex of transportation, communication and other facilities) – is different from that of small-scale industry.[44]

This analysis provides a crude but realistic impression of a world in which trade and monetary exchanges occur between unequal centres of activity in which the strongest can, by collectively exploiting locationally specific scale economies, generate a *cumulative* process of uneven development at the international level. Given the critical role of the state in providing many of the necessary services and in guaranteeing the general conditions for production in the private sector, it is evident that the resulting dynamic is inherently political and national in character. The neoclassical representation of a political world in which exchanges take place between formally equal, individualistic actors subjected to diminishing returns and perfect competition takes on the quality of an elegant and rigorous science fiction when compared to it. Yet the conclusions derived from this exposition of the interactions which might be taking place on some other planet are being used by the IMF and the majority of national governments to justify policies which must have the most damaging consequences in the world we do inhabit. What we have now to do, therefore, is show how the introduction of these considerations into the neoclassical trade model causes it to collapse, and thereafter to develop the implications of this collapse for of our understanding of the disintergration of the post-war economic order.

Free Trade and Uneven Development

Orthodox trade theory assumes the international immobility of factors, perfect competition, full employment and constant or diminishing returns to scale. In perhaps the most reproduced example in all economic literature – that devised by Ricardo – it is possible to demonstrate that the principle of comparative advantage operates in these circumstances to ensure that both parties benefit from trade even where absolute costs are higher in all sectors in one than the other. Haberler has provided us with a very condensed exposition of the example:

> In England a gallon of wine which costs 120 and a yard of cloth 100 hours of work, while in Portugal the real cost (labour cost) of wine and cloth amounts to 80 and 90 hours of work respectively. Portugal thus has an absolute advantage over England in the production of either commodity, but a comparatively greater one in the production of wine, since 80/120 < 90/100. Without trade the internal ratio of the prices of wine and cloth... would be proportional to their costs of production, that is, 120:100 in England and 80:90 (or 88.8:100) in Portugal. Thus cloth is comparatively cheap in England and wine is comparatively cheap in Portugal. After trade is opened between the two countries, England will export cloth and import wine. Ignoring transport costs, an equilibrium price ('real exchange ratio' or 'terms of trade') will result which will lie between the limits of 120:100 and 88.8:100. Let us assume, for example, that the equilibrium ratio of exchange is 100:100. If England now specialises in the production of cloth *and transfers labour from agriculture into industry*, it can produce 1.2 units of cloth for each unit of wine which it no longer produces. These units of cloth could now be exchanged for 1.2 units of wine imported from Portugal– with a resulting net gain of 0.2 units of wine for each unit of cloth exported. Alternatively, the same quantity of goods produced before trade occurred could now be produced at lower total real costs.[45] (emphasis added)

Thus strong and weak alike benefit from the move from autarchy to trade, free trade must produce the 'maximisation of world income',[46] and the extent and increase in international trade becomes 'the principal guarantee of the peace of the world'.[47]

The method of comparative statics is used here: an analysis of the dynamic processes implied in the transition from the conditions prevailing under autarchy to those of trade has to be derived from an examination of the probable changes in resource allocation given the existence of the original assumptions. To demonstrate the weakness of the analysis it is therefore necessary to describe these consequences in order to be able to demonstrate how they must change once new assumptions are introduced. We must thus first look at these processes with constant or diminishing returns, then with increasing returns to scale.

Before trade full employment prevails in both countries. Once it begins both wine and cloth producers in Portugal could sell their output at a higher price in England, where costs and therefore prices must be higher, but it is the wine producers who will benefit because they have the comparative advantage. They will therefore export a portion of the wine which was formerly sold locally, and will need to expand output to satisfy local demand. Given fixed proportions between labour and capital they will only be able to do this by a transfer of labour from the cloth sector and the country will then have to import the resulting shortfall in local cloth output from England despite the higher prices prevailing there. The increased returns on wine more than compensate the society as a whole for the resulting losses and the process goes on until Portugal's advantage in wine production over that of England has been fully exploited, with the outer limit being full specialisation in both countries. In England, meanwhile, the wine producers have had to cut their production because of their inability to compete with the new imports, but again an equivalent number of jobs become available in the cloth sector because of the expansion in demand. Temporary inconveniences are likely to emerge during the transitional period, but these will be more than compensated for by the long-term increases in efficiency.

Once external economies are introduced into this analysis, however, the processes change dramatically, more especially where these are of a labour saving kind. Let us now suppose that Portugal prior to trade has established a research programme in the field of viticulture which has generated new varieties and an associated production technology which dramatically increases output while reducing labour input and can only be introduced on a scale larger than that justified by the size of the domestic market. At this point England eliminates previous trade restrictions thus making it possible for the increased output to be sold there at an increased profit. The Portuguese wine producers now have more money to spend on cloth, but the Portuguese cloth producers can meet this increased demand by taking on the workers excluded from the agricultural sector as a result of technical change, and British exporters can make no headway in this market because of their higher costs. In Britain wine workers will be laid off and will remain unemployed; because of the decline in their demand cloth output will also begin to fall and a vicious deflationary cycle will ensue involving both a structural balance of payments crisis[48] and a loss in real welfare.

It is obvious that this process cannot continue indefinitely because eventually it must lead to the total impoverishment of English consumers and therefore to an end to their ability to consume imports when their supplies of foreign exchange ran out.[49] Here orthodox theory assumes that falling wages in England must lead to costs falling there to the point where one or other industry again becomes internationally competitive so that exports can be resumed and full employment and a balance of payments equilibrium restored. This therefore leads them to assume that it is *rigid wages* in deficit countries which constitute the key blockage to an effective international adjustment process,[50] and that all can be made well if what is euphemistically called 'downward flexibility' can only be produced – the clear implication of the thinking behind IMF adjustment programmes as we have already seen. If we consider the dynamic implication of the propostion we can see that it implies a constant labour/capital ratio in both countries. Where this exists the reduction in English wage costs will produce an equivalent fall in relative unit costs and increased penetration of Portuguese markets. But however rational this change might be for the system as a whole, it will neverthless be resisted by the Portuguese producers threatened with a reduction in output and potential bankruptcy. They will redouble their efforts to cut costs by introducing labour saving capital equipment since full employment will stop them from cutting wages. If they can increase the capital/labour ratio (that is to say increase the organic composition of capital) rapidly enough to offset falling English wages then the crisis will continue. The real world juxtaposition of long term surpluses and full employment at very high wages in the advanced countries, and of long term deficits and large-scale unemployment despite what are little more than starvation wages in the backward ones, suggests that wage rigidities, while perhaps contributing to the problems of adjustment in some countries, have very little to do with the general problem of unequal trade. This stems from inequalities in *unit wage costs* determined largely by the social productivity of labour stemming from levels of capital investment per worker, rather than from unequal wage *rates* which bear very little direct relation to them given the immense scale economies to be derived from modern machinery and organisational skills.[51]

The orthodox literature is largely silent on these matters though there have been periodic attempts to consider some of their implications during periods of international instability when the inadequacies of equilibrium models are being clearly exposed. Thus Neild demonstrates that

> there is the possibility that when one country, gaining the benefits of increasing returns, encroaches on the markets for manufactures of another, the latter because of diminishing returns in agriculture and the non-tradable nature of most services, may have difficulty in maintaining employment and may lose from trade.[52]

He therefore justifies a policy of managed trade. In a recent paper Krugman sets out a model where, with external economies in the industrial sector, 'a small "head start" for one region will cumulate over time, with exports of manufactures from the leading region crowding out the industrial sector of the lagging region'.[53] In the early 1950s when the dollar deficit was still a real possibility Balogh was producing the vigorous critiques of orthodoxy to which reference has already been made, and Hicks, from a far more orthodox perspective, also entered the discussion with an examination of the effect of the continuing improvement in the productivity of American industry on the position of Britain's import and export sectors. Making very few modifications of the Ricardian assumptions, he argued that if productivity gains were uniform across all industries the effect would not be harmful to Britain, but demonstrated that the weaker country must lose where productivity gains, instead of being uniform, were concentrated in the industries in the stronger country 'which compete most closely' with the exports of the weaker one.[54]

Perhaps most interesting of all is the debate initiated by 'Graham's paradox' in an article emerging out of the depressed and unstable conditions immediately after World War I. Here, by introducing diminishing costs onto one of Ricardo's boxes he shows that free trade can 'bring a situation in which the citizens of B get less reward for their efforts than if they had never carried on international trade at all',[55] again demonstrating the potential rationality of a policy of import substituting protection based on something much stronger than the pure infant industry case. Graham's argument was sufficiently powerful to elicit a response from Knight and Viner with the latter's refutation' becoming authoritative in a standard textbook,[56] despite serious deficiencies. Firstly, Viner argues that Graham failed to make an adequate distinction between internal and external economies, and accepts that a case can be made out in the latter area, although one whose applicability is 'extremely limited'.[57] However, our earlier analysis suggests the real significance of these variables in generating at the international level monopoly tendencies which create situations in which the private money cost ratios do deviate from true social real cost ratios, which are 'numerous, persistent, large and, last but not least, practically recognisable and calculable'.[58] Secondly, he sets aside Graham's numerical demonstration of relative losses in the sphere of internal economies using an entirely fallacious line of argument. Thus, while he concedes that competition must, with increasing returns, lead to monopolisation 'by a *single* concern', he claims that 'marginal rather than average cost remains the determining factor of price and no resources will be transferred from watchmaking to wheat growing if a loss in value of product results therefrom'. While competition still continues:

> Any producer of watches in country B who reduces his output of watches to produce wheat instead loses thereby the marginal output of watches and gains only the marginal increment of wheat.[59]

His fundamental error lies in the assumption that in this situation the marginal watch producer will continue to produce despite falling prices, whereas, by his own admission competition will have wiped him out in the process of turning the more efficient producer in the strong country into the 'single concern' left in the field. The fact that he is now forced to accept lower returns in wheat production (if it is possible to transfer into that sector at all rather than remain unemployed – the fate, for example, of the Indian cotton weavers in the nineteenth century destroyed by the scale economies of British power driven looms[60]) is exactly the 'recognisable and quantifiable' loss which demonstrates the deviation between individual and social gains and losses in this situation.

Given, instead, the tendency towards monopolisation in a *single country*, (and here, using the arguments relating to external economies and agglomeration developed above, we can see that this can apply to the evolution of whole centres of industrialisation monopolising productive capacity across a wide range of modern industry), this will 'bring about a situation in which the citizens of B get less reward for their efforts than if they had never carried on international trade at all'.[61] The result is clearly the need for 'a tariff to build up industries of decreasing unit cost in these countries', and hence the establishment of a 'scientific' basis for a 'commercial policy ... [to] modify the principle of comparative advantage'.[62] With equal insight Graham notes that where these conditions apply the 'relatively successful' countries have an even larger interest in free trade than they do in a Ricardian situation as their very high wages and profits depend on their ability to maximise productivity gains by saturating foreign markets, *if necessary at the expense of existing producers there*.[63] Looking at the matter in this way the paradoxial juxtaposition of free trade economists, in contrast to a protectionist world identified by Emmanuel[64] becomes explicable. The orthodox economists speak for the dominant industrial interests in the dominant countries – it is these countries, after all, which can afford the universities and even provide grants to students from countries where these conditions do not exist to acquire the 'scientific' skills required to persuade their own governments to adopt the same policies. 'The bulk of tariff policies', however, often 'blindly adopted' by politicians responding to the immediate pressures of unemployment and increasing import penetration, are actually directly concerned to achieve the results which Graham's analysis suggests.[65]

To conclude this chapter we can now attempt to consider some of the implications of this line of argument for our understanding of the process of uneven development and of its corresponding implications for international trade and monetary relations. Thus far the argument has done no more than demonstrate that free trade will lead to *uneven* development when scale economies apply to the production process in internationally traded goods. It does not necessarily imply that countries would be better off without trade since the *absolute* gains accruing from trade could outweigh those resulting from autarchy.[65] This case is at its strongest where the expansion of the leading industrial sector is strong enough to generate a rapid increase in the demand for commodities that can be produced in the primary producing sector where even the bulk of theorists who do look at increasing returns, feel that 'there will be decreasing returns to the application of extra resources'.[66] Here, in the absence of significant inelasticities in demand for primary products internationally, and with no limits to the absorption of the labour displaced from industry, it becomes possible for the weaker country to give up industry, adopt an 'agreeably' rural existence, and achieve welfare gains by constantly exchanging its output for the increasingly efficient and therefore cheaper production of foreign industry. Because in these circumstances, as Graham concedes, the total production of the whole system increases,[67] we have a confirmation of Johnson's view that trade must maximise world income (note 47) and a good 'second-best' case for remaining in the framework which presupposes trade to be optimal and that the burden of proof rests upon those who wish to introduce obstacles to it. Here we are confronting orthodox theory on its strongest ground, from which it is still possible to sustain many of the assumptions that support current national and international monetarist policies and institutions. Yet the problems are fundamental.

Firstly, even in the most favoured situation where full employment can be sustained in the weaker country, the latter is still likely to be able to benefit from some degree of protection to generate industries where productivity is greater than in agriculture yet where it is somewhat less than that which can be obtained in fully developed foreign centres able to trade world wide. The balance of advantage will depend upon a number of factors, notably the size of the domestic market, but it is impossible to say in advance that free trade will be best. Such tariff barriers will no doubt reduce welfare in the strong country and total global production, but the weaker ones can no more be expected to take this into account than they can expect the wealthy country to share some of the benefits which it secures by penetrating the markets of the poor ones. Here we do have a situation which could theoretically meet the neoclassical welfare test relating to the measurement of gains from trade, in that it produces a state in which 'everyone could be made no worse off and some be made better off than they would be in the alternative [ie. no-trade] situation, by means of appropriate compensations of income',[68] since, given the greater total world income with trade, it is technically possible for the rich to compensate the poor for the losses they incur by giving up the right to protection. Here orthodox theory legitimately assumes the likelihood of a general commitment to free trade in a situation where 'if a unanimous decision were required in order for trade to be permitted, it would always be possible for those who desired trade to buy off those opposed to trade, with the result that all could be made better off'.[69] Here we arrive at the formal statement of the problem set out in Chapter 1, that of the inadequate nature of the international political structures which attempt to reconcile the interests of the competing national entities involved in the struggle for markets and profits. We saw there that the legitimacy of the system, and the ability to forestall nationalistic interventions by governments depends directly upon the ability to compensate the weak by transferring surpluses to them in order to offset the costs that they incurred in opening up their markets in this way. And we also saw there, and will see more clearly in subsequent chapters, that the strong countries have consistently refused to make such compensations on an adequate scale and therefore made the development of adequate institutions at the international level virtually impossible. In these circumstances weak centres can legitimately adopt policies of planned or managed trade (not, of course, autarchy since we have already conceded that they depend on trade even more than the strongest centres) through which they can attempt to secure the optimum balance between the use of domestic productive resources and those they can obtain most effectively from abroad.

Secondly, the case becomes dramatically weaker when we move

from the situation where full employment applies to the much more likely case where it does not. Say's law tells us that the increased watch production in Graham's strong country will generate enough demand to ensure continued employment in the primary sector in the weak one, but this depends upon a number of untenable assumptions. These will be considered systematically in Chapter 4; here it is only possible to make a number of assertions. Firstly, the familiar terms of trade argument tells us that it is quite likely that the income elasticity of demand for primary products will be less than unity, and that the increased expenditure will go on other industrial goods which will no doubt be produced in the advanced centre where the necessary external economies exist. Secondly, with land and mineral deposits a finite resource in the primary sector, it is quite possible that it will not be able to absorb any further employment and the displaced workers will either have to become a net drain on the productive resources of those who remain in work, or will starve to death. Thirdly, scale economies are perfectly possible in the primary sector, notably in mining, but also in agriculture where immense improvements have been made in seeds, fertilisers and agricultural machinery some of which depend directly upon large scale operations and all of which dramatically increase the productivity of the labour of those who can afford to adopt them. These are mainly available in the developed regions, where, in addition, agricultural protectionism is also strong. Thus, exports from weaker producers are likely to be excluded or devalued, generating a problem of unemployment or super-exploitation on the land there. Thus Ugandan cotton producers using hand hoes must compete directly with Americans using tractors and mechanical harvesters and therefore can only be paid a few pence an hour.[70] Finally, the expectation that the level of employment in primary production can be sustained depends upon the maintenance of a very rapid rate of international growth. When this declines these areas must suffer disproportionately as they did in the 1930s and are doing again now.

Where these conditions apply the possibility of real absolute losses from trade apply and the case for controlled trade becomes overwhelming in the absence of massive real transfers of resources from rich to poor countries. Without these trade will result in a process of 'cumulative causation'[71] which will lead to continuous relative, and eventually absolute, decline in which import penetration will initiate the process of decline (or smother a potential industrial or agricultural 'take-off'), cause falling incomes and lock the population into more and more marginalised forms of activity. Unable to participate in fully developed industrial activities or to find work on the land, the population attempts to survive by various forms of hustling which are then given a formal academic status by being termed the 'informal sector' and chosen as the unlikely vehicle for a policy of redistribution with growth.[72] Once this stage is reached, of course, the strong surplus countries will find their markets collapsing because of the poverty of their potential customers, and a desperate attempt will be made to keep these in existence by international lending. But this, of course, by having to be repaid with interest, merely postpones the crisis but intensifies its effect when it finally arrives.[73] Once this situation is reached it is no longer possible to sustain all of the relationships, set out in Chapter 1, which depend upon the ability to achieve balance of payments equilibria without the use of systematic policies of import controls for nationalistic reasons. The system of both trading and monetary relationships is irreparably damaged and there must be a reversion to the autarchic and beggar-thy-neighbour policies which characterised the previous period when the capitalist world confronted the problem which resulted directly from its inability to reconcile the increasingly social nature of its forms of economic organisation with the inherently atomistic and competitive nature of its process of distribution and appropriation.

Notes

1. W. Leontief, 'Postulates: Keynes's *General Theory* and the classicists' in *Essays in Economics*, New York, Oxford University Press, 1966, p. 93.
2. I. Steedman, 'Introductory essay', in I. Steedman, ed., *Fundamental issues in trade theory*, London, Macmillan, 1979, pp. 1–2. It should be pointed out that Steedman does not make the simplistic criticism of neoclassical theory which I am identifying here.
3. M. Corden, *Recent developments in the theory of international trade*, New Jersey, Princeton University Press, 1965, p. 25.
4. See J.S. Bain, *Industrial organisation*, 2nd ed., New York, Wiley, 1968, p. 166.
5. Ibid., p. 170.
6. See E. Robinson, *The structure of competitive industry*, Cambridge, Cambridge University Press, 1958 edn., Chapter II.
7. A.A. Young, 'Increasing returns and economic progress', *Economic Journal*, Vol. 38, 1928, pp. 533–4.
8. M. Bienefeld's, 'Externalising problems in a future EEC', (mimeo), Institute of Development Studies, Sussex University, p. 21.

9. For a brilliant exposition of the problem in relation to location theory see R. Murray, 'Underdevelopment, international firms and the international division of labour', Society for international development, *Towards a new world economy*, Rotterdam, Rotterdam University Press, 1972.

10. Ibid., p. 171.

11. I am indebted to Dimitris Yannopolis, a graduate student at Sussex University, for clarification of this point.

12. For a discussion see E. Robinson, *The structure of competitive industry*, op. cit., Chapter 2.

13. K. Marx, *Capital*, vol. III, London, Lawrence and Wishart, 1972, p. 236. There is, of course, a direct relationship between the variables discussed here and Marx's 'Counteracting influences' against the 'Laws of the tendency for the rate of profit to fall'. (Ibid., Chapter XIV). Its nature will not be directly considered here, but should be clarified in the next section.

14. J.M. Blair, *Economic concentration*, New York, Harcourt Brace, 1972, p. 114.

15. A. Marshall, *Principles of economics*, 9th edn., London, Macmillan, 1961, p. 317.

16. For example, I.M.D. Little, 'Import controls and exports in developing countries', *Finance and Development*, Vol. 15, no. 3, 1978.

17. S.S. Kuznets, *Economic growth of nations*, Cambridge, Mass., Harvard University Press, 1971, p. 34.

18. S.S. Kuznets, *Economic growth and structure*, New York, Norton, 1965, p. 144.

19. A.J. Dolman, ed., *Reshaping the international order*, New York, Dutton, 1976, p. 12.

20. Marx, op. cit., pp. 71–2, 145; T. Weisskopf, 'Marxian crisis theory', *Cambridge Journal of Economics*, Vol. 3, no. 4, 1979, pp. 342–4.

21. K. Marx, *Capital*, vol. I, Harmondsworth, Penguin, 1976, especially Chapters 15 and 16; the most considerable modern treatment is H. Braverman, *Labour and monopoly capitalism*, New York, Monthly Review, 1974.

22. M. Barratt Brown, *From labourism to socialism*, Nottingham, Spokesman Books, 1972, p. 31.

23. J. deConinck, *Artisans and petty producers in Uganda*, PhD, Sussex University, 1980; S. Langdon, 'Multinational corporations, taste transfer and underdevelopment: a case study from Kenya', *Review of African Political Economy*, Vol. 2, 1975.

24. R. Nurske, *Equilibrium and growth in the world economy*, Cambridge, Mass., Harvard University Press, 1961, pp. 321–2.

25. C. Pratten et al. *The economies of large scale production in British industry*, Cambridge, Cambridge University Press, 1965, p. 99.

26. J. Schumpeter, *Capitalism, socialism and democracy*, London, Allen & Unwin, 1962.

27. Blair, op. cit., p. 101.

28. Ibid., p. 69.

29. S. Holland, *The socialist challenge*, London, Quartet Books, 1976, p. 49.

30. C. Vaitsos, *Intercountry income distribution and transnational enterprises*, Oxford, Clarendon Press, 1974, p. 3.

31. For example Murray, op. cit., and 'The internationalization of capital and the nation state', *New Left Books*, Vol. 67, 1971; Vaitsos, op. cit.; H. Radice,

International firms and modern imperialism, Harmondsworth, Penguin, 1975.

32. O. Sunkel, 'Transnational capitalism and national disintegration', in C.M. Meier, *Leading issues in economic development*, 3rd edn., New York, Oxford University Press, 1976, p. 696.

33. G. Adam, 'Multinational corporations and world wide sourcing', in Radice, op. cit.

34. R. Murray, *Transfer pricing and the state*, Brighton, Harvester, 1981.

35. Documented for the colonial period in E.A. Brett, *Colonialism and underdevelopment in East Africa*, London, Heinemann Educational Books, 1973; for the recent past in D. Burch, *Overseas aid and the transfer of technology*, PhD, Sussex University, 1979.

36. cf. P. Jalée, *The pillage of the third world*, New York, Monthly Review, 1968.

37. S.S. Kuznets, *Modern economic growth*, New Haven, Yale University Press, p. 302.

38. R. Murray, 'Underdevelopment, international firms,' op. cit., p. 171.

39. Bienefeld, op. cit., pp. 17-18. Here he is describing the mechanism which brought Japan to the fore in the late 1960s; the counterpart of this process is clearly the relative decline of the USA and UK. For an examination of the decline in the relative industrial strength of the UK see the work referred to in Chapter 2, notes 115-118.

40. Murray, 'Underdevelopment, international firms', op. cit., p. 171.

41. Notably A. Emmanuel, *Unequal exchange*, New Left Books, 1972; for a systematic critique see D. Evans, 'Unequal exchange theory', in D. Evans, *The political economy of trade*, Brighton, Harvester, forthcoming.

42. T. Balogh, *Unequal partners*, Oxford, Blackwell, 1963, pp. 13, 16, 31, 39, 56.

43. W. Leontief, *Input_output economics*, New York, Oxford University Press, 1966, p. 49.

44. S. Kuznets, *Economic growth and structure*, op. cit., p. 195.

45. G. Haberler, *A survey of international trade theory*, Princeton, Princeton University Press, 1961, pp. 7-8; for another excellent presentation see Emmanuel, op. cit., p. xii.

46. H.G. Johnson, 'International trade: theory', *International Encyclopedia of the Social Sciences*, Vol. 8, p. 88.

47. J.S. Mill, *Principles of political economy*, London, Longmans, 1900, p. 352.

48. Meade himself provides an account of something very like this process stemming from 'a spontaneous change in productivity' in one country, and demonstrates how this must lead to a reduction in prices there and an increase in unemployment and balance of payments problems in the other. (J.E. Meade, *The balance of payments*, London, Oxford University Press, 1951, pp. 82-4).

49. I am indebted to Rob Eastwood, Lecturer in Economics, University of Sussex, for clarification of this point.

50. Thus Lal, in response to an excellent exposition by Neild of the unequal trade case being put forward here, emphasises wage rigidity as 'crucial to the demonstration that free trade may decrease welfare'. (D. Lal, 'Comment' on R.R. Neild, 'Managed trade between industrial countries' in R. Major, *Britain's trade and exchange rate policy*, London, Heinemann Educational books, 1979, p. 29). Yet this argument, as Neild has pointed out, assumes full employment and is therefore

irrelevant to a consideration of unemployment (personal communication, 22 September 1980). Further it ignores the employment and wage effects of all of the dynamic production possibilities being considered in this paragraph.

51. Emmanuel, op. cit., would also seem to have overlooked the fundamental importance of this point.
52. Neild, op. cit., p. 11.
53. P. Krugman, 'Trade, accumulation and uneven development', Yale University Discussion Paper no. 311, May 1979, p. 1.
54. J.R. Hicks, 'The long-run dollar problem', American Economics Association, *Readings in international economics*, London, Allen & Unwin, 1968, p. 447.
55. F.D. Graham, 'Some aspects of protection further considered', *Quarterly Journal of Economics*, Vol. 37, 1927, p. 200.
56. F. Knight, 'Some fallacies in the interpretation of social cost', *Quarterly Journal of Economics*, Vol. 38, 1924; J. Viner, *Studies in the theory of international trade*, London, Allen & Unwin, 1960, pp. 475-80.
57. Viner, op. cit., p. 481.
58. This is Haberler's rule for determining the significance of any demonstration of the proof that social costs exceed benefits under free trade in a standard article which makes virtually no concessions to the case being made here. (G. Haberler, 'Some problems in the pure theory of international trade', American Economics Association, *Readings in international economics*, op. cit., p. 227).
59. Viner, op. cit., p. 429. Here he also claims Graham would not have obtained his results using marginal costs and returns, and entirely ignores Graham's explicit justification for not doing so. Graham, op. cit., pp. 207ff.
60. Their bones, according to Marx were 'bleaching the plains of India' in 1834-5, as a result. *Capital*, Vol. I, op. cit., Chapter XV, Section 5.
61. Graham, op. cit., p. 207.
62. Ibid., p. 217.
63. The fact that this must destroy the long-term viability of this market in these countries is something that the individual capitalist cannot take into account. This process lies at the heart of the apparently irrational nature of the current attempts by strong industrial countries to externalise their problems by 'running a persistent trade surplus'. Bienefeld, op. cit., p. 1.
64. Emmanuel, op. cit., p. xiv, cited in Chapter 2, note 107.
65. I am heavily indebted here to comments from Rob Eastwood, Tony Venables and David Evans of Sussex University on an earlier draft of this chapter.
66. Neild, op. cit., p. 9; this article provides a concise description of a three sector model which takes the relationship between trade and sectoral development further than I am in a position to do here.
67. Graham, op. cit., p. 211.
68. Johnson, op. cit., pp. 85-6.
69. M.C. Kemp, *The pure theory of international trade and investment*, Englewood Cliffs, N.J. Prentice Hall, 1969, p. 254. Kemp has nothing at all to say about the problems of arranging the agreement he refers to in a world of competing nation states.
70. D.J. Vail, *The public sector as a stimulus innovation adoption in a small-holder agriculture*, Yale, PhD, 1971, gives the figures on hourly earnings in Uganda.

71. Here one must acknowledge a general debt to Myrdal's pioneering development of the concept of 'circular and cumulative causation', *Development and Underdevelopment*, Cairo, National Bank of Egypt, 1956.

72. Notably in International Labour Organisation, *Employment, incomes and equality*, Geneva, International Labour Organisation, 1972; and H. Chenery et al. *Redistribution with growth*, London, Oxford University Press, 1974; for criticisms see M. Bienefeld, 'The informal sector and peripheral capital, the case of Tanzania', *IDS Bulletin*, Vol. 7, no. 2, 1975; C. Leys, *Underdevelopment in Kenya*, London, Heinemann Educational Books, 1975, pp. 267 ff.

73. For an account of the early phase of this process see R. Luxemburg, *The accumulation of capital*, London, Routledge & Kegan Paul, 1963, Chapter 30; for the recent phase, see Chapter 6 below.

4 Uneven Development, the Long Wave and Crisis

Depressions occur immediately after capital capacity has been fully rebuilt. When a peak in the long wave is reached, industrial countries are capable of producing more than they have ever produced before .... It should be a golden age, the time towards which society has been striving.

Instead the end of rebuilding has always led to depression, a time of economic disaster, with hunger, unemployment, and social breakdown.

(J.W. Forrester, *Innovation and the economic long wave*, MIT, 1978)

Chapter 3 attempted to demonstrate that uncontrolled capitalist competition must generate an international division of labour based upon an uneven rather than even distribution of productive capacity world-wide. It conceded that this process, given favourable circumstances, might produce absolute gains for even the weaker countries and therefore justify their support for a unified monetary and trading system despite real increases in relative inequality. But it concluded by asserting that the discontinuous nature of the processes involved in generating the inequalities would also be very likely to lead to a disjuncture between supply and demand with a corresponding growth in unemployment and systemic instability which would place unmanageable strains upon an international political and economic order which was without adequate redistributive mechanisms to offset them.

Can we now move from assertion to argument and produce an adequate theoretical demonstration of these claims? Can the capitalist system based upon unregulated competition, achieve the balance between supply and demand postulated for it by Say's law at the domestic level, and between imports and exports required for the stability of the system at the global level through market allocations alone? Or do the inequalities and discontinuities it must generate require so large an increase in social control over the allocation of resources that its nature must be fundamentally transformed? This chapter will attempt to answer this latter question in the affirmative by demonstrating how the literature on the monopoly problem and more especially Marx's analysis of the accumulation process under capitalism deny the long-term feasibility of the equilibrium conditions postulated for capitalist exchange by orthodox theory.

Before moving to this exercise some preliminary points must be made. The disequlibrium theory to be considered here has been developed to deal with the relationship within a closed economy and does not take account of the specific problems introduced into the analysis when one moves to the international level. This approach sees accumulation not as a 'constant flow of economic activity'[1] based upon perfect competition between formally equal agents in an increasingly interdependent system, but as a process of cumulative and uneven development in which the growth of monopoly power on the part of some agents at the expense of others necessarily leads to disequilibria which put the long-term feasibility of the system itself at risk. At the national level the tendency towards monopoly can be treated relatively simply as a function of the increase in the market power of the dominant firms in each sector. At the international level, however, competition again occurs between private firms, but firms which sometimes operate internationally and sometimes not, and, perhaps more significantly, always operate from differentiated national locations whose levels of development decisively influence the terms on which their goods enter the international market. Here we can see the emergence of monopoly on a locational basis, where the outcome of the process of uneven development must be a tendency towards the concentration of productive power at particular points in space as a result of the effects of the locationally specific external economies described in Chapter 3. If this is accepted, then it follows that the disequilibrium tendencies in international exchange have to be seen as the outcome of the attempt by both private firms and national 'centres of accumulation' to maximise their degree of control over the international market. This then implies that an adequate theory of international integration and disintegration must be based upon a clear identification of the role of each and the relationship between them.

Incorporating both the firms and locational dimension into the analysis is therefore a necessary task, but one for which I do not have either the capacity or the space. Instead the problem will be evaded by treating the capitalist world as a single closed economy, leaving the political/locational dimension out of the account, and treating the tendency towards monopoly in a spatially undifferentiated way.[2]

This chapter therefore starts from the assumption that capitalism has become an increasingly unified system since World War II, that it has attempted to sustain its integration by increasing recourse to non-interventionist market mechanisms that presuppose an automatic tendency towards equilibrium, and that it has thereby allowed a series of disproportionalities to develop which make it increasingly difficult to maintain the balance between its component parts. It is therefore concerned to develop a theoretical basis for an understanding of the dynamics of integration and disintegration by treating the crisis as the outcome of an endogenous tendency towards uneven development stemming from the *normal* process of capital accumulation with free competition and not as the outcome of a series of exogenous 'dysfunctions' or 'rigidities' as orthodoxy does. To do this we must first look at certain general aspects of crisis theory – notably the definition of equlibrium provided by Say's law and the nature of the business cycle; secondly develop the main features of the Marxist theory of crisis and add to it some important contributions provided by non-Marxist monopoly theorists; and finally consider very briefly the relationship between these views and the prospects for inducing a new upturn and offsetting the present tendencies towards international inequality and conflict.

The Conditions for Stability or Crisis

Capitalism moves into a state of crisis when an imbalance emerges between supply and demand which is 'cumulative and self-reinforcing'.[3] This possibility arises out of the nature of capitalist commodity production which separates production and consumption through the intervention of a market mechanism which is not directly responsive to any form of overriding social control. Yet this separation occurs in a context of 'reciprocal and all-sided dependence'[4] between producers and consumers in an international division of labour which makes each directly dependent on the other. Thus the stability of this system, and with it the maintenance of the conditions of existence for its component parts, depends upon its ability to solve the most complex equations by producing an appropriate volume of each of the billions of things required to sustain this system of interdependent activity, and at the same time to guarantee that all of the potential consumers have the appropriate buying power at their disposal to acquire them. For a purchase always to coincide with a sale to the point where the market is cleared and a new round of production can get under way involves a massive achievement in social organisation whose continued existence can never be simply taken for granted, especially given the lack of any form of conscious control over the market mechanism through which it is now managed. Thus Marx writes:

> the act of exchange split[s] into two mutually independent acts: exchange of commodities for money, exchange of money for commodities; purchase and sale. Since these have now achieved a spatially and temporally separate and mutually indifferent form of existence, their immediate identity ceases. They may correspond or not; they may balance or not; they may enter into disproportion with one another. They will of course always attempt to equalise one another; but in the place of the earlier immediate equality there now stands the constant movement of equalisation, which evidently presupposes constant non-equivalence. It is now entirely possible that consonance may be reached only by passing through the most extreme dissonance.[5]

In this situation, as Sweezy says, 'a rupture in the process of circulation ... can spread from its point of origin until it affects the entire economy', produce a 'coexistence of stocks of unsaleable commodities and unsatisfied wants', and lead for the first time to 'that peculiarly civilised form of economic crisis, the crisis of overproduction'.[6]

Now we have already noted that classical and neoclassical theory rejects this possibily by arguing, in the guise of Say's law, that supply creates its own demand. Thus according to Mill:

> Each person's means of paying for the production of other people consists of those [commodities] which he himself possesses. All sellers are inevitably, and by the meaning of the word, buyers. Could we suddenly double the productive powers of the country, we should double the supply of commodities in every market; but we should, by the same stroke, double the purchasing power.[7]

He concedes that this would not guarantee an appropriate level of demand for everything produced, but that in the long run the operation of the market would be bound to ensure that 'the supply will adapt itself accordingly' and an effective equilibrium be established.[8] The argument depends upon the further assumption that money, as a possible 'store of value', will not be hoarded and thus separate sale from repurchase. Instead it is assumed that it will, in Say's words, be held only 'momentarily' to avoid possible losses,[9] and, that where it is not spent on direct consumption, it will be invested and thus create an additional demand equivalent to the value of the commodities sold in order to bring it into the possession of its latest owner. According to Marshall, 'a man purchases labour and commodities with that portion of his income which he saves just as much as he does with that he is said to spend'.[10]

Now we have already noted that a critical component in Keynes's repudiation of Say's law was his belief that the existence of money as a store of value made hoarding possible, and that the social and economic conditions of late capitalism made it possible that individuals could save an excessive amount of their incomes for 'psychological' reasons, while the tendency for large firms and official agencies to set up sinking and amortisation funds on a huge scale would have the same effect upon an even larger scale. Indeed he went so far as to argue that 'this [latter] factor alone was probably sufficient to cause a slump', and continued to offer 'a serious obstacle to recovery' in the 1930s.[11] Hence we can see that his conception of the 'liquidity trap' discussed in Chapter 2 depended directly upon the possibility that savings could exceed the opportunities for profitable investment and thus produce a cumulative and self-reinforcing decline in demand and output.

This view, as we have seen, was subsequently challenged by the monetarists who argued that 'flexible prices and wage rates' in all sectors (and including here those of 'financial assets' of all kinds) would lead to an adjustment process which would bring supply and demand back into equilibrium with full employment (Chapter 2, notes 27–30). The second half of Keynes's analysis, and the most powerful, argued that once a decline in demand had set in, the 'animal spirits' of the entrepreneurs would be dampened and would only be revived where the state could intervene to guarantee its further expansion and thereby recreate a cumulative and self-reinforcing tendency towards growth. This argument, as we have already demonstrated, depended upon the existence of underemployed resources in the economy which could be brought into play through expansionary policies without inflationary effects; it also implied the existence of deflationary conditions in which output must be constrained because of an absence of spending power. Now Mill himself points to the irrationality of the assumption that individuals will continue to work, generate commodities to be sold, and steadfastly refuse to invest or spend the proceeds or increase their leisure in a passage which Keynes failed to acknowledge in his examinaition of Mill's elucidation of Say's law.[12] More significant in the present context is the continuation of unemployment and surplus capacity in conditions of rapid inflation and therefore potentially increasing demand. If there were no *structural* obstacles to the increase in production, these conditions should be incompatible with growing unemployment especially since, as Bienefeld points out, the very rapid increase in Eurocurrency and related credit facilities should provide 'adequate sources of international liquidity'.[13] In these conditions the usual Keynesian remedies of state induced demand expansion are ruled out as they can only exacerbate the inflationary problem, so that the whole theoretical structure falls to the ground with devastating intellectual and political consequences.

The most obvious consequence of this dethronement of the one-time 'saviour of western capitalism' has been the reinstatement of the classical and neoclassical analysis which does recognise that the problems lie not in some generalised failure of demand, but in structural rigidities which have depressed the rate of profit to a point where it rules out resumed investment and which stand in the way of the adjustments required to restore it to an adequate level. Thus, unlike Keynes, they do recognise the need for interventions at the micro level to restore the rate of profit, but see this as a process of eliminating rigidities and distortions in wages, working practices, investment opportunities and the like stemming from the strength of trade union organisation and the extent of state intervention. They can therefore account for the failure to invest and provide remedies that are obviously related to the symptoms of the problem, which the Keynesians cannot, and have therefore been able to re-establish their intellectual dominance. In doing this, however, they have ignored all of the problems of unequal competition and uneven development considered in Chapter 3, and assumed that the Say's law relationships will hold provided that the rigidities they identify can be eliminated. Indeed, Young's 1928 article dealing with the effects of increasing returns argues that the existence of scale economies does not involve any necessary disruption of the relationship between supply and demand since, following directly from Mill, in conditions where there is increasing demand, 'an increase in the supply of one commodity *is* an increase in the demand for other commodities, and it must be supposed that every increase in demand will evoke an increase in supply'.[14] Given that we can neither accept this optimistic orthodox view and its repressive monetarist policy consequences, not the adequacy of the hitherto dominant explanation, it is evident that we require a theory of dislocation which focuses upon the emergence of structural rigidities on the supply side which create the juxtaposition between massive excesses in productive capacity and growing areas of unfulfilled needs which are so obvious a feature of the present economic situation.

Now Say's law explicity denies the possibility identified by Marx that the creation of commodity exchange separates consumer from producer to the point where it permits the possibility of a 'constant non-equivalence' between the two. It assumes that the seller of any commodity must purchase an equivalent very soon thereafter and, further, that the existence of a developed credit mechanism will generate the necessary purchasing power to clear the market when the actual holders of money attempt to save rather than spend it. Because of the extent of the modern credit system, interest rates close to or even below the rate of inflation, and a constant increase in money prices, it is indeed impossible to attribute the recession to a voluntary propensity to save or refusal to consume. What we see instead is a general collapse in profit margins, most pronounced in weaker centres such as Britain, but generalised throughout the system,[15] which make it impossible for firms to maintain levels of output from existing capacity or to consider new investment on a sufficient scale to absorb the excessive supplies of labour and liquidity available by means of the credit system. Monetarist theory assumes that it can restore the rate of profit by bringing down wages and state expenditure; it fails to recognise that its attempt to do this must precipitate a *real* failure in demand resulting from the absolute impoverishment of the society and a return to a classical depression with large-scale unemployment coexisting with depressed wages and impoverished public services in a cumulative and self-reinforcing symbiosis.

The alternative to the monetarist position is not Keynesianism with its assumption that 'the classical theory comes into its own again' once the state has intervened at the macro level to guarantee 'an aggregate volume of output corresponding to full employment',[16] for the present crisis has emerged out of the period in which this strategy has been actively followed in all the advanced industrial countries. It involves instead a structural critique of the capitalist accumulation process which recognises that the failure to invest stems not from exogenous variables, but from the uneven and uncontrolled nature of capitalist competition with its tendency to produce monopoly controls over prices and output, its inability to maintain an appropriate balance between the demand for producer and consumer goods, its constant tendency towards the overexpansion of capital investment and corresponding tendency to push down the rate of profit, and its inability to relate wages and the demand for labour rationally to changes in productivity and technology. Because of the inability to resolve these problems the equilibrium between supply and demand collapses and a crisis of overproduction and underconsumption emerges which disrupts the accumulation process at both national and global levels.

Although orthodox theory prefers to ignore the fact, every schoolboy knows that the history of capitalism has never been characterised by stable equilibrium, but has always been marked by massive oscillations between prosperity and depression and by violent social and political crises. When these great upheavals are recognised in orthodox economic theory they are dealt with under the heading of 'business cycle theory' which, whether through a long-period or short-period analysis, views them as oscillations around a long-term upward sloping equilibrium (the 'natural growth rate') where each downswing must be followed by an inevitable and probably greater upswing. Underlying this approach is the assumption that these movements are the necessary consequence of capitalism's constant need to incorporate new technology and organisational forms into the production process and dispense with new ones. Here one theory simply attempts to identify their incidence without explaining their origins,[17] while another attempts to move beyond comparative statics and generate a growth theory, generally of a neo-Keynesian kind.[18] Here the primary concern has been with the problems involved in maintaining a stable relationship between savings and investment on the one hand and a growth path that satisfies a macro balance between technical change and the supply of labour on the other. Perhaps the most relevant contributions to the problem we are concerned with here, however, were made in the 1930s by Haberler and Schumpeter who attempted to go beyond pure description into an examination of relationships and causes.[19]

Against these tendencies we must look at the Marxist analysis which places crisis at the centre of its system, but which tends to examine it in a relatively ahistorical manner, as the outcome of a series of disjunctures identified through the analysis of a theoretical model of the accumulation process in the capitalist mode of production (CMP). Here the starting point is usually the assumption that competition must lead to a falling rate of profit which is closely associated with a rising organic composition of capital and to breakdowns in equlibrium conditions variously characterised as the outcome of a realisation failure, a rising strength of labour, and the emergence of a disproportion between the consumer and capital goods sectors.[20] Marxist theory will provide the core of this chapter, but it is important to note at the outset that it has generated a great deal of dispute between theoretical tendencies within Marxism mainly concerning the particular weight to be placed on each of the sources of breakdown outlined above. This chapter will attempt to initiate a synthesis between these tendencies by attempting to show how the problem itself cannot be approached in the abstract (through a 'dialectical materialism') but must be related concretely to the specific phases through which the capitalist trade cycle must pass as it moves from depression through an expansion and into depression again (through a 'historical materialism'). Mandel's work has made the greatest contribution in this respect, and will be incorporated directly into this analysis,[21] but closer attention still needs to be paid to the precise nature of the relationship between particular aspects of crisis and the phase in the cycle when they exert their main effects. To do this we require a brief description of the nature of the trade cycle and an indication of how an understanding of its structure can serve to clarify both the theoretical problems generated by both Marxist and bourgeois theories of crisis, and the practical problems associated with the attempt to sustain a successful international monetary system during a period of intensifying recession.

Haberler's major work on trade cycles, originally written during the 1930s, provides us with a useful starting-point. He defines 'the business or trade cycle' as 'a wavelike movement affecting the economic system as a whole',[22] representing 'an alternation of periods of prosperity and depression'.[23]

> depression means a state of affairs in which real income consumed or volume of consumption per head, real income produced or volume of production per head and the rate of employment are falling or are sub-normal in the sense that there are idle resources and unused capacity, especially unused labour.
>
> Prosperity, on the other hand, means a state of affairs in which the real income consumed, real income produced and level of employment are high or rising, and there are no idle resources or unemployed workers, or very few of either.[24]

Within this framework he then defines 'crisis' in two ways, as the 'turning point which marks the passage from prosperity to depression', where the word is used technically, and, where it is used in 'everyday language', to mean 'an acute financial crisis'.[25] Having marked out the high and low points in the cycle Haberler also notes that this implies the existence of two corresponding periods of transition between them, the 'upswing', from depression to prosperity, and the subsequent 'downswing' back to depression again.[26] In the period since World War II we can produce a rough periodisation with the upswing out of depression, war and an intially halting recovery really getting underway after about 1947; with reconstruction completed, currency convertibility established and trade liberalised period of prosperity existed from the early 1960s until perhaps the early 1970s; the downswing then decisively emerged in 1974/5 and continued despite some upward tendencies into the late 1970s.[27] At present we are clearly trapped in the continuation of the downswing, what remains to be seen is whether this will generate a sustained period of depression comparable to the one which prevailed for the most part between the Wars, and, if not, what mechanism will be responsible for initiating a new upswing. If this broad outline, crude as it is, is accepted, we can move on to the theoretical analysis by making some final methodological points.

Firstly, the distinction which it establishes between the nature of the conditions operating at the peak as opposed to the trough can be seen to clarify some fundamental theoretical issues. The current policy debate between monetarist and Keynesian theories cannot possibly be understood outside this context, since the former takes 'the full employment equilibrium' position as a starting point and fails to consider either the possibility or the consequences of an 'un-employment equilibrium'.[28] Keynes, on the other hand is concerned entirely with the conditions prevailing in the trough and clearly states that his analysis ceases to apply once full employment has been reached when 'there is no objection to be raised against the classical analysis'.[29] Thus the simplistic popular debate about the relative merits of the two theoretical tendencies posed in the abstract entirely misses the point and also fails to recognise the close similarities between the two.[30] More significantly, given the focus of this analysis, it is also the case that the relevance of the different aspects of the Marxian analysis emerge in relation to particular phases of the cycle and disappears in others. Thus, it is likely that the problem of a rising share of labour is likely to be a phenomenon of the upswing and more especially of prosperity; we will attempt to demonstrate that the problem of disproportionality is a function of the attempt to move from the rate of growth achieved during the upswing to that possible once full employment has been reached; and that the problem of underconsumption and overproduction emerges in one form in the latter phases of the prosperity and then must cumulatively intensify in the downswing and change yet again in the depression. Once these links between theory and the phases of the cycle are established a great deal of argument attempting to establish the 'fundamental' importance of one or the other by reference to 'classic' texts can be dispensed with.

Secondly, this orientation also serves to clarify the source and nature of the policy problems which have to be resolved in practice at the domestic and, more importantly from our point of view, at the international levels during the post-war period. Thus the problem of the 'dollar deficit' of the 1930s and 1940s, and of the need to externalise US resources through official action associated with it (as for example developed in Keynes's Bretton Woods proposal) was clearly a function of the depression. On the other hand the continuation of the 'dollar surplus', which resolved the earlier problem, into the prosperity of the 1960s generated inflation rather than increased output and created a crisis in international monetary management. Here it is only possible to establish a viable basis for relating policy decisions to their effects in practice (and hence to provide the theoretical underpinning for the substantive section of this book) by relating these decisions directly to the phase of the cycle in which they were taken.

Thirdly, it should be possible to simplify greatly the resulting analysis by focusing primarily upon the problems associated with two key points in the cycle – those related to the problem of sustaining the full employment phase and thereby postponing the crisis, and those relating to the possibility of generating a new upswing once that attempt has clearly failed. Orthodox theory tends to assume that the conditions prevailing during the prosperity constitute a normality that must continue indefinitely through the operation of Say's law provided that 'external' interferences with the market mechanism are avoided. Keynesians assume that it can be sustained indefinitely through limited forms of intervention ('fine tuning') which need in no way threaten the basic feasibility of the capitalistic system itself. The former can now blame the downswing on the negative consequences of the interventions recommended by the latter and have therefore been able to capture the centre of the stage since the latter have no explanations or solutions for a series of events which fall outside the limits of their model. Marxists, on the other hand have always argued that the capitalist system lacked the necessary planning capacity to sustain the balance between conflicting interests during the prosperity which must therefore necessarily give way to crisis sooner or later. Thus our task with respect to this aspect of the problem must be to use this theory (and with it some important developments in monopoly theory emerging out of more orthodox sources) to demonstrate that it is indeed these endogenous variables which have created the problem rather than the exogenous ones postulated by orthodoxy.

Having done this, however, we then have to confront an associated but distinct problem with respect to the reversal of the downswing and the solution to the crisis. Once the depression has been consolidated with the emergence of conditions of chronic unemployment the Keynesian critique of the inability of the Say's law mechanisms to regenerate an upswing would appear to come into its own again. For Marxist theory, on the other hand, structural obstacles resulting from the anarchic nature of capitalistic production itself necessarily preclude a rational solution to the problem and require the intervention of essentially negative external variables (such as imperialistic expansion or the 'permanent arms economy') to generate the initial impetus required to move the system into the upswing. To the extent that we are able to establish that it is indeed internal variables that generate the crisis, we will wish to argue that only external interventions are going to succeed in reversing it. This part of the analysis will be of central importance to the interpretation of the first phase of the post-war cycle immediately after Bretton Woods, and to the diagnosis of current prospects for the system; the earlier argument with respect to the problems involved in attempting to sustain the prosperity from the mid-1960s onwards.

Finally, it is important to keep in mind the centrality of the 'scale economies' argument developed in Chapter 3, even though it may appear to disappear in the specific arguments that follow. Most important here is the need to associate it directly with Marx's conception of the rising organic composition of capital (ROC), and hence to establish its importance in explaining both the dynamic nature of the capitalistic growth process and the corresponding structural distortions which make it impossible for it to sustain a desirable balance between supply and demand, and between sectors during the boom, and to regenerate a new upturn after the downswing. It is precisely because this tendency is internal to a growth process arising out of capitalistic competition (as are the changes in technology and scale through which it operates[31]) that the orthodox explanation collapses. Hence we can directly attribute the failure of their explanation not to logical inconsistencies in their model, but to its rejection of scale economies as an assumption, and we can recognise the importance of the contribution made by the small group of bourgeois theorists (Graham, Means, Schumpeter, and others) who were willing to come to terms with some aspects of the problems that it generates.

Towards a Theory of Crisis
In capitalism a crisis emerges when the rate of profit becomes too low to sustain existing levels of investment, and recedes when it becomes high enough to generate a significant expansion. Thus we can say that 'the defining characteristic of a Marxian theory of capitalist economic crisis may be identified as the focus on a falling rate of profit as the source of the crisis'.[32] Marxism does not treat capitalism as an equilibrium system but as one in which competition constantly drives profits downward and thereby induces major structural changes in the organisation of production and the balance between classes. It attempts to develop a general understanding of the problem by identifying the nature of the forces which exert this downward pressure, how they relate to each other, and how they are offset or intensified during particular phases in the business cycle. This section will therefore look first at the general effects of competition on profits and structural change, then at the more specific problems that emerge at the critical points in the cycle identified earlier.

Falling profits and monopoly capitalism
In conditions of perfect competition all existing producers using machinery and organisational structures of average productivity will be able to achieve the average rate of profit. Given continuous innovation in both mechanical and organisational spheres as an intrinsic aspect of the system itself, however, all new investment, whether to replace worn machinery or to set up a new plant, will be based upon superior equipment and will therefore reduce unit costs and threaten to drive down prices and undermine the profits of existing firms. It is through this constant downward pressure on existing profit levels through the constant emergence of more efficient producers that 'the immanent laws of capitalist production' assert themselves 'as the coercive laws of competition'[33] and force every capitalist constantly to reduce his existing cost structure either by increasing the direct exploitation of his workers or by investing a large enough portion of new capital to enable him to achieve levels of productivity comparable to those generated by the new entrants. If individual capitalists or, at the international level, national aggregations of capitals, fail to sustain the average rate of profit in the face of this downward pressure they will ultimately be unable to generate a sufficient surplus to maintain their competitiveness and will be faced with bankruptcy. Orthodox theory would not seek to deny this tendency, but assumes that continuous innovation is possible without

altering the balance between the supply of and demand for labour and capital, consumption and investment goods, savings and expenditure. Here perhaps the most developed analysis takes the form of Harrod's growth theory which does recognise the possibility of disequilibria emerging but fails to develop this into a theory of an internally generated tendency towards crisis.[34] Marxist theory, however, asserts that this continuous downward pressure on profits must generate a constant search for scale economies in the production process which will lead to monopoly, to intensified pressures on the profits of existing firms, and to imbalances between the demand for and supply of labour, capital goods and savings. This argument begins from the conception of the rising organic composition of capital.

To simplify matters here we will treat the ROC as Weisskopf does, as a 'rise in the real capital/labour ratio'.[35] Because of continous downward pressures on profits the capitalist can attempt to reduce costs by increasing direct exploitation (through 'absolute surplus value') or by investing in new technology which increases the mass of profit without the necessity for reducing wages or increasing the length of the working day by increasing the productivity of labour.[36] With full employment during the prosperity this will be virtually the only means of counteracting falling profits; during the downswing it will continue if technological progress is rapid enough to sustain a real 'difference between the value of the machine and the value of the labour-power replaced by it'.[37] This incentive will continue to exist even with falling real wages (though in a less powerful form), suggesting that it is not merely downward wage rigidity which causes unemployment. The result must be a continuous rise in the capital/labour ratio to enable the actual rate of profit to be sustained and accumulation to continue, something that has in fact been directly associated with 'the long-run growth of capitalist economies'.[38]

Given the operation of this process, competition will constantly tend to redistribute profits from capitalists using the least efficient to those using the most efficient technology and will destroy the most marginal of the former in the process. On the face of it this need not reduce the actual rate of profit in the next phase since the survivors with their higher organic composition will still be able to achieve the average rate which prevailed before. To assume that this tendency does not impose major structural changes on the system and threaten it with dislocation however, is to ignore some critical long-term implications. The most important of these would seem to be the further intensification of the general downward pressures on profits described above, the growth of scale economies and monopoly, and an increase in unemployment leading to a crisis of unemployment and overproduction.

The fundamental argument connecting the fall in the rate of profit with rising organic composition is to be found in the third volume of *Capital* where Marx demonstrates that because surplus value and therefore profit is derived from the exploitation of living labour, a decline in the labour/capital ratio means that 'the rate of surplus value, at the same, or even a rising, degree of labour exploitation, is represented by a continually falling general rate of profit'.[39] Mandel provides a succinct description of the workings of this process:

> if the average organic composition of capital increases for *all* enterprises the average rate of profit falls, all other things being equal. If, for example, between one decade the next, the value of annual production grows from 300 million c + 100 million v + 100 million s =£500 million, to 400 million c + 100 million v + 100 million s = 600 million, the increase in organic capital from 3 to 4 entails a fall in the rate of profit from 100/400 = 25 per cent to 100/500 = 20 per cent. 'As a system accumulates more and more productive plant and equipment, the rate of return on new and existing capital becomes depressed'.[40]

And since, as we have seen, competition constantly forces the capitalist class to push up organic composition, we can see why the ROC should be 'the basic tendency of the capitalist mode of production', and why it is correct to argue that '*the tendency of the average rate of profit to fall* is thus a law of development of the capitalist mode of production'.[41] Given the operation of this pressure, it follows that capitalists wishing to sustain the average rate of profit cannot simply re-equip using existing technology, but must constantly produce innovations which enable them to secure exponential increases in output through a continuous increase in scale economies. What are the causes and effects of this pressure?

The fall in the rate of profit occurs because of the increase in the capital/labour ratio. The effect of the operation of this additional capital, however, is to increase the mass of commodities sold and thereby to increase the total *mass* of profits generated in the system as a whole and accruing to the most advanced producers. And the greater the compression of the profit rate, the more rapid must be the increase in the productivity of capital to compensate. Thus, as the labour/capital ratio declines, 'an ever larger quantity of capital is required to employ the same, let alone an increased, amount of labour-power'.[42] Now this expansion requires a continuous increase in the output of the firms concerned where the actual number of workers employed might decline (depending on the nature of the technology involved), but where their scale of operation would necessarily be greater than older firms using more workers to produce fewer commodities.[43] It is on the basis of this analysis that we have to accept Marx's assertion that it is the 'normal case of modern industry' to generate 'an increasing productivity of labour and the operation of larger quantity of means of production by fewer workers'.[44]

The connection between these processes and the conception of scale economies used earlier can be established through Schumpeter's brilliant formulation of the theory of innovation which he sees, as does Marx, as an '*internal* factor' of capitalist production and the basis for his 'model of the process of economic change'.[45] Here what distinguishes his notion from the forms of change examined in orthodox equilibrium theory is that it involves not merely a variation in the quantity of product in relation to variations in the quantities of factors, but a variation in the 'form of the function' itself.[46] And where change is occuring on this basis the effect must be to eliminate the tendency to a decrease in the 'physical marginal productivity of every factor', and substitute for it another which 'displays higher increments of product throughout'.[47] Here we find a powerful conception of scale economies, constantly regenerated by the fact that the entrepreneur's profit derived from their creation constantly vanishes 'in the subsequent process of competition and adaptation',[48] which produces a process of discontinuous change not on the basis of 'falling long-run cost curves', but by destroying 'the old total or marginal cost curve', and putting 'a new one in its place'.[49] Thus

> what dominates the picture of capitalistic life and is more than anything else responsible for our impression of a prevalence of decreasing cost, causing disequilibria, cut-throat competition and so on, is innovation, the intrusion into the system of new production functions which incessantly shift existing cost curves.[50]

And with this analysis at our disposal it is possible to identify the source of two sources of disequilibrium in late capitalism, the tendency towards monopoly and the growth of overproduction.

Our earlier examination of scale economies in international trade suggested that they must produce a tendency towards uneven development and, given the emergernce of unemployment, would lead to absolute losses from trade. If we now look more closely at the problem in a closed economy, we can see first that there must be a strong tendency towards monopoly where they prevail and that this in turn must disrupt all of the equilibria presupposed by Say's law. Even the most orthodox of economists accept that the effect of competition on any process where continuous 'technical economies with increase in the scale of operations' exist must be to 'eventuate either in monopoly or in leaving the tendency behind and establishing the *normal relation* of increasing cost with increasing size'[51] (emphasis added). The difference between their position and ours therefore resides mainly in their denial of its predominance in the actual capitalist growth process at the empirical level, as Knight does here. In these circumstances the competitive strength of the largest units will constantly increase, the autonomy of smaller units will be as constantly undermined, and ever higher 'barriers to entry' against newcomers will develop.[52] Once this situation has developed the Say's law assumptions are undermined because dominant producers are no longer totally subordinated to the market, but can, in Sraffa's words, 'radically affect the market price' of what they sell and thereby influence the extent to which the system can adjust effectively to any disequilibrium in the overall relationship between supply and demand.[53]

Now this problem is not considered in orthodox theory or in Keynes, but it did generate an important discussion in the 1930s among non-Marxist economists who recognised that the breakdown of the market mechanism resulting from monopoly capital's ability to 'administer' prices could lead directly to a breakdown in the aggregate relationship between supply and demand. Here the most influential figure was probably Gardiner Means whose paper on 'administered prices' at the start of 1935 provided the Roosevelt administration 'with its first intellectual basis for ignoring the received wisdom of Say's law ... which for years had paralysed the will of governments to combat massive unemployment'.[54] The diagnosis which Means and his associates provided for the administration was then based on three major postulates – that organisational and technological advances related to mass production had replaced the market-centred economy with 'an administered system, privately planned and directed by a few industrial leaders' in 'industry after industry'; that this had hindered appropriate adjustments in prices, savings, wages and investment opportunities; and finally that the problem could not be solved by the traditional anti-trust approach as this would 'impair efficiency and lower the standard of living' so that the only alternative was a transfer of private 'power over economic decisions to new agencies of control' of a fully representative kind.[55]

The radical implications of this analysis are therefore very considerable in that it leads to a demand for central intervention which far transcends that suggested by Keynes. Indeed Keynes himself, responding to these influences, strongly advised Roosevelt in 1938 against a policy of direct intereference with business and in favour of one based purely on a general expansion in demand.[56] Its strength has certainly not diminished and is now complemented by an analysis of the pricing practices of the multinationals – the characteristic form assumed by the large-scale corporation since World War II – which demonstrates an ever greater autonomy than before resulting from the extended use of transfer prices.[57] Thus it is hardly surprising that the case is again being widely canvassed as an explanation for the failure of Keynesian interventionism and as the basis for a radical increase in state intervention and democratically controlled planning.[58] It is also being used to provide the most convincing explanation for the contemporary juxtaposition between inflation and rising unemployment which Kahn argues stems directly from monopoly controls over prices, production and profits and which therefore lead to the 'inducement or aggravation of a downswing, resulting in needless unemployment and substantial underutilisation of resources'.[59]

Secondly, the process of structural innovation described here must make it increasingly difficult to sustain full employment and freedom of access to the market for small firms. Given the exponential growth in output generated by the rising productivity of labour, an equivalent expansion in demand is required to absorb it without creating unemployment. The possibility of achieving this in accordance with Say's law, as Young, for example considers to be perfectly possible (see note 14), then depends upon the extent to which the expansion in output can be sustained not through a growth of demand in general, but through an increase in the demand for the particular types of commodities which the system is producing at a particular point in time. Given the complete lack of overall planning in the system, no social means exist to guarantee that these proportions will be maintained, while the qualitative changes in production relations induced by 'innovation' in Schumpeter's sense almost guarantees that serious disproportionalities will constantly emerge. A subsequent section will consider the problem posed by uneven changes in the relation between the consumer and producer goods sectors; here it is important to notice that this will have serious consequences for the labour market as well.

A crude explanation for unemployment can be found in the Marxist

literature on unemployment which attributes it to the underconsumption generated by the fact that all capitalists are driven by
competition to maximise output yet minimise wages. Mandel clearly
demonstrates the inadequacy of this view,[60] but this does not eliminate
the problem of excess capacity and unemployment itself. When this is
considered more closely, in relation to the arguments developed
above, it becomes clear that the underlying problem is not so much
the repression of wage *rates*, but the constant attack on wage *costs*
through the constant reduction in the labour/capital ratio. Thus the
creation of an effective new labour saving technology will increase
output and reduce the level of employment; it may also reduce the
total wage bill and hence the demand for wage goods despite rising
wages for those workers who remain in employment. The effect of
this will then be an increase in 'structural' unemployment and a
breakdown in the balance between supply and demand which will
induce cumulative deflationary pressures tending to push the system
out of prosperity into the downswing, that is to say the creation of
what Marx calls a 'realisation crisis'.[61] This situation may well co-exist
with the problem of a 'rising share of labour' examined in a later
section, where there are structural rigidities in the labour market.

These tendencies towards monopoly and unemployment arising
from the ROC operate continuously throughout the trade cycle as
generalised pressures, but their effects are likely to be very different
in each phase. During the upswing and prosperity, while it *is* possible
to sustain demand at an adequate level, it will be possible for the
downward pressure on profits to be contained and even for small-
scale, high cost firms to remain in existence, often in a direct symbiotic
relationship with the monopolies who may use them as distributors or
suppliers of goods and services in sectors where scale economies are
difficult to achieve. Yet the tendency towards concentration will
continue as we saw from the evidence presented in Chapter 3, leading
to the creation of a dual economy containing a monopoly sector able
to make super-profits during booms and to resist downward pressures
in the recessions, alongside a competitive sector forced to respond to
downswings by reducing prices and profits more substantially and
therefore constantly finding itself at a structural disadvantage in
relation to the growing monopoly sector.[62] During the post-war
upswing and prosperity some very radical theorists began to argue
that the downward pressure on monopoly profits had been eliminated
and attributed problems of underconsumption and structural dislocations to this factor alone.[63] But this view ignored the fact that the

transformation of the production process induced by competition was continuing unabated so that as soon as the realisation problems identified above (and other problems to be discussed below) began to threaten the prosperity, the downward pressure on profits came to be felt with increasing severity in both the competitive sector, *and that occupied by the monopolies themselves*. Here Mandel again provides an excellent analysis of the problem, showing both that the effect of competition on the structure of production must always subject 'monopoly surplus-profits ... to erosion'[64] in the long run, and that their constant need to expand will drive them constantly to attempt 'to annex formerly non-monopolised branches of production',[65] thus constantly reducing the scope for small-scale competitive production.

Once the downswing has begun, of course, these pressures will be increased as a result of falling aggregate demand which will further intensify the competitive struggle, drive up the capital/labour ratio and turn the downward pressure on profits into an actual decline. Once this occurs there will be a collapse in investment opportunities with falling wages merely intensifying the decline in aggregate demand without creating any likelihood of new investment. This is the phenomenon identified by Keynes and ignored by monetarism, but we can see that it owes little to any voluntary 'propensity to save' on the part of individuals, or to the decline in the 'animal spirits' of the enterpreneurs, but stems directly from structural imbalances arising out of an accumulation process based upon a constant growth of scale economies and monopolistic competition. And although this analysis has operated purely in the context of a closed economy, there appears to be no difficulty in applying it to the international conditions set out in Chapter 3 where the emphasis is upon a monopolistic tendency towards regional agglomeration with corresponding pressures upon employment and profit margins in weaker centres unable to push their overall cost structure down below that of the stronger ones. Here the result must be the structural imbalance between surplus and deficit countries attributed by orthodox theorists to 'mercantilist' policies on the part of the strong countries, but in fact the outcome of the uneven nature of the capitalist accumulation process on the global level.

Sectoral imbalances and the business cycle
Say's law requires not merely a balance between an undifferentiated 'aggregate' of supply and demand, but one between sectors and, in particular, between the inputs and outputs of the capital and consumer

goods industries, Departments I and II. Given an economy with a high and growing capital/labour ratio, the output of the capital goods sector (Department I) must correspond to the demand for new equipment required to replace existing machinery and produce the new capital goods needed to sustain a particular rate of growth. With stable growth rates and no fundamental changes in technology the relationship between the demand for and supply of capital equipment would not be problematic. But given the existence of the trade cycle and of discontinuous changes in technology this balance can no longer be taken for granted. In these circumstances the possibility will always exist of fundamental changes in the demand for the output of existing sections of Department I (with corresponding changes in its demand for the output of Department II) which, given the large-scale nature of the production processes involved, must lead to fundamental imbalances. Here we can deal with two major problems – the need for a transition from one growth path to another resulting from a movement into a new phase of the trade cycle, and the difficulties of integrating a wholly new productive technology into the cycle without entirely disrupting the balance between savings and investment postulated by orthodox theory.

During a transition from depression (or the after-effects of a world war) to full employment a very rapid growth rate can be sustained without inflation and previously underemployed resources can be brought rapidly into the production process. During this phase Department I will expand to the size determined by that rate of growth and its demand for consumer goods will grow accordingly. Once the full employment equilibrium is reached, however, it is unlikely that it will be possible to sustain the same rate of growth without generating inflationary pressures. According to Hicks:

> Until [the Full Employment level] limit is reached, output can expand, both by natural growth and by a reduction in the percentage of unemployed resources. Once, however, the limit is reached, only natural growth is possible.... [Thus] *having reached its full employment limit, the system must begin to turn round again and output to go down, at least relatively to the trend.*[66]

At this point, given the lack of planning in capitalism, two serious problems must emerge. Firstly, the transition to a lower level of output in Department I justified by the lower growth rate cannot be organised through a rational reallocation of resources to other uses, but must occur through the intensification of the competitive struggle, an actual fall in the rate of profit, and extensive bankruptcies. Individual firms, with costs depending heavily on scale of output, will be unable to organise a programmed reduction in output, but will respond by attempting to expand their market share and, where monopolistic conditions prevail, by pushing up prices. Hence the result must be an intensification of conflict and the generation of inflationary pressures until the excess capacity is eliminated. Secondly, the initiation of a contraction in Department I will, if no external variables intervene, then set off a 'process of contraction' which will be 'cumulative and self-reinforcing',[67] because of the integrated nature of the production process. Haberler provides us with a vivid description of this process which is difficult to reconcile with the optimistic equilibrium assumptions in his more abstract work. Once the downward process has 'continued for a while', he writes:

> The profit rate will be reduced all along the line, and new investment or reinvestment of amortisation quotas will be curtailed. Nobody dares to embark on ambitious schemes of investment; and this will intensify the tendency to reduce commodity stocks and to increase money stocks, that is to hoard – the counterpart of the tendency to dishoard during expansion.
>
> It is important to note that such a contraction process can happen even in a pure cash economy with constant quantity of money. In a modern banking and credit economy, powerful intensifying factors come in....
>
> Owing to the rigidity of a number of cost items, each decrease in the total demand for goods in terms of money is followed by a certain shrinkage in production, and any reduction in the production of finished goods tends to be transmitted with increasing violence to the preceding stages of production, which again tends to reduce the demand for finished goods, and so on in a long and painful process.[68]

Here it is plain that 'hoarding' emerges not as the result of a *voluntary* propensity on the part of consumers and large firms, as Keynes assumes, but as the outcome of the collapse in the balance between Departments I and II which stems directly from the discontinuous nature of the capitalist growth process; that is to say from endogenous variables which could only be controlled *by controlling the operation of the market mechanism itself*.

As if this difficulty were not sufficient, Marx's examination of the relationship between sectors in Volume II of *Capital* also demonstrates that fundamental imbalances must occur in the full employment situation where there is rapid technical change in the capital goods industry. Attention has been diverted away from this analysis by the emphasis on the scheme of 'extended reproduction', notably by Luxemburg who fails to recognise that the problem of the full employment equilibrium has to be looked at through the scheme of 'simple reproduction' involving development without the qualitative expansion in demand and supply possible during the upswing.[69] Marx's exposition involves a complex and tedious analysis of the exchanges which must take place between capital and labour and producer and consumer goods sectors as production proceeds through its various cycles. What is critical to the analysis and, more especially, to the demonstration that a long-term equilibrium is all but impossible, is the fact that serious imbalances are bound to emerge in the production processes where 'innovative' technical change is occurring in the capital goods sector. Only the main points of the argument can be developed here.

In any given period a certain portion of the value embodied in current output will be derived from the value of the constant capital consumed in order to produce it. This capital will have been produced by the firms in Department I who must be able to rely on constant sales to all other producers if they are to be able to maintain their productive structures intact and are not to be faced with the need to maintain costly surplus capacity. Yet the actual capital consumed in current production by their customers will have been purchased in the past and will only be replaced at some time in the future. Thus the value product of a given year is greater than the value added to it 'by the labour of the current year', the increment being the value transferred to it through the use of the constant capital fabricated in the past.[70] Given the lumpy and discontinuous nature of the capital investment process, a potential problem always therefore exists of overproduction in the capital goods sector, especially where growth is limited by the conditions of the full employment equilibrium.

Technically this problem is dealt with through a transfer of value over time and space through the development of the credit system. Capitalists depreciating existing equipment establish amortisation funds to provide for subsequent re-equipment. This will only be spent in the future when re-equipment has to take place and therefore must 'settle down beside the productive capital and persist in the form of money'[71] where it forms 'a hoard' which 'is thus itself an element in the capitalist process of production'.[72] The existence of this hoard therefore creates the possibility of overproduction in the capital goods sector, as Keynes also realised.[73] The solution to the problem consists in a sufficiently even process of depreciation in the multitude of firms using the capital goods to generate an equally even level of demand for the output of that sector. This may be relatively unproblematic where capital equipment is relatively small and a multitude of firms make use of it, as was no doubt the case with competitive capitalism. It becomes progressively more difficult to sustain where production is concentrated into a very small number of giant plants making very discontinuous demands on their major suppliers.

But this is not the most critical problem, though its effects are being clearly felt at present by a substantial number of firms making very heavy capital goods. Given that the capitalist purchases his equipment at one point in time and replaces it at another, there is no guarantee that the savings accumulated over the period will not exceed the value of the new equipment *if the technical composition of capital has changed over the period*. If a computer-based firm obtained its original equipment for £1,000,000 in 1970, and found it could replace it in 1980 for £1,000 as a result of the micro-chip revolution, it would have generated a substantial body of savings which would have to be reinvested in other sectors if the overall level of demand for capital goods were to be sustained. Hence Marx argues that the 'law of reproduction on the same scale' must be the maintenance of 'a balance' between the value of the constant capital 'renewed in kind each year', and that of that 'which continues to function in its old bodily form', and whose 'depreciation in value ... is first to be compensated in money'.[74] Thus, where this condition is not met, and it *cannot* be, where 'innovative' change is taking place in the capital goods sector, rapid growth must occur if structural overproduction is not to emerge,[75] which will almost certainly be greater than the level which can be sustained in the conditions prevailing in the full employment equilibrium.

This problem of potential overproduction, as Marx points out, can exist even in a planned economy given the uneven nature of the investment process, and 'can be remedied only by a continuous relative over-production'.[76] But in capitalism this cannot be arranged, because the relationship between demand and supply is established through competition and not through planning. The firm confronted with a shortfall in demand in a particular year must attempt to expand its market share and eliminate other firms if it is to survive. The resulting destruction must create further imbalances and quite possibly initiate a 'contraction' of the sort described by Haberler earlier, with devastating results. The alternative to this anarchic mechanism is the planned maintenance of the level of surplus capacity required to generate a particular level of production over time which 'is tantamount to control by society over the material means of its own reproduction',[77] a level of social control which is impossible given the contradiction between the socialised form of production and the privatised form of accumulation which remains the characteristic feature of late capitalism.

If we now combine the two arguments presented in this section we can see the pressures on capitalists to continue to expand at the old, or even a more rapid, rate will continue when the full employment point is reached and a limited downturn becomes necessary. Here both Keynesian and orthodox theory will call for a limited deflation, without recognising that the imperative to expand makes this impossible without doing fundamental damage to the capital goods sector. Hence we can here establish that the full employment equilibrium can only be sustained through the constant expansion of the capitalist economy into new areas as Luxemburg argued, although the structure of the argument is somewhat different from the one which she presented. This, of course, corresponds very closely to the history of capitalism which has never been an equilibrium system but one which has been driven forward by a relentless seach for new areas to conquer from its first beginnings. It will also serve to explain the serious difficulties involved in sustaining the stability of the international monetary order from the end of the 1970s once the impetus imparted by the post-war upswing had begun to diminish and the problem of sustaining the earlier rate of growth emerged as a global problem. The resulting combination of surplus capacity and inflation are obviously closely linked to the sectoral imbalances described here which have always been an endogenous element in the capitalist growth process.

Rising wages and social services
Since orthodox theory fails to accept any of the analysis provided in the last two sections, it must use the monopoly power of labour and of the state to explain the failure of Say's law. If the preceding arguments are accepted, however, it is evident that they cannot be the sole, and are probably not even the most imporant source of the problem, especially given its existence even in countries where wages are constantly depressed and social services almost non-existent. Yet there is considerable evidence to suggest that these factors do play some part in pushing the system towards crisis during the boom and in restricting its ability to restructure during the downswing. What is at issue, therefore, is not so much whether wage pressures and state provision can be 'blamed' for the crisis, but the nature of the limits which their position in the system imposes upon its ability to sustain

the balance between consumption and investment required to maintain the full employment equilibrium.

If we begin with the problem of wages, we can see that there is considerable empirical evidence to support the assertion that their tendency to increase did impose downward pressures on profits in the industrialised countries in the 1960s and 1970s. Thus Glyn and Sutcliffe argued that the main reason for the falling rate of profit in Britain especially in the 1960s lay in 'the squeezing of profit margins between money wage increases on the one hand and progressively more severe international competition on the other',[78] and further that this tendency existed 'in all the major capitalist countries'.[79] Secondly, Weisskopf concluded that the 'rising share of labour' was the most significant of the factors depressing profits in the USA during the whole of the post-war period.[80] Finally, Boyer demonstrated for France that while profits were able to increase in line with wages in France through high productivity gains, the growing strength of the unions, notably in the 'monopoly' sector, enabled them to push wages upwards 'largely independently of the degree of competition on the product market',[81] and to ensure that there would be a growth in unemployment rather than a decline in wages should any downturn begin.[82]

When we attempt to relate these broad tendencies to the critical points in the trade cycle identified earlier, we find that the crucial importance of wage pressures lies not so much in any generalised tendency to undermine profits, but in the particular difficulties they create for any policy oriented towards maintaining or restoring the full employment equilibrium. During the upswing capital should be able to offset rising wages through increases in productivity and output. Once full employment is reached and a shift occurs to a lower growth rate these opportunities decline while the strength of labour continues to increase. In these conditions unions are likely to be strong, and, even if they are not, 'competition itself will lead to a secular rise in wages even in the absence of trade unions'.[83] The effect of this will be to force capitalists to attempt to continue to expand at the old rate even though the resource constraints are intensifying, pushing the system into 'over-full employment' and threatening inflation and bankruptcies. This is likely to generate calls for voluntary or compulsory wage restraint,[84] but these are unlikely to be effective in the long-term partly because of the possibility of working class resistance, more so because the upward pressure is mainly generated by the intensification of capitalist competition in the boom for the reasons set out in the previous sections. Once this fact is grasped by the ruling class it becomes clear that only a substantial increase in unemployment will serve to restore the rate of profit so that the capitalist class itself must connive in policies designed to move the system out of prosperity into a downswing in order to re-establish its control over the working class which cannot be effectively sustained without the existence of a substantial reserve army of the unemployed.[85]

During the downswing the situation becomes much more ambiguous. Here rising unemployment will tend to depress wages, and capital will press for actual reductions in order to restore the rate of profit on the assumption that this will generate a new upswing. Union organisation may now make it possible for the most favoured groups of workers to limit wage cuts in the monopoly sectors, as Boyer asserts, leading to the possibility that 'the refusal to accept lower wages will reduce the rate of profit still further, and thereby make the slump even worse than it already is'.[86] Yet, as Rowthorn points out, the further reduction in wages at this point will intensify the decline in demand and even place 'firms which would be highly profitable under normal conditions ... in great difficulty'.[87] The solution at this point, as Keynes also recognised, must be a high wage policy, but the competitive and antagonistic nature of the capitalist system precludes this since each capitalist *has* to reduce his own wage payments to a minimum in order to sustain profits in conditions of declining demand and intensifying competition. Where workers *do* attempt to keep up profits they must undermine these efforts and have therefore to recognise that the nature of the system itself now stands in the way of a rational solution to the contradiction created by the gap between 'the limited dimensions of consumption under capitalism and a production which forever tends to exceed this immanent barrier'.[88]

Closely associated with the problem of wage pressure is that of 'excessive' state spending which is blamed by theorists of both left and right for the falling rate of profit.[89] Here, again, great care is needed, since a number of the social services provided by the state are necessary for the reproduction of capital itself and can actually serve to increase profits where they can be provided more efficiently collectively than they could be privately.[90] Yet with full employment and strong social democratic parties, it is always likely that the demand for these services will exceed the limits strictly necessary for the reproduction of labour power and capital and constitute a net cost to the community. Any expansion will increase the competition for labour and therefore push up wages; if it is financed through taxation profits will be reduced, if through an increase in the money supply the result will be inflation and a balance of payments problem. Once the pressure on profit margins reaches critical levels the ruling class will be forced to intervene to reduce the proportion of social resources appropriated by the state in order to reduce their costs and hence to initiate an increase in unemployment. Yet this, too, will have ambiguous effects since it must also intensify the decline in demand once the downswing has started and push the system further and further into crisis, as the exponents of monetarist policies are now discovering.

Crisis, Uneven Development and State Intervention

The post-war upswing and prosperity sustained a version of reformist social democratic politics, in the advanced capitalist countries at least, which appeared to have replaced the class war with a continuous truce between capital and labour organised through the auspices of the interventionist state. In the present downswing the resources required to sustain this truce are becoming scarce and the politics of social compromise are being increasingly threatened at both the national and international levels. Reformist politicians such as Carter, Callaghan and Manley have found themselves increasingly driven to adopt unwelcome monetarist solutions by crises usually initiated through their international economic relations; their more uncompromisingly monetarist successors must intensify the pressures on popular consumption even further and generate major social confrontations. No policy in any sphere is unaffected by the downswing and the corresponding attack on wages, job security and social services of all kinds. This demonstrates yet again the organic connections between objective economic variables and the choices available to politicians attempting to respond to popular demands for a return to the favourable conditions existing a few years ago. But the monetarists are quite right in asserting, with Marx, that 'there is no such thing as a free meal',[91] and that if the present conditions do not provide capital with the rate of profit required to re-establish the upswing, there will be no means of sustaining the existing level of wages, employment or social services. Thus the fundamental question for the coming decade must be the objective possibility of restoring the rate of profit without a fundamental restructuring of the nature of the capitalist mode of production itself. If this possibility really exists we can afford to treat the present situation as an uncomfortable but temporary phase and wait confidently for the upturn once the appropriate adjustments have been made. If not we must expect the crisis to deepen and we will have to accept the necessity of adopting far more drastic remedies.

The object of the preceding analysis of uneven development and capitalist accumulation was to provide the theoretical tools required to understand the inability to sustain the boom, that of the next will be to demonstrate their applicability to our understanding of the evolution of the international monetary system since World War II. It now remains to consider very briefly the implications of the preceding analysis for the resolution of the crisis on the one hand and to indicate its relevance to our understanding of the political economy of crisis management in the international monetary system on the other.

Controlling the downswing

Thus far we have argued that the crisis must occur when the rate of profit is depressed to unmanageable levels by the intensification of the competitive pressures generated by the discontinuities inherent in the process of capitalistic accumulation outlined above. Following the same logic, the possibility of an upturn can be seen to depend upon an increase in the profit rate to levels which allow a new phase of investment to take place. Thus our problem becomes that of identifying the extent to which the change in conditions produced by the transition from full employment to recession tend to reduce or increase costs of production and thereby prepare the system for a new upturn. Optimists often seem to assume that this is an automatic process, but the evidence to substantiate this belief seems far less certain.

The substance of the monetarist case lies in the assumption that the downswing will reduce the demand for labour and thereby push down the rate of wages; if this is associated with a deliberate programme of reducing unproductive state services, tax payments will also fall. Since the effect of these changes will also be the elimination of the least efficient firms in the system, the market shares of those which remain will expand, thereby preparing the way for an expansion in the output of the survivors. Once the profit rate has been raised in this way and the 'rigidities' shaken out of the system, new investment will begin and a new upswing can be generated starting from a more efficient base and therefore capable of pushing the whole system to a new equilibrium at an even higher level than before.

There is, no doubt, some truth in these assertions, but they nevertheless omit a number of critical variables identified in our earlier analysis which suggest that the deflationary tendencies emerging in the downswing will generate countervailing cost increases and new rigidities which may more than offset them and keep the system in a state of semi-permanent stagnation. Here we can do no more than allude to the elements of a very complex argument:

1. Because of the importance of scale economies and the capital/labour ratio in determining average costs, any decline in demand must tend to increase costs more rapidly than a decline in wages and taxes. Given the increase in the monopoly power of the dominant firms arising out of their exploitation of scale economies, the possibility also exists of a response to declining demand based upon monopoly power capable of inducing 'extreme inflexibility in large areas of the price structure' and thus pushing the system towards 'severe depression'.[92] This factor will keep large amounts of surplus capacity in the system long after it would have been eliminated in a regime of perfect competition, and act as a permanent obstacle to new investment.

2. The transition from a low rate of growth during full employment to a much smaller or even negative rate during the downswing will further intensify the pressure on the capital goods sector. This, in turn, will deflate demand even more and hence intensify the realisation crisis and the downward pressure on profits for the whole system.

3. Cuts in state spending may marginally reduce taxes, but the growth in unemployment will then tend to force up unproductive state spending very rapidly. Attempts to cut it may then lead to social unrest and to the need for increased expenditure on the repressive apparatuses. Actual cuts in expenditure will reduce demand and increase costs in the same way as cuts in wages and the decline in the activities of the less efficient firms.

4. Given the rigidities arising out of monopolistic competition and the cumulative nature of the decline in demand engendered by these processes, entrepreneurial optimism may disappear as Keynes argued, and new investments fail to materialise even after objective conditions have altered sufficiently to make them possible.

5. Given the intensely competitive nature of the conditions created during the downswing, new investment during this phase may be even more capital intensive than during the boom when markets were expanding and high cost producers still survived. The effect of this could well be to worsen the unemployment problem while generating an increase in productive capacity. Unless this process were associated

with some effective redistribution mechanism (made increasingly difficult through the reduction in state spending resulting from monetarist policies) the effect would be a substantial increase in inequality without a lessening of the problem of unemployment.[93] The current stress on 'de-manning' in most of the core industries of the advanced countries points in this direction; the increasingly capital intensive nature of foreign private investment in the third world has been having this effect there for some time as Vaitsos's work clearly demonstrates.[94]

Our view of both the source of the downturn and the difficulties involved in inducing an upturn confirms the view that the problem of overproduction and unemployment stem directly from *internal* contradictions in the capitalist accumulation process. Thus, though the manner of getting there differs, it confirms Luxemburg's fundamental belief that 'the realisation of the surplus value for the purposes of accumulation is an impossible task for a society which consists solely of workers and capitalists',[95] and that long-term stability therefore requires 'that there should be strata of buyers outside capitalist society'[96] if a desirable balance between supply and demand is to be sustained. We have spent so long attempting to establish this proposition because it is of fundamental importance to the substantive interpretation of the evolution of the post-war monetary system which follows. There we will attempt to demonstrate how the upswing of the 1940s resulted directly from the external impetus given to the world economy through the externalisation of the American surplus in the form of official lending and more especially of unproductive defence expenditure, and how the subsequent instability emerging in the late 1960s stemmed from the exhaustion of this possibility. If this analysis is accepted it then becomes possible to understand 'the failure of world monetary reform' in the eighties not as the result of a lack of political will and technical inadequacy as neoclassical theory does,[97] but as the outcome of a fundamental contradiction in the operation of the capitalist world economy itself.

(ii) *Crisis and the International State System*

To conclude this section we must consider briefly the effects of the crisis on the ability to maintain the international economic equilibrium which the first chapter treated as essential to the viability of the institutional structures which sustain the existing level of international monetary cooperation. This chapter has assumed an integrated world capitalist economy in which the effect of the downswing must be a continuous attack on the viability of all of the weaker fractions of capital. If we now draw on the discussion of the locational effects of uneven development presented in Chapter 3, we can see that this process must also operate to intensify the deflationary pressures on all of the weaker national centres in the system since a disproportionate amount of the less viable productive capacity will be located there. The cuts in state expenditure enforced by monetarist policies are likely to be largest in these centres and must serve to weaken all of those socially provided services which, as external economies, we saw to be critical to the ability of particular locations to attract and sustain a viable productive base. Thus, in the downswing competition ceases to be a means of allowing capitalists to maintain the 'identity' of their interests and instead 'becomes a fight among hostile brothers',[98] and this necessarily translates itself into an international struggle between national centres of accumulation all attempting to save as much of their own productive capacity as possible by expanding their share of a constantly shrinking world market.

In these circumstances one of the sources of external demand identified by Luxemburg was the existence of non-capitalist markets in the colonial world. Now, given the almost complete domination of these markets by the capitalist mode of production, these opportunities no longer exist and the current effects of the crisis are being experienced as a constant reduction in the capacity of the third world to import western output and even to sustain its payments for past debt. Against this it remains perfectly possible for the strongest centres to continue to expand, to worsen the overall balance of payments crisis and thus continually to intensify the problems being experienced by the weak. This decisively exposes the inadequacy of the neoclassical view (ever more stridently propagated by the political representatives of the strongest countries) that a reversion to the use of untrammelled market forces will serve to restore an equilibrium favourable to all. If the system is not to collapse as a result of these increasing inequalities it is evident that the central political structures must find some means of redistributing resources from strong to weak in order to offset these imbalances along the lines set out in Chapter 1. But because the pressures on the producers in even the strongest centres are also intensifying, the possibility of organising this process through voluntary political agreement diminishes in direct proportion to the increase in the need for it.

The implications of these arguments for our interpretation of the past evolution and future prospects of the post-war monetary system are very serious as they suggest that the reformist measures now being attempted can do nothing to resove its problems for these arise from structural contradictions internal to the system itself. We have now to attempt to confirm this assertion through a direct examination of the evolution of key aspects of that system and of the problems that it now confronts.

Notes

1. For an excellent statement of the presuppositions of the orthodox equilibrium model, and its theoretical relationship to the examination of dynamic processes see, J.A. Schumpeter, *Business cycles*, New York, McGraw Hill, 1964, Chapter 2.
2. Here it is perhaps worth noting that Marx himself treated 'the whole world of trade as one nation', in his own analysis of capital accumulation. (K. Marx, *Capital*, Vol. I, Harmondsworth, Penguin, 1976, p. 727).
3. G. Haberler's phrase: *Prosperity and depression*, Cambridge, Harvard University Press, 1958, p. 323.
4. K. Marx, *Grundrisse*, Harmondsworth, Penguin, 1973, p. 156.
5. Ibid., p. 148.
6. P. Sweezy, *The theory of capitalist development*, New York, *Monthly Review*, 1970, p. 135.
7. J.S. Mill, *Principles of political economy*, London, Longmans Green, 1900, p. 338.
8. Ibid.
9. J.B. Say, 'Of the demand or market for products', in H. Hazlitt, *The critics of Keynesian economics*, Princeton, van Nostrand, 1960, p. 15.
10. A. Marshall, 'The pure theory of domestic values', cited in J.M. Keynes, *The general theory of employment, interest and money*, London, Macmillan, 1973, p. 19.
11. Keynes, op. cit., p. 100.
12. Mill, op. cit., p. 338. I am indebted to Donald Winch, Professor of Economics, Sussex University, for this point.
13. M. Bienefeld, 'Interpreting excess capacity', (mimeo), Institute of Development Studies, Sussex University, p. 6.
14. A.A. Young, 'Increasing returns and economic progress', *Economic Journal*, Vol. 38, 1928, p. 534.
15. For some of the relevant figures see E. Mandel, *The generalized recession of the international capitalist economy*, Brussels, Imprecor, 1975, p. 7.
16. Keynes, op. cit., p. 379.
17. This approach is most closely identified with the work of N.D. Kondratieff and the debate which it initiated in the 1930s. See the article on his work in the *International Encyclopedia of the Social Sciences*, Vol. 6, 1968, by G. Garvey; for a useful and critical account of the 'long wave debate' see J. Clark et al., 'Long waves and technological developments in the 20th century', Science Policy Research Unit, Sussex University, 1980.

18. Notably R. Harrod, *Economic dynamics*, London, Macmillan, 1973; J.R. Hicks, *Capital and growth*, Oxford, Clarendon Press, 1965; and E. Domar, 'Capital expansion, rate of growth and unemployment', *Econometrica*, Vol. 14, 1976.

19. Haberler, op. cit.; Schumpeter, op. cit.

20. For a review of the historical development of the debate see E. Mandel, *Marxist economic theory*, Vol. 1, New York, *Monthly Review*, 1962, Chapter 11; for an excellent synthesis of the elements of Marx's theory see T. Weisskopf, 'Marxian crisis theory', *Cambridge Journal of Economics*, Vol. 3, no. 4, 1979.

21. Notably in E. Mandel, op. cit., pp. 344–60, and *Late Capitalism*, London, Verso, 1975, Chapters 4 and 17.

22. Haberler, op. cit., p. 257.

23. Ibid., p. 264.

24. Ibid., p. 259.

25. Ibid., pp. 257–8.

26. Ibid., pp. 268–9.

27. Mandel locates the beginning of the downswing (the 'crisis' in Haberler's technical sense) in 1967 (*Late Capitalism*, op. cit., p. 132). I would accept that the underlying tendency was clearly downward from this point onwards, but that this was conceived by various inflationary external factors, notably the expenditure generated by the Vietnam war. It was the oil crisis, together with the ending of the war which brought these underlying tendencies out into the open.

28. Note here the statements of Friedman and Johnson, Chapter 2, notes 30 and 33.

29. Keynes, op. cit., p. 378.

30. Note in particular the comment on Friedman in Chapter 2, note 36.

31. Note here Schumpeter's insistence that 'technological progress was of the very essence of capitalistic enterprise', (op. cit., p. 5) and his excellent examination of the nature of innovation and its dramatic effects upon orthodox equilibrium theory (Chapters 2 and 3).

32. Weisskopf, op. cit., p. 341.

33. K. Marx, *Capital*, Vol. I, Harmondsworth, Penguin, 1976, p. 433.

34. Harrod, op. cit.

35. Weisskopf, op. cit., p. 344. Here I am accepting the value of his attempt to reduce the Marxian 'value-theoretical framework ... into a price framework', (p. 343) though this does involve some simplifications which might be rejected by the purists.

36. Reductions in the cost of inputs or increases in price have been excluded from the argument here.

37. Marx, *Capital*, Vol. I, Harmondsworth, Penguin, 1976, p. 515, for a discussion of the relationship between technical change and the trade cycle see Clark et al., op. cit.

38. Weisskopf, op. cit., p. 344.

39. K. Marx, *Capital*, Vol. III, London, Lawrence and Wishart, 1972, p. 213.

40. Mandel, *Marxist economic theory*, op. cit., p. 166; the internal quotation is from L.R. Klein, *The Keynesian revolution*, p. 68.

41. Ibid.

42. Marx, *Capital*, Vol. III, op. cit., p. 223.

43. Hence the emergence of 'small' firms employing very limited numbers of workers made possible through the emergence of automated technology would not offset this tendency since their very large output would now require an increasing share of the existing market.

44. Marx, *Capital*, Vol. III, op. cit., p. 58.
45. Schumpeter, op. cit., pp. 61, 62.
46. Ibid., p. 62.
47. Ibid.
48. Ibid., p. 50.
49. Ibid., p. 64.
50. Ibid., p. 66.
51. F. Knight, 'Some fallacies in the interpretation of social cost', *Quarterly Journal of Economics*, Vol. 38, 1924, p. 597.
52. Here see J.S. Bain, *Barriers to new competition*, Harvard University Press, 1962; and *Industrial organisation*, 2nd edn., New York, Wiley, 1968; E.T. Penrose, *The theory of the growth of the firm*, Oxford, Blackwell, 1966, Chapter XI; and J. Eaton and Lipsey, 'Freedom of entry and the existence of pure profit', *Economic Journal*, Vol. 88, 1978, p. 466.
53. P. Sraffa, 'The laws of returns under competitive conditions', reprinted in P.C. Newman et al., *Source readings in economic thought*, New York, Norton, 1954, p. 598.
54. J.M. Blair, *Economic concentration*, New York, Harcourt Brace, 1972, p. 420.
55. E.W. Hawley, *The new deal and the problem of monopoly*, Princeton, Princeton University Press, 1966, pp. 174–5.
56. J.M. Keynes to F.D. Roosevelt, 1 February 1938 (I owe this reference to Donald Winch, Professor of Economics, Sussex University).
57. C. Vaitsos, *Intercountry income distribution and transnational enterprises*, Oxford, Clarendon, 1974.
58. Notably in S. Holland, *The socialist challenge*, London, Quartet Books, 1976.
59. A. Kahn, 'Market power inflation', in G. Means et al., *The costs of inflation*, London, Wilton House, 1975, p. 544; here see also Lance Taylor, *Macro models for developing countries*, New York, McGraw Hill, 1979, Chapter 5.
60. Mandel, *Marxist economic theory*, op. cit., pp. 361–6.
61. Marx,, *Capital*, Vol. III, pp. 244–5, 255–6; *Capital*, Vol. I, Chapter 25, deals more directly with the problem of the proportions between capital and labour and the resulting growth of the 'reserve army of labour'.
62. Means's work in the 1930s was of critical importance in the identification of this process. See in particular National Resources Committee, *The structure of the American economy*, Part 1, edited by G. Means, 1939, reprinted New York. Kelley, 1966.
63. Notably Holland, op. cit.; P. Baran and P. Sweezy, *Monopoly capital*, Harmondsworth, Penguin, 1966.
64. E. Mandel, *Late capitalism*, op. cit., p. 531.
65. Ibid., p. 537.
66. J.R. Hicks, 'Mr Harrod's dynamic theory', in American Economic Association, *Readings in business cycles*, London, Allen & Unwin, 1966, p. 31; another account of this process can be found in Haberler, op. cit., p. 288.
67. Haberler, Ibid., p. 323.
68. Ibid., pp. 325–6.
69. R. Luxemburg, *The accumulation of capital*, London, Routledge and Kegan Paul, 1963. Although I find this aspect of the argument misplaced I would agree with her overall view that capitalism requires a constant expansion in demand from external sources to sustain its necessary growth rate once full employment has been

reached. Hence I agree with her identification of the *consequences* of the inevitable failure to remain at this level, much of which has yet to be bettered.

70. K. Marx, *Capital*, Vol.. II, London, Lawrence and Wishart, 1970, p. 441.
71. Ibid., p. 454.
72. Ibid.,p. 455.
73. He argued that the sinking funds set up in the US by 1929 were so 'huge' that it became 'almost hopeless' to find sufficient new investment to 'absorb these financial provisions'. Hence he felt that 'this factor alone was probably sufficient to cause a slump', (Keynes, op. cit., p. 100).
74. Marx, *Capital*, Vol. II, op. cit., p. 469.
75. See in particular, Ibid., p. 472.
76. Ibid., p. 473.
77. Ibid.
78. A. Glyn and B. Sutcliffe, *British capitalism, workers and the profit squeeze*, Harmondsworth, Penguin, 1972, p. 65.
79. Ibid., p. 75; confirmation can also be found in BIS, *Annual Report*, 1980/81, p. 41.
80. Weisskopf, op. cit., esp. pp. 362ff.
81. R. Boyer, 'Wage formation in historical perspective: the French experience,' *Cambridge Journal of Economics*, Vol. 3, no. 2, 1979, pp. 116–7.
82. Ibid., p. 113.
83. B. Rowthorn, 'Marx's theory of wages', in *Capitalism, conflict and inflation*, London, Lawrence and Wishart, 1980, p. 220.
84. Note here, for example Harrod's assertion that wage controls are essential given permanent full employment to avoid a 'wage–price spiral'. (Harrod, op. cit., pp. 116–7). Note also the Confederation of British Industry's call for compulsory wage restraint in the context of a call for a return to 'market disciplines' with respect to all other areas of policy. (CBI, *The road to recovery*, London, CBI, 1976, p. 20.)
85. This is clearly the strategy being followed by the Thatcher government in 1981, thus confirming Marx's assertion of the necessity for a 'reserve army' to subject the class 'to the dictates of capital'. (*Capital*, Vol. I, op. cit., p. 789.
86. Rowthorn, op. cit., p. 220.
87. Ibid.
88. Marx, *Capital*, III, op. cit., p. 256.
89. Here see J. O'Connor, *The fiscal crisis of the state*, New York, St. Martin's Press, 1973, for a Marxist view, and R. Bacon and W. Eltis, *Britain's economic problem: too few producers*, London, Macmillan, 1976, for an orthodox view.
90. Rowthorn, op. cit., p. 210; here, instead, we can locate many of the publicity provided 'external economies' identified in Chapter 3 as a major source of competitive power for the industries located in particular regions.
91. Compare this statement, attributed to Friedman, with Marx's assertion that 'if society wants to satisfy some want, and have an article produced for this purpose, it must pay for it'. (*Capital*, Vol. III, p. 187).
92. H. Simon, *A positive program for laissez-faire*, cited in Blair, op. cit., pp. 541–2.
93. I owe this point to Luke Sute, Fellow, Science Policy Research Unit, Sussex University.
94. Note in particular his assertion that multinationals have actually employed no more than 2½–4 million people in the whole of the third world. C. Vaitsos,

Employment problems and transnational enterprises in developing countries: distortions and inequality, Geneva, International Labour Organisation, 1976, p. 1.
95. Luxemburg, op. cit., p. 350.
96. Ibid., p. 351.
97. Notably in J. Williamson, *The failure of world monetary reform, 1971–1974*, London, Nelson, 1977.
98. Marx, *Capital*, Vol. III, op. cit., p. 253.

Part III
Integration and Disintegration in the International Monetary System, 1945–1981

Prologue

all science would be superfluous if the outward appearance and the essence of things directly coincided.
(K. Marx, *Capital*, Vol. III, London, Lawrence & Wishart, 1972, p. 817)

This book attempts to provide an explanation of the collapse of the international monetary order which transcends those hitherto provided for us by orthodox or Keynesian theorists. Because of the importance of theory in any interpretation of concrete events, a great deal of space was devoted to the development of an alternative theoretical structure in the preceding chapters. It now seems equally essential that we link these abstract arguments to a concrete account of the period in order to secure the 'reintegration of theory and history'[1] fundamental to the scientific method established by Marx and those who have followed him. This decisively rejects both idealism and a mechanistic determinism by developing categories that enable us to comprehend the nature of the objective possibilities which confront people who, living in the real world, must attempt to make their own history, but can never make it entirely as they choose.[2]

The critical significance of these methodological issues emerges clearly from even a cursory examination of the political consequences of the general acceptance of bourgeois explanations of the post-war monetary crisis. In the orthodox view this stems directly from the Keynesian interventionism which has disrupted the rationality of the market and thus allowed rigidities and indisciplines to develop which preclude the operation of the automatic mechanisms which would otherwise have maintained both prosperity and equilibrium. For Keynesians, however, there is no automatic tendency towards equilibrium at the international level, and the tendency towards crisis can only be intensified by the attempt to reimpose the neoclassical disciplines. These conflicting views, considered in detail in Part I, have in fact provided the capitalist world with the intellectual basis for political mobilisation in the post-war period, so that the bulk of the struggles over monetary policy which have occurred at the national and international levels during these years have in fact been conducted in the form of a debate between these two bodies of thought.

The extended analysis of these views presented in Part I was a response to their importance in this ongoing policy debate. The critique then presented in Part II attempted to demonstrate that neither considered certain fundamental aspects of the development process under capitalism, and that neither of them could therefore serve to provide us with an adequate explanation of its current inability to solve its fundamental problems. This critique took the form of an attempt to substantiate a series of fundamental assertions – that free trade leads to uneven, not even, development; that this must eventually destroy the balance between supply and demand unless some exogenous source of liquidity can be found; that capitalism can generate a powerful upswing in productive capacity if such a source can be found, but that this must sooner or later run up against objective limits and culminate in a crisis of overproduction and underconsumption. These views suggest that the need for a far more radical political response to the crisis than those which have predominated hitherto; they also suggest the need for a fundamental reinterpretation of the events of the post-war period that have brouhgt about the present situation. It may help to clarify the following attempt to do this if we begin here by relating the main features of the period as a whole to the theoretical arguments that have been developed thus far.

Post-war economic development, looked at in relation to the trade cycle theory developed earlier, can be seen as a recovery in the 1940s from depression and war, an upswing in the 1950s, a period of prosperity in the 1960s, a crisis in the 1970s and a likely return to depression in the 1980s. Looked at in relation to monetary policies, we see a period of close nationalist controls in the 1940s and 1950s giving way to an increasing liberalisation and internationalisation in the 1960s and 1970s. Superimposing these two tendencies, we can see that the development successes of the 1940s and 1950s produced the context within which it was actually possible for the liberalisation of the 1960s and 1970s to occur. For bourgeois theory this combination of liberalisation and growth serves as the major validation of their commitment to the structures which sustain the open world capitalist economy. So powerful was the tendency, indeed, that few thinkers stopped to ask whether the actual processes involved derived their shape from the relationships assumed by orthodoxy or could be the outcome of other, very different variables. The subsequent collapse of the equilibrium conditions combined with the evident failure of monetarist prescriptions now strongly suggests that this was indeed the case. When we actually look at these earlier events in the light of this knowledge a number of glaring inconsistencies immediately emerge which will provide the remainder of this book with its substance and will be briefly anticipated here.

The recovery and upswing owed little or nothing to liberal theory and a great deal to exogenous variables – notably a substantial level of direct government control over trade and monetary variables and a massive level of American overseas defence and aid expenditure in response to Soviet expansionism in Eastern Europe and the Chinese threat in Asia. Secondly, the resulting US deficit which sustained this expansion produced, by the start of the prosperous 1960s, a surplus of dollars overseas combined with a relative decline in American productive superiority which was quickly seen to constitute a long-term threat to the viability of the Bretton Woods system itself. This problem, again, could not be comprehended through orthodox theory (it took the work of Triffin, a political scientist, to bring it to the surface[3]), since it was essentially the outcome of the fact that growth took uneven rather than even forms. The early attempts to deal with it in the 1960s therefore made little impression, thus paving the way for the crisis in the system initiated by Nixon's cynical repudiation of America's Bretton Woods obligations in August 1971. Finally, the increasing stresses involved in maintaining the prosperity, arising out of the variables discussed in Chapter 4, emerged dramatically in the mid 1970s with the first major downturn in production initiated by the oil price increase in 1973/4, and the continuation of uncontrolled inflation combined with increasing unemployment in response to the contradictory nature of official attempts to maintain output without moving towards the direct planning of money, trade and investment. These problems, and their effect on monetary and financial variables, remain entirely unresolved and are now likely to initiate a period of prolonged depression. This book, ambitious enough as it stands, makes no attempt to spell out any alternatives, but instead concludes by attempting to demonstrate how the arguments presented here can be directly related to those presented in Lenin's seminal work on the problems of the international capitalist economy, leading to a confirmation of his conclusion that short of some very fundamental changes the outer limits of the capitalist system have now very probably been reached.[4]

Notes

1. E. Mandel, *Late capitalism*, London, Verso, 1978, p. 19.
2. The paraphrase is from K. Marx, 'The eighteenth Brumaire of Louis Bonaparte', in K. Marx and F. Engels, *Selected Works*, 1968, p. 97; the concept of 'objective possibility' is derived from G. Lukacs, *History and class consciousness*, London, Merlin, 1971, p. 51.
3. See R. Triffin, *Gold and the dollar problem*, New Haven, Yale University Press, 1960.
4. V.I. Lenin, *Imperialism*, Moscow, Progress Publishers, 1970.

5 The System and its Flaws: an Overview

Chapter 1 argued that the success of the attempt to unify the international monetary system initiated at Bretton Woods required a general commitment to the creation of an essentially open trading system. This implied the renunciation of the right to use protectionist measures, hitherto closely associated with the assertion of national sovereignty in the economic sphere, which involved the application of monetary controls to secure competitive balance of payments advantage, and a willingness to allow policy in this critical sphere to operate within the limits set by the Articles of Agreement of the International Monetary Fund. The possibility of sustaining these commitments, together with the feasibility of the monetary arrangements based on them, were then shown to depend upon the ability to maintain an overall balance of payments equilibrium at the global level based upon an even rather than uneven development of the world's productive capacity.

The central debate at Bretton Woods took the form of a struggle over the actual resources to be put at the disposal of the new monetary agency to enable it to intervene positively to promote this latter process by assisting the weaker countries to develop their productive powers rapidly enough to enable them to compete more effectively with the strong. Here the US, the key surplus country, was only willing to allow it the controls necessary to promote unfettered trade and the minimal supplies of credit required to induce deficit countries to adjust without resorting to protectionism; the deficit countries, led by Britain, felt that it should also incorporate mechanisms capable of controlling the tendency to accumulate surpluses in strong countries and of reallocating them productively to stimulate the development of weak ones. The outcome of this unequal struggle was the establishment of the IMF (International Monetary Fund) as an agency which owed almost all of its form to the interests of the US as the only country capable of providing it with its resources. It entered the world with a fundamental commitment to liberalisation and only limited powers of direct intervention in the form of an ability to provide short-term balance of payments financing in exchange for an obligation to adopt the foreign and domestic economic policies most conducive to the resolution of the problem within the framework of the liberal trading and monetary system most favoured by the surplus countries.

If the assertions about the uneven nature of unmanaged capitalist development made in Chapters 3 and 4 are correct, the outcome of this solution should have been a very rapid process of disintegration followed by a reversion to the autarchic policies which had dominated the economic life of the 1930s. Thus the first problem that we have to consider in this chapter is the apparent failure of this prediction manifested in the upswing engendered after 1947, the relative decline of American economic superiority in relation to the leading European countries and Japan, and the corresponding ability to eliminate most monetary controls and substantially reduce protective barriers from the late 1950s onwards. We have thus to provide a convincing explanation for the very substantial achievements of the post-war capitalist system which have been the foundation of its ability to sustain a relatively stable democratic political structure in the advanced countries and to extend some form of political independence to the third world. On the other hand, we have also to consider that this process of expansion and integration culminated in a period of increasing stress in the late 1960s which led to the collapse of certain critical components of the Bretton Woods settlement in the 1970s – notably the ending of dollar–gold convertibility and the transition from fixed to floating exchange rates. These changes, the outcome of the eventual reassertion of the law of combined and uneven development, have also to be considered here if we are to understand the issues involved in the attempts to reform the system which will be considered below.

This chapter, therefore, will contain a necessarily problematic attempt to explain an entirely contradictory process – the evolution of a system of international economic organisation which initially sustained a massive increase in integration, but only achieved this through processes which, because of their uneven nature, undermined the foundations on which it was based and hence produced structural changes which initiated a new period of crisis once they had fully matured. To do this it will be necessary to consider two things – the factors which offset the tendencies to uneven development and allowed the recovery and upswing to occur and their effects, and the effect of these structural changes on the workability of the monetary arrangements established at Bretton Woods. Because there is a wide range of historical accounts of these processes, they will only be considered in the broadest detail here.

The American Deficit and International Economic Restructuring

In 1945 the US controlled some 70 per cent of the world's financial assets and had survived the war with its productive equipment massively expanded; Western Europe and Japan returned to demolished cities and diminished productive capacity; most of the rest of the world was locked into the underdevelopment resulting from colonial subordination. If Hume and his successors were to be believed these massive imbalances should have produced an automatic tendency towards equalisation. Full employment in the USA should have led to a rapid increase in relative prices and to an outflow of capital to the weaker centres. These, taking advantage of this flow and of an almost infinite supply of low cost, disorganised labour power, should then have been able to generate a rapid growth in both production and in exports to the US to pay for the capital transfers involved. This process could be expected to continue until their productive resources were fully deployed when the tendency would begin to reverse itself.

In the event, however, the enormous superiority of the American productive investment more than offset the low wage advantage of its competitors, and it ran substantial surpluses in 1946 and 1947 with the result that 'the rest of the world used about $6 billion of its gold and dollar holdings to finance its deficit with the United States'[1] and Europe's reserves fell by one fourth as a result. Those concerned with monetary affairs rather than monetary theory quickly recognised that Hume's nostrums had little relevance to this situation. Solomon, an eminent American banker thus reports that:

> It was believed that American products would remain especially attractive, in terms of price, quality and availability, and would easily outcompete those Europe and Japan in their own markets, in other countries, and in the United States.[2]

The possibility of a continuation of this situation if 'natural' market forces were allowed to continue to operate unchecked, of course, threatened the viability of far more than some central tenets of orthodox economic theory – it put the very creation of a successful post-war capitalist order at serious risk.

Looked at from the perspective of the US, the hegemonic international power of the day, the problem manifested itself concretely in the emergence of three imminent threats. Firstly, American industry itself, having completed the early re-equipment of domestic industry, now faced a problem of potential surplus capacity if it were unable to find expanding foreign markets. Thus full employment would quickly be threatened unless some means could be found of providing the rest of the world with the dollars required to enable it to re-equip itself with the capital goods being produced in such abundance by America.[3] Secondly, the intensification of the foreign exchange squeeze in 1946/7 strengthened the position of left-wing political forces which were still very influential in western Europe and were committed to policies of economic nationalism and centralised planning likely to preclude the creation of the liberal international economic order which the Americans wanted. These tendencies manifested themselves clearly in the international debate over the creation of the proposed International Trade Organisation during these years, and in the incorporation of such strong commitments to planning and economic nationalism in the Havana Charter that American interests were forced to repudiate it by blocking its passage through Congress.[4] Finally, and most dramatically, the failure to produce an adequate solution to the problems of weaker countries manifested itself in a series of communist victories in eastern Europe and Asia which intensifed both the economic and the military threat to the system itself. In these circumstances liberal solutions had to be jettisoned in favour of a massive direct intervention in which American economic and military power could be marshalled in a form capable of overcoming the tendency to uneven development which threatened the system itself.

The source of these critical problems was seen at the time as the 'dollar shortage', the monetary expression of the relative weakness of the productive capacity of the old world in its dealings with the new. The problem was then resolved as an act of central policy, not market realignment, through the establishment of a 'dollar deficit' which has lasted almost uninterruptedly to the present and was created mainly by American aid and defence expenditure abroad. Thus Balogh wrote:

> It took $84,000 million of grants and loans ... or 15 times the original dollar component of IMF and 6½ times the total maximum lending power of the [World] Bank; and military expenditure and supply grants abroad of an average of well over $5,000 million per annum since 1952 to restore balance. American domestic demand was buttressed by military expenditure which between 1951 and 1961 amounted to $451 billions.[5]

This process was extended in 1950 when the effect of the 'rearmament and stockpiling programmes in the United States' induced by the Korean War 'was to increase the volume of their imports and reduce the availability of goods for export'.[6] Once the advanced industrial economies had been rebuilt the threat of communist penetration in the third world continued, serving as a stimulus to aid programmes in the 1950s and initiating a renewed increase in the US deficit in the 1960s once it had become fully involved in the Vietnam war. It should be noted in passing, that the majority of the so-called Newly Industrialised Countries (NICs) of the third world have been major recipients of these favours which must have had at least as much to do with their successes as their supposed adoption of liberal economic policies.

The creation of this deficit was in fact almost entirely attributable to the effects of overseas defence and aid expenditure. The American trade account remained in credit (although on a progressively diminishing scale) until the end of the 1960s, while foreign private investment abroad, although substantial, has been in continuous surplus. During the 1960s, for example, Robinson asserts that US corporations exported $33 billion, but obtained $64 billion in return.[7] The effects of these interventions were dramatic – the stimulation of the 'economic miracles' of Germany and Japan and the creation of an expansionary impetus which carried the world economy triumphantly into the prosperity of the 1960s and 1970s.

If we can thus explain the success of the upswing as the outcome of the defence and aid commitments forced on the US by the post-war crisis, we can also understand the subsequent instability in the system as the outcome of the resulting weakening of its relative productive capacity. Here we see the classic exemplification of the contradiction embodied in the attempt to use a national currency as the basis for international liquidity examined in Chapter 1 (pp. 30ff). American aid and defence expenditure stimulated rapid economic development in weaker foreign countries without producing the negative balance of payments effects of direct private foreign investment as they did not generate subsequent financial obligations of the same magnitude. At the same time it weakened the relative productive capacity of the central country by diverting resources from productive investment in the domestic economy to productive investment abroad or into unproductive foreign and domestic military expenditure. There can be little doubt that the latter factor was the major element in the American – and, in all probability, British – relative decline. According to Solomon:

Defence spending was of much smaller importance in Europe (and Japan) than in the United States. Of the increase in GNP from 1950 to 1969, almost 15% went to defence spending in the United States, whereas comparable figures in the larger European countries ranged from 2.8% in Germany to 6.4% in the United Kingdom.[8]

The imbalance meant that Europe and Japan could devote much larger percentages of annual output to productive investment than the US and UK so that they were able to sustain much higher rates of productivity growth right through into the 1970s.[9] As a result the productive superiority which originally guaranteed the international position of the dollar had disappeared by the start of the 1960s, creating the need for a radical restructuring of the system as the most far-sighted theorists quickly realised.[10]

The attempts at reform which began in the 1960s as a result will be considered in Chapter 6. We can now conclude this section by pointing briefly to the major consequences of this change in the balance of international economic power. By the 1960s America was no longer the most productive world economy, its foreign exchange and gold reserves no longer matched its external obligations and its now permanent deficit had ceased to perform the benign role of guaranteeing the stability and expansion of the system, and become instead a source of inflation and a tax upon the productive capacity of the surplus countries. By the early 1960s the deficit had reduced gold reserves below the value of external dollar holdings, thereby producing the 'dollar overhang'; they then fell from $17.8 billion in 1960 to $11 billion in 1970 despite the very powerful pressures exerted on countries which, like France, attempted to transform their dollar assets into gold in order to forestall the possibility of an American devaluation.[11] The vulnerability of the dollar to crises of confidence as a result can be gauged from the fact that American gold and monetary reserves 'were sufficient to cover 32 ¢ on the dollar of its liabilities' at the start of 1971, only 18 ¢ at the end as a result of capital outflows and speculative movements.[12]

This decline and the corresponding instability could only have been halted through a return to surplus on the part of the US economy, together with a transition to deficit on the part of the now surplus industrial economies. Again orthodox theory suggests that this should have occurred automatically as a result of the upward cost pressures being imposed upon the strong countries by full employment and expansion. But again their predictions were falsified by the continuing ability of these countries to offset these pressures through the greater productive investment which their international successes made possible for them. Having overcome the relative disadvantages from which they suffered in the 1940s, they had now entirely reversed the situation which had existed then. In the conditions of open exchange, fully established by the 1960s, their competitive power would continue to grow at the expense of the now relatively weaker centres of the US, the UK and, it must also be noted, of the third world as well. Again the *normal* tendency to uneven development in capitalism could only be offset by some external intervention sufficiently powerful to divert resources from strong centres to weaker ones and thereby restore the equilibrium.

But while the conditions of the 1940s forced the US to adopt this role in response to the direct threat of socialist expansionism, those of the 1960s simply intensified the problem. Having taken on the expensive and contradictory role of defender of the international capitalist order, the US was forced to continue to maintain its defence commitments and, indeed, to test their power against the resistance organised by the peasants of Vietnam. The immense success of this apparently puny opposition decisively exposed both the moral and the structural weakness of the system itself. On the monetary side American aggression massively escalated its deficit, creating a situation in which they were importing more and more real resources in exchange for paper tokens whose backing was becoming increasingly devalued, but which the rest of the world was forced to accept by the terms of the Bretton Woods agreement. The result was a rapid escalation of monetary instability and a clear indication that the apple of the prosperity was being actively consumed from within.

The overt manifestation of the problem was a rapid escalation of inflation in both the surplus and the deficit countries. Thus an IMF expert wrote in 1976:

> any consideration of the intensification of inflation in recent years needs to start with the large US budget deficits at the time of the Vietnam war. Because of the size of the US economy, these deficits represented a major inflationary shock to the whole international system.[13]

Because of the relative lack of competitiveness of the US economy this increase in demand led to an increase in imports from the strong countries whose surpluses therefore increased rather than diminished as they should have done. As a result US consumption could be sustained and working class opposition to the war contained; the surplus countries, however, found themselves holding more and more dollars in exchange for their own output. These, automatically entering the domestic money supply in a situation of overfull employment, had immediate inflationary effects, leading an eminent German banker to accuse the system of 'forcing monetary debauchery on surplus countries'.[14] In effect the system was operating to impose a tax on the non-combatants for the payment of the war; the exact size of this became clear after 1971 when dollar devaluation led to a substantial cut in the value of their reserves and hence absolved the Americans from meeting their obligations in full.

A break in the prosperity could certainly have been expected at the end of the 1960s in response to the tendencies examined in Chapter 4 – indeed, Mandel locates the start of the downturn as early as 1967.[15] But the structure of the post-war capitalist system, with its extensive mechanisms for national interventions and international recycling of surpluses, made it possible for growth to continue for a time, albeit on a reduced scale and in an increasingly unstable way. During these years the inequalities already outlined continued to intensify, an actual downturn occurred in 1974/5 in response to the first oil price increase, and growing structural imbalances came to be reflected in an intensification of price inflation and balance of payments deficits. We can now briefly consider some of these broad changes, firstly with respect to the relations between the industrial countries, secondly between them and the third world.

Looking at some of the key indicators of economic performances set out in Table 5.1, we can see that the inequalities between the RU and RS countries continued to increase, with productivity and output growing more rapidly, inflation and unemployment less rapidly in the latter than the former. Between 1976 and 1978 the US was partially able to offset these tendencies by taking advantage of its structural ability to increase its balance of payments deficit by exporting dollars while the strong countries were having to adjust to the negative effects of the 1974/5 recession, and grow more strongly than Germany and almost as fast as Japan, but this improvement was not to last. Towards the end of 1978 the American authorities finally accepted a commitment to arrest the 'steep slide of the dollar' which had followed the growth of the deficit and in 'a new departure in US policy' began to enforce greater restraints, mainly through increases in interest rates and credit controls.[16] As a result growth was much slower in 1979 and the first half of 1980 saw a substantial regression. The RS countries, on the other hand, grew relatively strongly in 1979 and entered the recession a good deal later than the US in 1980. Britain, however, now bereft of external means of offsetting internal weak-

Table 5.1 Key economic indicators for four industrial countries

		Annual average growth in productivity (%)		Growth in real GNP (%)			Inflation measured by GNP deflator* (%)			Unemployment (%)	
		1960–73	1973–79	1963–72	1973–79	1979	1963–72	1973–79	1979	1957–73	Early 1980
Relatively unsuccessful countries	USA	2.1	0.2	3.9	3.0	2.3	3.6	7.4	8.9	5.0	7.0
	UK	3.1	0.7	2.9	2.1	0.9	5.1	14.6	14.4	2.2	6.0
Relatively successful countries	Japan	8.8	3.4	10.5	3.7	6.0	4.9	8.1	2.0	1.1	1.9
	FDR	4.4	3.2	4.5	2.8	4.4	4.1	4.9	3.9	1.4	3.6

*Defined as 'a comprehensive indicator of total domestic unit costs'. (IMF, *Annual Report*, 1980, p. 5).

Sources: Productivity and Unemployment from Bank for International Settlements. *Annual Report*, 1979/80, pp. 31 and 53; Growth and Inflation from IMF, op. cit., p. 8.

nesses, performed uniformly badly over the whole period and would now, but for the fortuitous discovery of oil, be involved in a depression of massive proportions. Externally the period was mainly characterised by balance of payments surpluses for the strong and deficits for the weaker countries; here the major change appears to be a strong movement towards deficit in the case of Germany[17] and towards surplus in the US. But while this long awaited reversal has had the positive short-term effect of reducing the deflationary effect of the 1979 oil price increase, since Germany could largely finance its increased imports out of savings, it would be a mistake to assume that it would be likely to initiate any process of long-term expansion for the world economy where an intensification of the recession is now almost certain.

Several reasons can be adduced for this. First, the movement towards surplus in the US is the outcome of the restrictive policies of the last few years which must not only intensify the recession inside the country, but also serve to deflate international demand with negative consequences for the rest of the system. Secondly, the deterioration in the German (and to a lesser extent Japanese) positions is not the outcome of forces which are likely to boost growth in the same way as the American deficit did in the 1950s. Here an exception might be made for the increases in tourist spending abroad, but not for the growth in foreign private investment which must soon serve to re-establish the surplus once the returns begin to flow back. Equally important, the weakening of export growth results mainly from declining demand abroad, particularly for investment goods which in the German case constitute more than half of manufactured exports,[18] and is hence a sign of weakening conditions abroad rather than a change in relative competitiveness favouring the weaker centres where productivity continues to grow more slowly. Finally, the most important single negative item has been the renewed increase in the cost of energy imports which, far from redistributing resources to weaker areas, has mainly led to an increase in surpluses held by the most favoured OPEC countries. Because the overall response to the increase in inflation and payments imbalances which have now emerged (and in which the strong countries are again doing much better than the weak) is an intensification of the deflationary monetarist policies examined earlier, we can see that there is little prospect of any improvement.

These problems of instability and recession become even more significant, however, when they are related to the structural imbalances and deflationary tendencies being confronted by the greater part of the third world. Here again important distinctions have to be drawn between the fates of the strong in contrast to the weak performers – the OPEC countries and NICs on the one hand and the low income countries on the other. While conditions in the first two are relatively favourable, serious problems exist for all of them which could, in certain circumstances precipitate a major crisis for the whole of the world economy; on the other hand conditions in the latter are almost uniformly disastrous pointing towards a period of extended regression and instability.

The OPEC countries have been major beneficiaries of the relative growth in the demand for energy stemming from the rising organic composition of the capitalist production structure. Their special advantages have made it possible for them to increase their income without increasing production and thus to appropriate large monopoly rents which have been used to finance an orgy of personal consumption on the part of their ruling classes and a reasonably rapid growth in domestic production. While this growth is likely to continue, its stability is by no means assured. It is possible, though not likely, that the surpluses may decline as rapidly as they did between 1975 and 1978 (when the OPEC countries as a whole were in net deficit) if demand continues to decline, Iran and Iraq are able to settle their differences and restore their lost output, and new producers, notably Mexico, begin to increase theirs. If this occurs the level of demand for imports from OPEC countries will decline, negatively affecting some exporters, but the deflationary consequences of existing price levels will also be removed. Equally significant from the point of view of the system as a whole, is the danger of a major social upheaval, equivalent to the one that occurred in Iran, in one of the major suppliers, notably Saudi Arabia. This would further reduce supplies, push up prices and tighten the deflationary noose around the rest of the world's productive capacity. Finally, the present build-up of oil surpluses is increasing the stress on international credit institutions, pushing up inflation and exerting a downward pressure on demand. If it continues the global situation can only worsen, especially that of the low income third world countries.

During the 1970s a number of middle income LDCs – notably the small countries benefiting most directly from US aggression in Asia – were able to expand relatively rapidly by increasing their industrial exports and finance investment through a substantial increase in external inflows, especially from the Eurodollar market. Their experience has been taken as a model for the rest of the third world by neoclassical theorists,[19] and has provided a growing market for industrial exports from the centre. Whether they will be able to maintain their impetus (and thus continue to serve as an attractive advertisement for the benefits of orthodox policies) is now increasingly open to doubt, given declining demand and protectionism in the industrial centres, the possibility of reduced access to private credit as a result of their build-up of debt, the growing cost of financing this debt and the escalating price of energy. Further, they, too, are now suffering from spiralling inflation and having to attempt to control wage increases. Hence their generally repressive regimes are having to act with even greater violence and could initiate a political crisis at almost any time – recent upheavals in South Korea involving the occupation of a whole city suggests that this is a real possibility. Here the critical risk to the stability of the system as a whole results from the effects that such a crisis in a heavily indebted country (particularly in Brazil or in Mexico which hold about 40 per cent of third world Eurodollar debt) would have upon an international banking system which is already greatly over-extended. A major country default could initiate a financial crisis of substantial proportions, especially given the increasing provision having to be made for bad domestic debts by the major international banks.

Finally, there can be no doubt that the low income countries have experienced the second half of the 1970s as a period of sustained, structural recession. With escalating balance of payments problems, slow or negative rates of growth and increasing levels of internal inequality and unemployment, they have been able neither to provide for their own populations, nor to sustain any increase in demand for foreign producers. They have not been able to make much use of commercial credit facilities and have had to rely on the stagnant supply of official concessional lending. Their exports have confronted declining growth in the industrial centres, and their own attempts to modernise have largely collapsed in a welter of corruption, incompetence and repression. Their immediate prospects are even bleaker, since the recession must push down concessional funding (notwithstanding the appeals made in the Brandt Commission[20]) and reduce raw material prices while inflation continues to push up the price of their industrial and energy imports. Their current balance of payments situation is entirely unmanageable (an increase in the deficit of all developing countries from $53 billion to $70 billion is anticipated between 1979 and 1980[21]) so that many of them cannot sustain their supplies of essential capital equipment, spare parts and medicines and are suffering a real decline in productive capacity as a result, while inflation is now running at an *average* of 30 per cent. Political instability is now endemic, with potentially revolutionary movements being able to make stronger and stronger appeals for mass support, while the ruling classes find it more and more difficult to generate resources sufficient even to retain the loyalty of middle income and entrepreneurial strata. After their experience in Vietnam the Americans have been loath to intervene and have even allowed Somoza to be evicted from Nicaragua. Clearly the relative stability of the old *pax Americana* is a thing of the past.

The overall impression that emerges from this account is, on the surface at least, one of great variation where a few countries have been able to maintain or even improve their relative competitive positions by exploiting their favourable endowments of capital or natural resources, while the majority of the others have suffered the bulk of the losses stemming from the recession. It is thus impossible actually to assert that the position of particular countries *must* deteriorate in this situation, since, given its fluid, competitive nature, it will always be possible for some to improve their positions, albeit at the cost of worsening those of others. If one merely looks at the problems of individual countries, it is therefore still possible to advance monetarist remedies for the lack of internal demand which involve a futher intensification of deflation where it is assumed that the resulting increase in competitiveness will secure a larger share of an external market.[22] When the recession is world-wide, however, as it now is because of the problems of over-production and under-consumption set out in Chapter 4, the contradictory nature of the strategy becomes self-evident for it is impossible for everyone, with the limited exception of the surplus OPEC countries, to increase their exports and reduce their domestic consumption simultaneously. Surplus capacity exists in all of the industrial countries in the form of the high levels of unemployment and low capacity utilisation, especially in key manufacturing sectors such as shipbuilding, steel and motor manufacturing. In this context global deflation is entirely irrational even on the basis of the limited critique of these measures provided by Keynes in the *General Theory*. Thus even the Bank for International Settlements, not a notably radical institution, now considers that the extensive application of these policies might 'push the western industrial world into an outright recession', that the effect of this will be to 'shift the burden of the current account deficits from the stronger industrial countries to the weaker ones and, in particular to the non-oil LDCs', and that the persistent problems of inflation, public sector deficits and oil imbalances might therefore put us back 'on the road to stagflation – but with even more inflation, less growth and wider imbalances than after the first oil shock'.[23] The report concludes its analysis with an outline of its own policy proposals which can only intensify the problems which it outlines here; clearly something more than reforms are now required to rescue a system whose inner logic is producing such disastrous consequences.

The Breakdown of Bretton Woods
The Bretton Woods system was based upon four key commitments – to the US dollar as a universal currency convertible into gold at a fixed price; to fixed exchange rates in the rest of the system, adjustable only in extreme circumstances; to open monetary and trading arrangements; and to the creation of the IMF as an agency capable of maintaining the stability of the whole system by supervising these general obligations and providing short-term balance of payments financing to countries facing serious external deficits. Only the latter two have survived the 1970s, and then in an increasingly untenable form as protectionism grows,[24] while the effects of IMF interventions are subjected to fundamental criticism from the representatives of the deficit countries which are supposed to be their principal beneficiaries.[25] Having looked at both the theoretical reasons for these changes in Chapter 1, and at the changes in economic conditions that produced them in the previous section, we can now document very briefly the actual events which led to the breakdown of the arrangements themselves.

The termination of dollar_gold convertibility
We noted in Chapter 1 how any international monetary system must create a universal currency which is both stable in value and universally available, how the hegemonic position of the US at Bretton Woods made it possible for the dollar to take on this role, and how this then created a contradiction for the system itself. While the stability of the dollar depended upon the overwhelming strength of the American economy itself, its external availability required that foreign countries be in a position to maintain a continuous balance of payments surplus with it in order to be able to acquire the resources required to finance imports from the US and their trade with third

parties. The previous section showed how this problem was dealt with through the growth of American foreign credits and defence spending. Tables 5.2 and 5.3 give a clear indication of the actual changes in the balance of payments and foreign reserves that occurred as a result.

Table 5.2 The US balance of payments, 1945–79
($ billion 1946–64; SDR billion 1968–79)

	Trade balance	All payments		Trade balance	All payments
1946	6.6	1.4	1969	0.6	−5.5
1947	10.0	3.8	1970	2.2	−2.7
1950	1.0	−3.4	1971	−2.7	−19.8
1955	2.8	−1.2	1975	7.4	−3.9
1960	4.8	−3.9	1977	−26.4	−30.03
1964	6.6	−3.1	1979	−22.8	8.7
1968	0.6	−2.5			

Sources: 1946–50, H. Lary, *Problems of the US as world trader and banker*, National Bureau of Economic Research, 1963, p. 164.

1955–64, H. Piquet, *The US balance of payments*, Washington, American Enterprise Institute, 1966, p. 11.

1968–71, IMF, *Balance of Payments Yearbook*, Vol. 25, 1968–72, United States, p. 3.

1975–9, IMF, *Balance of Payments Yearbook*, Vol. 31, no. 8, 1980, p. 21, lines 1A.C4, F1.X4.

The figures in Table 5.2 and 5.3 show how US reserves grew rapidly in the 1940s until they contained 71 per cent of the capitalist world's 'monetary gold stocks' in 1949,[26] declined relatively slowly in the 1950s until external liabilities exceeded reserves in 1961, and then increasingly rapidly in the 1960s until, by 1968, it had become evident that they would fall below the $10 billion mark which was widely considered to be the lowest level which the authorities would consider acceptable. At this point, with military activity intensifying in Vietnam, it became clear that the external deficit could not be sustained without some fundamental change in the structure of the system itself. During this period negotiations were going on which were directed at the limited reforms which will be discussed in Chapter 6, but none of these were radical enough to influence the developments which resulted from the fundamental weaknesses which were now exposed.

Table 5.3   US reserves and external liabilities, 1945–79 (end of period, $ billion)

	Gold	All reserves	External liabilities	Liabilities to central banks		Gold	All reserves	External liabilities	Liabilities to central banks
1937	12.79	13.44	1.89	—	1969	11.86	16.96	45.91	16.00
1945	20.08	20.47	6.01	4.18	1970	11.07	14.49	46.96	23.78
1949	24.56	26.02	6.41	3.36	1971	10.21	13.19	67.81	50.65
1955	21.75	22.80	13.03	8.26	1975	11.60	16.23	126.55	80.71
1960	17.80	19.36	18.69	11.64	1977	11.72	19.31	192.32	126.03
1965	14.06	15.45	25.18	14.17	1979	11.17	18.93	268.36	143.17
1968	10.89	15.71	38.47	17.34	1980*	11.17	23.00	278.50	149.19

* Third quarter

Sources: 1937, 1945, IMF, *International Financial Statistics*, Vol. VII, no. 12. December 1954.
1949–65, IMF, *International Financial Statistics, Supplements to 1966–7 Issues*, United States tables.
1968–71, Ibid., Vol. XXVI, no. 12. December 1973.
1975–9. Ibid., *Yearbook*, 1980.
1980, Ibid, Vol. XXXIV, no. 1, January 1981.

The expanding gap between reserves and foreign liabilities now persuaded outsiders that the dollar must be devalued sooner or later to bring American costs into line with those in the stronger countries, leading to substantial losses for all of those holding dollar denominated assets. The resulting loss of confidence led to an immediate intensification of the pressures on a system which had now come to depend more directly upon confidence than upon the solid backing of real gold and productive capacity. Thus the private demand for gold increased, its price went up and the authorities were forced to create a two-tier gold market in 1968; in 1965 de Gaulle appeared to threaten the system of gold convertibility itself when France 'initiated regular and substantial conversions of dollars into gold';[27] perhaps most significantly immense speculative movements began to occur into or out of currencies threatened with re or devaluation: this greatly intensified the costs of defending them and provided the speculators with an almost risk free source of personal enrichment. Without the old mechanisms of direct currency controls the authorities could do little to stem these movements except adopt politically difficult and usually deflationary policies to improve the balance of payments; the problem of the dollar in the international monetary system in the late 1960s resulted directly from the fact that the Americans were unwilling or unable to do this for reasons of both national and international policy, and were sheltered from the need to do so by the privileged position accorded to them by the dollar's position as the centre currency.[28] We can, perhaps, best understand the implications of this problem for the survival of the system, and the impossibility of resolving it satisfactorily by looking at the nature of the conflicts of interest which it created between the major protagonists.

So far as the US was concerned, its willingness to finance the deficit had enabled it to guarantee an external market to its leading exporters, to defuse the Soviet challenge and, incidentally, to enable its leading corporations to acquire a substantial share of the capital assets on which the expansion of western Europe and the third world was based.[29] Further, its ability to export dollars almost without limit gave it access to what was in effect an interest-free source of credit and thus largely overcome the difficulties which would otherwise have been involved in financing the Vietnam war from domestic sources. On the other hand, however, the commitment to dollar–gold convertibility and a fixed gold price made it impossible to devalue the dollar and this, by the late 1960s, was seen to be the main reason for the growing uncompetitiveness of the domestic American economy and the decline in the trade surplus. Thus the senior American negotiator at the Jamaica conference on monetary reform in the 1970s argued that:

> the Bretton Woods system of exchange rates ... produced a situation in the second half of the 1960s in which the US was at a particular disadvantage as a result of the definition of the dollar in terms of gold and our inability to change the value of the dollar relative to other currencies while at the same time other countries were able to adjust their parities relative to the dollar. I think this produced a situation which was reflected in the erosion of the US current account, of our merchandise trade position'.[30]

In 1968 the US apparently attempted to devalue in response to 'the second big gold crisis' in the first quarter, but was told by the European countries that they would simply follow suit and stop the change from taking effect.[31] In response the Americans adopted their policy of 'benign neglect' which meant that they could 'just let the balance of payments go where it may, which meant a $20 billion deficit in 1971, at which point then the Europeans and the Japanese were somewhat more inclined to accept the fact that the dollar was overvalued'.[32] Thus, when Nixon unilaterally announced the decision to go off gold and to devalue in 1971,[33] the strong countries were unable to resist any further because they would otherwise be faced by an escalation of the deficit and an intensification of the inflationary pressures described in the previous section. The coercive nature of this process was described by an economist from the Federal Reserve Bank to a Senate Sub-Committee, who concluded by noting that 'two devaluations and the subsequent managed float have helped to improve the US competitive position to the point that the merchandise trade balance swung from a $6.4 million deficit in 1972 to close to a $1 billion surplus in 1973, to a huge $20 billion surplus, excluding trade in oil and petroleum products in 1974'.[34]

Having thus broken the connection between the dollar and the value of gold the US could now both continue to sustain a deficit and devalue at will. The improvement in its balance in 1974/5 was short-lived as its imports of oil increased dramatically – its deficit exceeded $30 billion in 1977 and the dollar depreciated continuously against the strong currencies over the whole decade as Table 5.4 shows.

An immense transfer of real resources was now clearly taking place from the surplus countries to the US which they were powerless to control – to argue, as Williamson does, that 'there were no deep-seated conflicts of interests' in this situation 'that compelled countries to adopt incompatible positions'[35] therefore seems to be little short of naive.

From the point of view of the surplus countries the continuation of

Table 5.4   Effective post-Smithsonian exchange rates
(mid-year figures, indices – 21 December 1971 = 100)

	1975	1976	1977	1978	1979
Swiss franc	136	153	148	185	193
DM	116	122	132	141	149
Yen	100	101	112	140	130
Dollar	97	97	97	88	86

Source: Derived from Bank for International Settlements. *Annual Report*. 1977/8. p. 113; 1978/9, p. 138.

the dollar deficit did, indeed, have some advantages. It provided their industries with an expanding market for their output in a period when competitive pressures were beginning to intensify; it enabled the US to take almost the full weight of imperialist defence and thereby spare them both the financial and moral costs of an equal involvement in the policing of the global capitalist order. Thus proponents of the American position could, with some justice, accuse the Europeans of 'glaring incongruities' in that their demand that the US should balance its trade was accompanied by 'blind refusals to pay the full costs of their own defences and to revalue their currencies against the dollar.'[36] In a Ricardian world of equal competition and even development it would have been rational for the strong countries to have made these concessions in 1967/68 when they were asked to do so, but their exporters understood the workings of the system much better than the economists they employed to provide the rationalisations for its operation. Revaluation was resisted for as long as possible, exports to the US were maximised while every effort was made to persuade the Americans to react to their problems by a domestic deflation rather than by adopting the protectionist measures which they had used in the 1940s and 1950s to create their own relative strength. Once the break with gold had been made, however, they were powerless to resist the negative working of a 'dollar standard' system in which there were no effective limits on the ability of the centre country to debase the value of the tokens in pursuit of its own military or economic objectives. This system, Williamson argued, 'necessarily implies a degree of asymmetry in power which, although it actually existed in the early years, had vanised by the time the world found itself sliding into a reluctant dollar standard.'[37]

Thus the outcome of this struggle was the emergence of a 'non-system' from which the Americans could draw substantial short-term advantages, which enabled expansion to continue in the strong countries, albeit in an increasingly inflationary way, which devalued the dollar reserves held by LDCs and subjected them to arbitrary variations in their value and which made it increasingly difficult to believe that the whole system could continue to operate indefinitely with any degree of stability or continuity. From 1971 onwards it has been subject to continuous high level investigation organised mainly through the IMF along lines which will be looked at in Chapter 6. However nothing has emerged to reduce the conflict of interests or the structural imbalances which produced the original collapse so that it seems more and more likely that the changes which do come will move the system back to the protectionism of the 1930s with all that that entails by way of monetary disintegration.

From fixed to floating exchange rates

The fixed parity (or 'adjustable peg') system adopted at Bretton Woods eliminated the possibility of currency manipulation for competitive balance of payments purposes, and provided a stable basis for the conduct of international trade and balance of payments transactions. As we say in Chapter 1, it could only be maintained for as long as most countries, and most especially the centre country, were able to maintain a reasonable balance of payments equilibrium without resorting to damaging interventions in the domestic economy. We can therefore trace the collapse of this component of the system to the same processes of uneven growth that were considered in relation to the ending of convertibility in the preceding section.

In the 1940s the strength of the dollar made it impossible for the weaker countries to adopt convertibility, and forced a general devaluation in 1949. During the remainder of the upswing stable rates were sustained until the late 1960s when the competitive pressures involved in maintaining full employment began to manifest themselves in growing instability. Britain was forced to devalue in 1967 after a long and damaging attempt to defend the existing parity; France did so in 1969 in response to the pressures generated by settlement of the strikes and disturbances of May 1968. But most problematic was the evident desire of the US to do so for the reasons already given – at the Smithsonian Conference in December 1971 the dollar was actually devalued by about 9.7 per cent against the strongest currencies, and by 7.5 per cent on an overall basis.[38] This amount proved too small and a further currency crisis developed at the end of 1972 which was only resolved by the middle of 1973 with a revaluation taking the strong currencies about 17.5 per cent higher.[39] At this point the costs of attempting to continue to defend the adjustable peg system were considered too great (mainly those of defending parities against speculative flows) and a system of 'managed floating' emerged which has continued to the present.

This change was opposed by the IMF itself until the last, partly because of its belief in the usefulness of fixed parities as a means of enforcing domestic policy 'disciplines' on surplus countries, more so because of the difficulties involved in avoiding the use of currency manipulation for competitive purposes once they were removed.[40] The breakdown of the system required an amendment to their Articles of Agreement, which was finally agreed in 1976 and ratified and introduced in 1978. Thus, whereas the old Article IV forebade changes in par values without prior consultation and agreement from the Fund, the new one merely gave it 'firm surveillance' over exchange rate policies, and the obligation to establish 'specific principles for the guidance of all members' in this area.[41] Backed by real powers this change might have given the IMF a substantial increase in its international role, but it was in fact only given the right to consultation and information. Given its failure to exert any influence over the collapse of 1971, it is clear that there are now no effective central controls over the operation of the system, as Witteveen himself more or less conceded at the time.[42] From 1 April 1978, as Abdulla argues, 'the foundations of the Bretton Woods system disappeared'.[43]

Notes

1. R. Solomon, *The international monetary system, 1945–76*, New York, Harper and Row, 1977, p. 14.
2. Ibid., p. 18.
3. See in particular D. Burch, *Overseas aid and the transfer of technology*, Sussex University, PhD, 1979, Chapter 3.
4. See K. Kock, *International trade policy and the GATT, 1947–1967*, Stockholm, Almquist and Wiksell, 1969; and W.A. Brown, *The United States and the restoration of world trade*, Washington, Brookings Institution, 1950, more especially the American Chamber of Commerce resolution cited above, Chapter 1, note 37.
5. T. Balogh, *Unequal partners*, Vol. 2, Oxford, Blackwell, 1963, p. 11.
6. B. Tew, *The evolution of the international monetary system, 1945–77*, London, Hutchinson, 1977, p. 37.
7. H.L. Robinson, 'The downfall of the dollar', *Socialist Register*, 1973, p. 409.
8. Solomon, op. cit., p. 21.
9. Between 1960 and 1975 the productivity of labour grew at an annual rate of 9.7 per

cent in Japan, 5.7 per cent in Germany, but only 3.8 per cent in the UK and 2.7 per cent in the US. (US Department of Labour, Bureau of Labour Statistics, *Bulletin no. 1958*, Washington DC, 1977).

10. Notably Robert Triffin in *Gold and the dollar crisis*, New Haven, Yale University Press, 1961.

11. Note J. Williamson's comment that 'conversion of dollars into gold became an act of political hostility to the United States, especially after de Gaulle launched his gold war in 1965' (*The failure of world monetary reform, 1971–74*, London, Nelson, 1977, p. 25).

12. Robinson, op. cit., p. 414.

13. A.R. Braun, 'Inflation and stagflation in the international economy', *Finance and Development*, Vol. 13, no. 3, 1976, p. 29; see also Solomon, op. cit., Chapter VI; and S. Strange, *International monetary relations*, London, RIIA, 1976.

14. O. Emminger, *Inflation and the international monetary system*, Basle, Per Jacobssen Foundation, 1973, p. 40.

15. E. Mandel, *Late capitalism*, London, Verso, 1978, p. 132.

16. Bank for International Settlements, *Annual Report*, 1979/80, p. 25.

17. For recent reviews see Morgan Guaranty Trust, *World financial markets*, May, October, 1980.

18. Ibid., October 1980, p. 10.

19. For a clear summary see I.M.D. Little, 'Import controls and exports in developing countries', *Finance and Development*, Vol. 15, no. 3, 1978; for an excellent survey article, D.T. Healey, 'Development policy: new thinking about an interpretation', *Journal of Economic Literature*, Vol. X, no. 3, 1972; for an outline of the problem of credit and money, R.I. MacKinnon, *Money and capital in economic development*, Washington, Brookings Institution, 1973.

20. Independent Commission on International Development, *North–South: a programme for survival*, London, Pan, 1980.

21. IMF, *Annual Report*, 1980, p. 17. These figures include the deficits for the NICs as well.

22. For an excellent restatement of these arguments see the most recent IMF *Annual Report*, 1980, pp. 34–9.

23. Bank for International Settlements, op. cit., p. 175.

24. See B. Nowzad, *The rise in protectionism*, Washington, IMF, 1978.

25. See in particular, 'The international monetary system and the new international order', *Development Dialogue*, Vol. 2, 1980.

26. W. Wisley, *A tool of power: the political history of money*, New York, Wiley, 1977, p. 167.

27. Williamson, op. cit., p. 21.

28. The ability of the Americans to continue running their deficit in the late 1960s by exporting dollars should be compared with the pressures imposed on the British both before and after devaluation in 1967. See especially Solomon, op. cit.

29. Note for example Fowler's statement, as Secretary of State for Commerce in 1965, when he claimed that it was 'impossible to over-estimate the extent to which private American enterprises overseas benefit from our commitments, tangible and intangible, to furnish assistance to those in need and to defend the frontiers of freedom', cited in Robinson, op. cit., p. 405.

30. USA Congress, House of Representatives, Committee on Banking, Currency and Housing, *Briefing on the IMF*, Washington, Government Printing Office, 1976, p. 3.

31. USA Congress, Senate, Committee on Foreign Relations, Sub-Committee on Multinational Corporations, *Multinational Corporations and United States Foreign Policy*, Part 13, Washington, Government Printing Office, 1976, p. 26.

32. Ibid.

33. The secrecy involved in the American decision was such that the Manager of the IMF was only informed of the decision 'in the few minutes' before Nixon's broadcast. (F. Southard, *The evolution of the International Monetary Fund*, Princeton, Princeton University Press, 1979, p. 38).

34. US Congress, Senate, op. cit., p. 24.

35. Williamson, op. cit., p. 172.

36. Wisley, op. cit., p. 234.

37. Williamson, op. cit., p. 37.

38. Wisley, op. cit., p. 299.

39. Details in Bank for International Settlements, *Annual Report*, 1972/3, p. 140.

40. The IMF's official position was set out in 'The role of exchange rates in the adjustment of international payments', in M. de Vries, ed., *The International Monetary Fund*, 1966–71, Vol. II, *Documents*, Washington, IMF, 1976; Williamson, op. cit., contains an excellent critique of their position.

41. Published in *Finance and Development*, Vol. 13, no. 2, 1976, p. 10; see also *Finance and Development*, Vol. 14, no. 2, 1977, and a supplement to the IMF Survey, 18 September 1978.

42. Witteveen noted in 1977 that the agreement lacked 'provisions on convertibility or asset settlement, or arrangement for the control of reserve creation and composition' and also established no 'rules for ensuring symmetry in the adjustment process' ('The emerging international monetary system', *Finance and Development*, Vol. 13, no. 3, 1977, p. 8).

43. I.S. Abdulla, 'The inadequacy and loss of legitimacy of the IMF', *Development Dialogue*, Vol. 2, 1980, p. 47.

6 Restructuring Monetary Relations, 1962–81

> The decadent international but individualistic capitalism, in the hands of which we found ourselves after the war, is not a success. It is not intelligent, it is not beautiful, it is not just, it is not virtuous – and it doesn't deliver the goods. In short we dislike it and we are beginning to despise it. But when we wonder what to put in its place we are extremely perplexed.
>
> J.M. Keynes, 'National Self-sufficiency', 1933.

The emergence of the 'dollar overhang' in the early 1960s and the continuation of the American deficit focused attention on the inherently unstable nature of the existing monetary structures and initiated a search for alternatives. Without the creation of some alternative to the dollar the system was confronted with the possibility of two diametrically opposed, but equally problematic options. On the one hand a 'long-run shortage of liquidity' would be bound to arise with deflationary effects if the centre currency countries equilibrated their balance of payments or found that central banks refused 'to pile up further IOUs from them';[1] on the other uncontrollable inflationary pressures would emerge if the deficit continued and the surplus countries were 'called upon to finance indefinitely US deficits through unpredictable accumulations of dollar claims'.[2] It was primarily the former possibility which stimulated change in the 1960s, the latter, an expanding reality, which pushed it forward in the 1970s. This chapter will therefore attempt to look very briefly at the attempts made to deal with this problem and to account for their inability to resolve it in any fundamental way.

An attempt to understand this process is intrinsically complex, not merely because of the difficulties involved in comprehending social processes which do not lend themselves to equilibrium explanations, but also by the fact that the actors involved were themselves attempting to deal with it through the application of the orthodox theoretical tools which, as we have seen, were quite incapable of doing so. Thus if Heckscher–Ohlin–Samuelson trade theory and the monetary theory of the balance of payments are to be believed, the problem itself should have been automatically overcome through a movement from deficit to surplus in the key currency and vice versa in the new surplus countries which would have taken the pressure off the dollar and made it possible for the currencies of the now surplus countries to replace it. But in the real world the market refused to perform this wondrous task so that even the most orthodox had to recognise the need for some extension of the powers of direct intervention to compensate for its failure, and this in a context where no 'adequate' form of international state existed to do so.

Thus the probelm of international redistribution addressed by Keynes in the 1940s and temporarily resolved through the extension of US aid and defence commitments in the 1950s had emerged again in another guise and in a totally different context in the 1960s. A dynamic centre currency had ben created, but one whose stability and availability could no longer be guaranteed within the limits of the present institutional framework. To solve this problem a new mechanism would have to be created capable of recycling resources from surplus to deficit countries in a manner that led to growth and not just inflation, and which also enabled existing dollar balances in overseas central banks to be run down gradually and replaced by assets based upon the creditworthiness of the new surplus countries. What was needed, therefore, was a technical monetary solution to the disequilibrium created by the process of uneven development, but the problems involved in producing it resulted directly from the fact that technical success must depend upon a real reallocation of global productive resources and hence upon a real alteration in the balance of economic and political power. Our understanding of this failure must therefore depend primarily upon an examination of the nature of these conflicts and more especially upon those between the elements which continued to benefit from a continuation of the existing system, and those which would have been better served by a fundamental reform.

A number of special interests in the US benefited directly from the operation of the system, despite the limitations which it imposed upon the growth of the American economy as a whole. Thus the arms industry depended directly upon foreign and domestic defence spending, finance capital upon the growth of an international Euro-dollar market, and American multinationals in general upon the maintenance of an international economy and upon easy access to the finance capital required to sustain their expansion on a global scale. Against these we can pose the interests of small and medium-sized 'domestic' capitals in the US and the working class which would in some limited sense have benefited from higher domestic as opposed to foreign, and greater productive industrial rather than unproductive defence, expenditure.[3] Despite the negative consequences of post-war policy for the growth of the domestic economy (a situation in direct contrast to that of American *capital's* foreign empire), there can be litle doubt that the interests most closely associated with it were most strongly placed in the political structure.

In the strong industrial countries, on the other hand, domestic industrial capital benefited directly from easy access to the US market and would have suffered directly from a reduction in the US deficit, or a substantial increase in imports to their own markets. Thus while their economies as a whole might have been suffering from inflation as a result of their economic surpluses, this would have been offset by the cost reductions secured through their ability to sell on a global scale and by the long-term security offered to both owners and workers by their continuing relative increase in competitive power in the world market. No doubt these advantages would have been less important during the upswing when there was some possibility that growth could continue even with a relative decline in their share of both the American and domestic markets, but this was much less likely to be so as competition intensified during the prosperity and more especially in the downswing. Thus, while the official representatives of the monetary structures of these surplus countries continuously opposed the Americans for their 'indiscipline' in maintaining the deficit, their leading manufacturers had no qualms about continuing to increase their sales on the American market as rapidly as they could.[4] Finally, it was the producers of the deficit countries, and more especially those in the poorest of them, which had most to gain from a reflationary solution to the liquidity problem, since their needs were of course qualitatively greater than those in the prosperous industrial countries, and their ability to initiate autonomous productive processes qualitatively smaller.

There can be little doubt that the long-term feasibility of the system as a whole has always depended upon its ability to stimulate a desirable investment process in the deficit countries, as their spokesmen have argued from Keynes in the 1940s to the Brandt Commission in the 1980s. It is also the case that the groups whose short and medium-term interests are best served by the maintenance of the existing relationships have always been most strongly placed in the political process at both the national and international levels. But it would be a mistake to attribute the policy failures of the recent past to the purely 'political' influence which they have been able to exert over the decision-making process, as reformist thinkers tend to do. This is to make a wholly improper distinction between the political and the economic, and to assume that voluntaristic interventions at the political level can serve to offset the long-term consequences of the uneven development generated by the international operation of the law of value.

Now both Marxist and orthodox theorists would accept that the stability of the system as a whole must depend upon the creation of some effective mechanism for the recycling of surpluses from strong to weak centres. Yet the arguments presented earlier in this book are all intended to suggest that the resolution of the problem of uneven development cannot simply depend upon a simple diversion of flows of financial resources, *but upon the creation of conditions in the weaker centres which make it possible for investment to take place there in direct competition with the production already in existence in the stronger ones.* If this were not the case the massive expansion and redistribution of international liquidity in the 1970s (when more new reserves were created than in the whole past history of mankind) would have been more than sufficient to resolve the problem which has continued to intensify instead. Orthodox theory has no explanations for this failure, apart from criticisms of the irrationality and incompetence of the policies followed by many of the governments involved. Marxist theory locates the problem at a more fundamental level, however, in the structural imbalances and uneven development created by the relationships examined in Part II. These, by weakening the relative competitive positions of the deficit in contrast to the surplus countries, constantly raise the barriers to effective new investment and ensure that financial flows ultimately find their way into an increasingly inflationary financing of consumption and leave the fundamental problem untouched. Only where recycling can be accompanied by effective policy interventions capable of offsetting these tendencies generated by free competition and intensified by orthodox policies will it have the required effects. It is no accident that the initial rebuilding of the old industrial centres took place in a post-war situation characterised by controlled trade and extensive interventions in the domestic economy, as the flow of American assistance would otherwise have led directly to an intensification of their relative dependence rather than to the creation of an autonomous domestic productive capacity.

Thus the following examination of the struggle over monetary reform will focus not merely on the direction and scale of the financial flows which it influenced, but also on the nature of the policy interventions that accompanied them. It will attempt to show how these, imprisoned within the constraints of orthodoxy, and always modified by the pressures imposed by the dominant interests which have benefited directly from the operation of the existing system, have constantly attempted to offer growing amounts of financial assistance, but have constantly been forced to do so on the basis of policy conditions that made it impossible to use effectively. In these circumstances the politics of international monetary reform had to become a chronicle of vain attempts, uneasy compromises and limited achievements which could never go to the root of the problem because of the fundamental inability to recognise that the consequences of free capitalistic competition are not the dynamic equilibrium predicted by Say's law, but the uneven and crisis-ridden evolution foreseen by Marx.[5] The rest of this chapter will now attempt to deal briefly with these attempts, looking first at official attempts to provide alternative sources of international liquidity, then at the growth of the private Eurodollar market as the major source of balance of paymets financing from the late 1960s onwards.

Official Liquidity Creation

The IMF and the World Bank
The debate over the future role of the IMF at Bretton Woods was resolved in favour of a solution which gave it limited powers of short-term intervention on the basis of resources allocated to it by its members. Quotas were allocated in accordance with levels of economic development, 25 per cent formerly payable in gold, now in SDRs or hard currencies, the rest in domestic currencies. These then became the IMF's own assets to be lent to deficit countries whose access to them is determined by the size of their own quota and subject to increasing degrees of 'conditionality' as the level of borrowing increases. Since deficit countries will not wish to draw their own or other unconvertible currencies from the Fund, its effective resources are confined to the 25 per cent of all quotas provided in gold or hard currencies, and to those provided by the hard currency countries themselves. Thus in the 1940s and 1950s its real resources were ultimately determined by the size of the US quota (the subject of much hard bargaining between the British and Americans before

Bretton Woods[6]), while from the 1960s onwards they have been more heavily dependent on those of the OECD countries as a whole. These quotas are subject to periodic re-negotiation, their growth and distribution can be derived from the figures in Table 6.1.

While the size of surplus country quotas determines the level of potential IMF lending, that of deficit countries determines their capacity to borrow. Thus it can be seen that the ability of the Fund to be used by third world countries is severely constrained by the fact that their quotas (when those of the smaller industrial countries are subtracted from the rest of the world) constitute no more than a third of the total.[7] Countries coming to the Fund are allowed to borrow the first 25 per cent of their quotas (the reserve 'credit tranche') without any conditions, the following 25 per cent is subjected to minimal conditionality, and subsequent borrowings involve direct and increasingly close controls before payments are agreed and for as long as the loans are outstanding. Initially it was assumed that members would only be able to draw up to 125 per cent of their quotas, now total drawing can go up to 600 per cent using both the normal credit tranches and the other credit facilities which have been developed to deal with particular problems over time. These include the Extended Fund Facility, established in 1974 to provide balance of payments support for longer periods than under the credit tranches; the Compensatory Financing Facility set up in 1963 to assist countries in difficulties as a result of temporary shortfalls in export earnings for reasons beyond their control; the Buffer Stock Financing Facility established in 1969 to assist in the financing of buffer stocks under international commodity agreements; a Trust Fund created out of profits from gold sales available only to low income countries;[8] and the Supplementary Financing Facility set up in 1977 (operational 1979/80) to provide resources to members 'facing serious payments imbalances that are large in relation to their Fund Quotas'.[9] Between 1974 to 1976 an Oil Facility existed to enable members to cover the increase in oil payments stemming from the 1973/4 price increase.

The actual contribution of these facilities to international recycling has, in fact, been very limited, confirming the arguments advanced earlier that the IMF's function was mainly to be concerned with regulation rather than with direct intervention. In the early years it made no contributions at all, making its first 'Stand-by' loans in 1953. Up to 1973 it had lent a total of only SDR 24.8 billion; under the pressures stemming from the first oil price increase it pushed up lending between 1975 and 1977 (notably through the creation of the

Table 6.1 IMF quotas, 1945–78 ($ million, 1945–71; SDR million, 1978)

	1945	%	1955	%	1965	%	1971	%	1978	%
United States	2750	36	2750	31	4125	26	6700	23	8405	21
Group of Nine	2550	34	3200	37	5582	35	10870	38	13544	35
Rest	2300	30	2800	32	6269	39	11237	39	17062	44
TOTAL	7600	100	8750	100	15976	100	28807	100	39011	100

Group of Nine contains Belgium, Canada, France, Germany, Italy, Japan, Netherlands, Sweden, and the United Kingdom.
At present negotiations are under way to raise this total to SDR 60 billion.
Source: 1945–71, J.K. Horsefield, *The IMF*, Vol. II, pp. 278–80; M. de Vries, *The IMF 1966–71*, Vol. I, pp. 206–8; 1978 from *IMF Survey*, Supplement, September 1979, p. 8/9.

low conditionality Oil Facility financed mainly by contributions from the OPEC countries), but then reduced its lending and has in fact received more in repayments than it has lent for the last three years as Table 6.2 shows.

Table 6.2 IMF lending and repayments (SDR million)

	1945–73	1974	1975	1976	1977	1978	1979	1980	1974–80
Drawings	24800	1058	5102	6591	4910	2503	3720	2433	26318
Repayments	na	672	518	960	868	4485	4859	3776	16138

Trust Fund and gold sale distributions excluded.
Source: IMF *Annual Reports*.

Within these limited confines more than half of all payments have been made to the weaker industrial countries, notably Britain, Italy, France and the United States which drew its entire reserve tranche entitlement as part of a dollar rescue programme in 1979. The organisation has been under heavy pressure both from the third world and from those concerned with the instabilities emerging in the private banking sector to increase its level of operation. In response to this the Fund is pressing for the 50 per cent increase in quotas now being negotiated, has agreed to increase the limits on borrowing to 600 per cent of quota and to extend the periods for payments, and had substantially increased the commitments made in 1980 over those made in the previous four years.[10] The overall distribution of lending as between regions and facilities is summarised in Table 6.3.

It would be incorrect to confine an evaluation of the recycling facilities created at Bretton Woods to the activities of the IMF, since the Conference also created the World Bank (the 'International Bank for Reconstruction and Development') and allocated it the 'developmental' role of providing credit for actual investments in member countries. Yet its role was initially confined to the provision of credit derived from commercial borrowing on private capital markets, and thus forced it to adopt very 'conservative lending policies',[11] a position reinforced by a desire to convince the American banking community that it was to be run on 'sound investment principles' and not as 'a political institution'.[12] Its operations tended to reinforce the maintenance of international property relations since it only lent to governments which had not defaulted on loans, expropriated foreign assets or failed to honour agreements with foreign investors.[13]

Table 6.3   Distribution of IMF lending, 1974–80 (SDR million)

	Third world	All others	Total
Tranches			
Reserve	1102	4810	5912
Credit	3515	4686	8201
Facilities			
Buffer stocks	55	24	79
Compensatory	2945	1515	4460
Extended	764	—	764
Oil	2736	4166	6902
TOTAL	11117	15201	26318
	42%	58%	100%

Supplementary Fund Facility of SDR 383 million in 1980 included in credit tranche figures.
Source: IMF *Annual Reports* and *Development Digest*, Vol. 2, 1980, p. 112.

This conservatism led to strong pressures in the late 1950s from the third world for some form of multilateral concessional aid which the industrialised countries accepted and organised under the auspices of the Bank where the same weighted voting system operated as for the IMF. As a result the International Development Association (IDA) was set up to provide highly concessional financing for the poorest countries, obtaining its funds from direct contributions from the industrialised countries, yet still applying 'the same rigorous standards' in its project appraisal that are applied to normal loans.[14] The growth of World Bank and IDA lending can be derived from the figures shown in Table 6.4.

Table 6.4   World Bank and IDA disbursements, 1947–80
($ million, annual averages)

	1947–50	1951–5	1956–60	1961–5	1966–70	1971–5	1976–80
World Bank disbursements	153	213	448	534	753	1361	3172
IDA disbursements				104*	265	545	1249

* 1962–5 only.
Source: World Bank *Annual Reports*.

During the 1960s the bank's caution was such that repayments exceeded disbursements, so that there was a reverse flow of resources from the industrial countries and stagnation in its lending to the third world. At the end of the 1960s Robert McNamara, presumably having learnt something of the costs of dealing with crises of underdevelopment during his supervision of the American war effort in Vietnam, assumed control of the Bank and initiated a period of dynamic growth which really got under way in IDA lending in 1972 and Bank lending in 1974. By the end of the 1970s McNamara had become the most prominent spokesman behind the international campaign to increase the provision of assistance to the third world, IDA disbursements had increased from $235 million in 1971 to $1411 million in 1980, and he had even announced the Bank's intention to provide long-term balance of payments financing, a direct intrusion on the role of the IMF.[15]

Despite these not unimportant increases in provision, the actual role of IMF/World Bank financing is of limited significance in a global context now entirely dominated by the activities of the private banking system. Yet their institutional role cannot be underestimated because of their central position in the regulation of the global economy where the absence of an adequate form of state imposes heavy responsibilities on them. The political influence of the IMF has become increasingly visible as the result of the growing number of interventions which it has been drawn into; that of the World Bank is more hidden, but probably more continuous and persuasive, especially in the poorest countries that now depend very directly on it for developmental resources. The nature of these interventions have been extensively reviewed elsewhere,[16] and will only be considered in broad outline here.

The influence over domestic policy exerted by the IMF derives directly from the 'conditionality' imposed on all drawings in the higher credit tranches and from the Extended and Supplementary Fund facilities. This influence has been consistently used in favour of the principles of the monetarist policy theory examined in Chapter 2, being concerned to increase the rate of profit by reducing wages and public spending; to restore external equilibrium by devaluation and deflation designed to reduce the consumption of imports; and to increase the overall efficiency of the economy by reducing levels of central intervention and placing much more emphasis on the market for both domestic and foreign exchanges. At present, perhaps as a result of the growing criticisms which it has produced,[17] there is some evidence that it is being reviewed with de Larosiere conceding recently that programmes must now 'address the structural aspects' of the underlying problem, and create 'conditions conducive to the improvement of supply'.[18] Yet this statement is accompanied by no examination of the variables examined earlier which stand directly in the way of the creation of these conditions, and is accompanied by a demand for 'supportive measures on the demand side' designed 'to keep the claims on resources in a sustainable relationship with their availability',[19] whose deflationary implications are perfectly evident.

The position in the World Bank is a good deal more complex, with support for the most conservative of the positions adopted by the IMF coinciding with a serious attempt to come to grips with the problems of reallocating resources to the poorest producers in contexts where uneven development has produced the coexistence of the most modern and capital intensive plants with backward and undercapitalised producers. The World Bank produces general country level analyses of economic policies and performances (distributed to only a select audience) which presumably inform its overall assessment of creditworthiness; it has recently engaged on a very extensive review of policy theory in a wide range of working papers, and it has addressed itself to the specific problem of getting aid to the poorest strata without reducing the rate of growth. Briefly, the overview presented in a number of country surveys to which I have had access suggests a broad commitment to exactly the same views as those held in the IMF. This analysis is strongly reinforced in general policy papers on the overall approach to planning and foreign economic policy,[20] which calls for the liberalisation of external trade, the encouragements of foreign private investment and a reduction in direct state intervention. On the other hand, an influential group in the economic research department has begun a critique of pure market theory, calling for a recognition of the 'rationality of small-scale domestic ('informal sector') producers, and for an active government role in transferring resources to them because of their strong propensity to increase employment and to use domestic rather than imported inputs.[21] This work entirely ignores the political problems associated with securing a change in policy of this kind, the nature of the contradictions between the large and small-scale sectors, and the super-exploitative nature of the relationship between workers and capitalists in the informal sector.[22] Yet this also represents the most important official initiative in the international policy debate in the 1970s, and places the Bank in direct conflict with many of the more reactionary interests in the third world countries which it is attempting to influence when it attempts to put these principles into effect. It is in any event by no means clear that the 'redistribution with growth' tendency represents the mainstream within the Bank in terms of the real allocation of its resources, and there is no evidence as yet that it has led to a significant breakthrough in the destruction of the structural barriers to the generation of cumulative growth among the world's poorest.

The general arrangements to borrow (GAB)
The emergence of the dollar overhang, that is the excess of American overseas liabilities to foreign reserves, at the start of the 1960s and the even more serious weakening of the pound sterling rendered the system operating with fixed exchange rates increasingly vulnerable to speculative movements[23] and threatened to expose the inadequacy of the resources available to the IMF to deal with them. Responding to these pressures, the 'Group of 10' leading industrial countries[24] came together in 1961 to establish the GAB as a 'network of "swap" arrangements (reciprocal credit facilities)'[25] between their central banks which placed $6 billion at the disposal of the IMF for allocations to the Group when these were called for. The arrangement has been renewed continuously since then, and now provides the IMF with the maximum of 'about SDR 6.5 billion'.[26]

Looked at from the point of view of the arguments being developed in this book about the need for redistribution and reflationary deficit financing, it is clear that the agreement created some serious problems. The Chairman of the group which created it argued that it would enable the industrial countries to 'provide resources to assist one of their number, and in this way all of the countries of the world'.[27] Now it might be true that an improvement in the ability of the central banks in the industrial countries to defend their currencies against speculative movements might have reduced the necessity to resort to domestic deflation and hence maintained the overall level of international economic activity. Yet this ability can also be viewed as an additional defence of an essentially conservative, strong country oriented economic order which weakened possible pressures for reform which might otherwise have had to be taken more seriously. Thus, even the more radical orthodox theorists such as Friedman considered the heavy commitment to the defence of the fixed exchange rate system to be mistaken because of the pressures which it imposed upon the domestic economic policies of the weaker countries.

Again, the fact that payments were confined to Group of 10 members who also took all the decisions about their use, thus confining the IMF's role to a purely administrative one, highlighted the inequality between them and third world countries which apparently led the latter to organise 'themselves into a coherent pressure group, which was first reflected in the creation of UNCTAD in 1964'.[28] Further, the organisation in fact was a reflection of the new international authority of the emerging surplus countries of the OECD who were concerned to use it 'to express their new-found power relative to the United States',[29] and were also concerned to ensure that the UK would not be allowed to draw from the IMF on 'less stringent conditions' than they would wish.[30] It is perhaps no accident that the last use made of the GAB was by the US for SDR 777 in November 1978,[31] the point, it will be remembered when it made the transition to a genuinely deflationary orientation to the domestic economy. Thus the additions which the GAB provided to international liquidity were being used to reinforce the conservative orthodox policies for which the IMF has been so severely criticised. Finally, the establishment of the agreement ensured that none of the surplus countries would be subjected to the effects of the Scarce Currency Clause in the IMF Articles of Agreement (VII Clause 3), thereby removing from it all vestiges of control over them. Keynes had always hoped that this clause could be used to ensure that the IMF could bring as much pressure to bear on surplus as on deficit countries to adjust, since it allowed the IMF to permit members to discriminate 'against them by being released from "any obligation to take [their] exports" '.[32] By agreeing to provide the IMF with additional supplies of their currencies through the GAB, and then confining their use to the leading industrial countries alone, the Group of 10 turned this clause into a dead letter and confirmed the asymmetrical nature of the treatment handed out to chronic debtors as opposed to creditors.

The GAB must therefore be treated as a highly contradictory response to the emerging liquidity problem which essentially consolidated the dominance of the position occupied by the leading industrial countries by allowing controlled lending to take place between them and thus stopped a structural weakness in any one of them from threatening the stability of them all. Equally important, it created the institutional basis for the initiation of the major official monetary innovation in the post-war period – the creation of Special Drawing Rights in 1969.

The creation of special drawing rights

Keynes's original Bretton Woods proposal envisaged an agency able to issue its own credit money backed by the foreign exchange reserves held by the surplus countries. By using it to recycle these to the deficit countries he was in effect envisaging a means of offsetting the deflationary effects of uneven development and creating the institutional mechanism at the international level required to overcome the problem of over-production and under-consumption which must otherwise emerge at the end of the upswing and prosperity. The theoretical analysis put forward earlier suggests that a good deal more would have been required to solve this problem than the creation of an asset operating in the purely monetary sphere, but it is also true that the development of a stable and reflationary international credit form would have made a significant contribution to it. The success and failure of the SDR must therefore be evaluated in relation to this overriding need.

The SDR, greeted perhaps justifiably as 'a momentous innovation in the international monetary system',[33] was described by the official historian of the IMF as 'a unique type of reserve ... issued by an international agency rather than by any national government, and used by governments, along with gold and foreign exchange, to settle international accounts'. As a result she could assert that a mechanism now existed 'for the deliberate creation of reserves to inject liquidity into the international monetary system, should the need arise'.[34] Her use of the term 'creation', however, conceals a crucial aspect of the process since it implies the illusory possibility of creating real resources by an act of will which both our own and the orthodox positions would reject. While the highly technical nature of the new asset made it possible to present it in this way and thereby to conceal the nature of the real transfers of resources which it made possible, a closer examination reveals that its function (and its very real significance) was not to *create* but to *redistribute* liquidity and thereby to transfer resources which would otherwise be hoarded from surplus countries incapable of using them to deficit countries where they could be used to generate a reflationary solution to the otherwise intractable deficit problem.

SDRs are in fact 'drawing rights' allocated in specified amounts (directly proportional to IMF quotas at present) to all the countries which belong to the IMF. Surplus countries will make no use of them since they can deal with their foreign liabilities through the use of their own reserves. Deficit countries, on the other hand, can transfer them to another country either by mutual agreement or to one 'designated' by the IMF which is then obliged to provide them with an equivalent amount of a 'currency convertible in fact' (Article XXV Clause 4) in exchange. Interest, initially of a fully concessional kind, now at 80 per cent of the combined rate prevailing in the five leading industrial countries, is paid by countries on the SDRs they have transferred to those whose holdings exceed their original quotas.[35] The SDR was originally valued in terms of gold, subsequently in relation to the combined values of a 'basket' of the currencies of initially the sixteen, now the five leading trading currencies,[36] and can therefore be used as a substitute for gold as an international standard of value relatively insulated from exchange rate fluctuations in any particular currency. Fifteen countries have now pegged their exchange rates to it. Without the technicalities, what we have here is a scheme which issues prommisory notes to 141 governments which can be cashed in for real assets at will. The political process involved in its creation has therefore to be viewed as a very concrete struggle over the scale on which it was to operate, the form it was to take and the controls to be maintained over its development.

The political/legal basis for the validity of the new tokens depends upon an *unconditional obligation* on the surplus country to provide convertible currencies (i.e. credits earned through the past export of *real* goods) to deficit countries on demand, and the corresponding obligation on the deficit countries to meet the interest charges on them and to redeem ('reconstitute') them in hard currency in due course. Unlike the most important of the other forms of IMF financing, therefore, SDRs provided an unconditional source of revenue, an essential feature of a scheme in which the acceptability of the monetary tokens depends upon the certainity that they will be exchangeable when central banks needed to use them to meet either domestic commitments or commitments to the IMF. The extent of the obligation imposed on the surplus countries was limited to the requirements that no country be asked to exchange hard currency for an amount equivalent to more than twice the value of the SDRs originally allocated to it. To limit the level of use by borrowers everyone had initially to maintain an average holding of 30 per cent of its cumulative allocation, since 1979 only 15 per cent.[37] The scale of operation and the impliction of these limitations will be considered in more detail below. What must be considered now is the political struggle involved in persuading the surplus countries to assume these obligations and thereby produce the corresponding resource transfers to those in deficit.

The protagonists in this struggle can be easily identified – the surplus countries whose resources were essential if it was to be created; the USA as the key currency country, now in deficit, whose position at the centre of the existing monetary system (and whose seigniorage derived therefrom) might be threatened as a result of its creation;[38] and the structural deficit countries mainly in the third world. Looked at from an orthodox or Keynesian perspective there should have been few deep-seated obstacles to the reconciliation of these interests. The assets to be redistributed were being stored, not used by the surplus countries, so no sacrifices in immediate consumption from their populations were required. The only losses would result from any difference between the interest rates paid on SDRs as opposed to alternative forms of investment, and ensuring an appropriate level should have been a matter for technical negotiation. In the 1960s dollar–gold convertibility still implied that the US would have to control its deficit at some point, so that it should have been likely to benefit from the creation of a mechanism that allowed it to do this without stimulating a decline in the level of activity in its foreign markets. Further, its own manufacturers could have been expected to benefit by an expansion in exports and a curtailment of imports which a commitment to the ending of the deficit would have required. Finally, of course, the deficit countries could be expected to be directly behind a scheme which would assist them 'to bridge the gap between export earnings and import needs', lessen the pressure on their foreign assets, and thus reduce the otherwise 'disequilibrating pressures of a long-term character on [their] balance of payments'.[39] Yet in the event intense resistance developed to any scheme which could have made a material difference to the overall situation, partly from the opposition from the surplus countries to an unconditional use of their resources by deficit countries, partly from an inability to persuade the US to accept the constraints which would have resulted from a substantial alteration in the relative position of the dollar in the system as a whole. While both of these problems were present during the whole period from 1962, the former was most important during its inception in the 1960s, the latter during the attempt to use it to resolve the monetary problems precipitated by the dollar crisis after 1971. These two periods generated different problems and must be considered separately.

The initiation and initial conceptualisation of the new asset was confined to the surplus countries, taking place between 1962 and 1966 through discussions between representatives of the Group of 10 countries in association with the IMF. The problem of development financing was excluded from the discussions which were concerned with the overall problem of monetary reform, including the general problems of 'adjustment', confidence in the main reserve currencies, and the growth of liquidity.[40] All of these can be seen to derive from the contradictory nature of the relationship between the industrial deficit and surplus countries, since the problem of adjustment related to the nature and the extent of the policies required to bring balance of payments into equilibrium, confidence in the reserve currencies on the likelihood that the US and UK would be willing and able to adopt them, and the problem of liquidity would then arise out of the elimination of the US deficit and the necessity to find an alternative means of guaranteeing the growth in reserves required to finance the expansion of world trade, Hence it seems legitimate, especially given the limited space available, to consider the problem in the unitary terms set out in the previous paragraph.

Both the deficit and the surplus countries recognised the nature of the fundamental contradiction between a more rapid increase in the demand for reserves than in the supply of gold, with a corresponding liquidity shortage 'unless the US continued to run a balance of payments deficit', which would then 'undermine confidence in the dollar', lead to an excessive demand for gold and precipitate a crisis.[41] Yet their different interests led them to important differences of emphasis, with the surplus countries mainly concerned to ensure that any new asset should not 'absolve deficit countries from the need to balance their accounts with the rest of the world', but should include a 'firm resolve by all countries in deficit or surplus but especially the former' to adopt, with greater alacrity than before, remedial policies appropriate to the treatment of the prevailing disequilibria'.[42] In the negotiations the French pushed this demand most strongly, calling for a new asset directly linked to gold which would create a system in which 'the US would be subject to the same balance-of-payments discipline as any other country';[43] the Germans, not pushing the argument to the same limits (since the effect would most probably have been to reduce liquidity rather than increase it) nevertheless operated from the same side of the fence, being more concerned about 'need for discipline rather than liquidity', and arguing that 'in financing deficits we "should pay more attention to price stability than to expansion and growth" '.[44]

On the other hand the US's position was highly ambiguous. It was constantly making firm verbal commitments to orthodoxy by asserting the need for the elimination of the deficit through a 'restoration of balance in our international accounts' in order to secure 'the position of the dollar'.[45] Yet in the years that followed its actual ability to do this was to be progressively undermined as the Vietnam war escalated, so that its intervention in the liquidity debate had necessarily to take the opposite form from that which characterised it in the 1940s when it still occupied a dominant position at the economic level. Now it appeared 'in the garb of a debtor and would reject the disciplinary rules it had demanded as a creditor when the Bretton Woods agreements had been drafted'.[46]

Now it was this ambiguity in the American position which enabled any degree of agreement between the competing interests to take place at all, since it made it possible for the conservative demands of the creditor countries to take precedence by taking a firm commitment to the elimination of the US deficit as the starting point for the whole exercise. Thus the Ministers of the Group of 10 reaffirmed this in 1966, saying: 'Large US deficits are not a satisfactory source of future reserve increases for the rest of the world nor are they acceptable to the US'.[47] Thus, given an inadequate increase in gold supplies, they were forced to accept the possible need for the 'deliberate creation of new reserve assets'[48] in order to avoid the risk of 'a harsh and abrupt adjustment process' which 'could endanger the objectives we all share for the growth and stability of the world economy'.[49] With the 'firm commitment' obtained from the US to eliminate its deficit this made it possible for the Group of 10 to agree among itself on the possibility of a scheme for 'the future creation of reserve assets as and when needed',[50] without accepting any real commitment at all to an overall increase in the resources moving from surplus to deficit countries, since the new assets were in fact intended to do no more than compensate for the expected loss of dollar outflows from the US. Had the US in fact brought the deficit under control as they were expected to do instead of allowing it to escalate, there can be little doubt that the downturn of the 1970s would have occurred much earlier, since the proposals included no provision at all for the creation of mechanisms to force surplus countries to increase their imports, or for Keynesian type developmental credits to go to the deficit countries to offset the resulting tendency towards uneven development and deflation.

The conservativism of their analysis is confirmed when we consider their attitude to the LDCs who were expressly excluded from the early and crucial phase of the debate. For lenders the most crucial element in any credit mechanism must be its ability to guarantee repayment with interest in due course, an ability which is inversely related to the prosperity of the borrower. In the Keynesian formulation, on the other hand, it is the poverty and weakness of the deficit country which determines the need for the consciously controlled redistributive mechanism both because such countries will be unable to obtain resources on purely commercial terms and because overall prosperity can only be secured if they are able to maintain their purchases from the stronger ones. The predominance of the creditor view in the Group of 10 emerges with admirable clarity from the Ossola report, their major technical examination of the problem. Here, arguing for the limitation of the scheme to 'a limited group of industrialised countries', they noted that an international asset 'must be based on credit and that the credit of those who back it must be unquestioned'; that these assets must 'initially be distributed without the recipients' having had to forgo real resources in order to earn them, but will thereafter 'command real resources', so that 'care is therefore needed in establishing the group in which they are to be used' since, if the assets are to be repaid in 'due time' they should 'be distributed only to countries whose balance of payments is likely to move between deficit and surplus and which are, therefore, able to assume the obligations as well as the rights entailed in the convention and its working'.[51] And with the optimism characteristic of the rich, they conclude by asserting that 'a system which meets the reserve needs of the larger nations will, in practice, benefit all countries'.[52] Further, on a more technical level (and entirely disregarding the central role of Marshall aid in the externalisation of the US surplus and the creation of their own 'development' reserves only a few years before) they rejected any link between 'the provision of capital to developing countries' and 'the creation of reserves' since this would conflict with the 'needs of flexibility required for monetary management', and thus 'impair the monetary quality of the asset'. Any concession in this area would, inevitably, put unacceptable pressures on the surplus countries:

> The difficulties might not be insuperable if ... the amount of reserve creation associated with development finance were kept at a modest fraction of the total creation of reserves. But it would be difficult to resist demands from developing countries, and internal pressures in the industrial countries to give aid in this form, which appears to avoid a cost in real resources. There would be a risk that, over time, more of the assets might be created than the surplus countries would be willing to acquire.[53]

Here we have a clear expression of the commitment in the surplus countries to the maintenance of the monetarist disciplines and the rejection of any significant redistributive mechanism of the kind which they had been advocating in the strongest terms in the 1940s when their objective circumstances required it.[54]

While, as we have seen, the US tended to support the campaign for 'discipline' at the verbal level, its own deficit position made it impossible for it to accept all of the implications of the argument and ensured that it acted as an ambiguous but significant obstacle to the conservatives. Thus the initial debate in 1963/4, centred around the possible creation of Composite Reserve Units (CRUs) as a multilateral substitute for the dollar and pound 'created by the deposit with the Fund of the main national currencies' to be issued 'to countries to hold in their reserves'.[55] The French suggestion was that CRUs should be directly linked to gold which, as the Ossola report pointed out, would probably lead to a 'shrinkage of total reserve assets', the main effect of which 'would fall mainly on US reserves',[56] and whose international consequences would be the adoption of 'excessively harsh policies in order to avoid deficits and a resultant loss of gold'.[57] Here the role of the US was certainly important in that it displayed 'a vehement negativism' in its opposition to the scheme,[58] and thereby forced the debate towards more liberal proposals, of which the SDR was the outcome.

Here, again, the fundamental issues remained – how many SDRs to create, how large an obligation to impose on the surplus countries, how strong a pressure to repay to impose upon the deficit countries, how widely to distribute them. As we have seen the surplus countries wanted a limited issue confined to the industrialised countries.

> But the United States and Britain shared with the developing countries an immediate shortage of national reserves and an interest – as Blessing [of Germany] had put it – in 'raising the tide level higher', an interest which gave a bias towards growth and expansion even at the risk of inflation. It was an inevitable alliance of debtors against the hard-nosed creditors.[59]

Thus, although a specific aid link was excluded, the scheme was eventually opened to all IMF members, despite surplus country fears that 'the United States and the developing countries might team up and vote for excessive reserves'.[60] The last stages of the negotiations were conducted through joint meetings of the executive directors of the Fund and of the Group of 10 in 1966 and 1967 at which roughly thirty delegates from the Group of 10 countries confronted nine from the third world who had been entirely excluded from the discussions until that point and could therefore be presented with a virtual *fait accompli.*[61] The final decision, largely agreed between Germany and France,[62] produced the unit distributed in accordance with quotas (and hence without reference to the need for reflation), with 30 per cent of the allocation to be held averaged over five years, and with a voting system in the IMF for key decisions in this area such that the new surplus countries were guaranteed a veto over any new allocations or changes in the fundamental rules. The final decision on the scale of operation was taken in 1969 and, at $9.5 billion spread over a three-year period starting in 1970, was relatively large, mainly for short-term reasons. Ironically enough, France had been forced into deficit and devaluation through the crisis of May 1968,[63] Britain was now moving into surplus as the result of the deflationary policies of the Labour government, the newly introduced regulations to control the private speculation in gold was increasing pressure on official gold holdings,[64] and the surplus countries were now having to consider the need for increased reserves to make it possible for 'their own balance of payments positions to reflect the improvements in the external positions of the US, France and Britain'.[65] Yet the linking of these issues to quotas ensured that less than 30 per cent would go to developing countries, and the 30 per cent requirement meant that a large proportion of this would be confined to very short-term uses. Thus the fundamental concession to the need for conscious intervention to control the flow of liquidity was matched by conditions which severely limited the scope within which it could be exercised.

The post-Smithsonian liquidity crisis
In the event the intense conflict over the level of liquidity creation through the SDR turned out to be entirely misplaced since, instead of the US deficit being curtailed with deflationary effects, it exploded immediately after the introduction of SDRs with the enormously inflationary results considered in the previous chapter. As the accompanying chart shows, global reserves more than doubled between 1969 and 1973 with the now irresistable outward flow of dollars ensuring that foreign exchange reserves grew from $32.3 billion to about $120 billion, as against the $9.4 billion increase in SDRs.[66]

The effect of this change, as we have seen, was to impose heavy taxes on the surplus countries through the depreciation in the value of their dollar reserves, to allow expansion to continue in the US and to some extent in other deficit countries, and, for reasons that will be considered in the next section, to ensure that the primary mechanism for international reflationary recycling would be the private banking

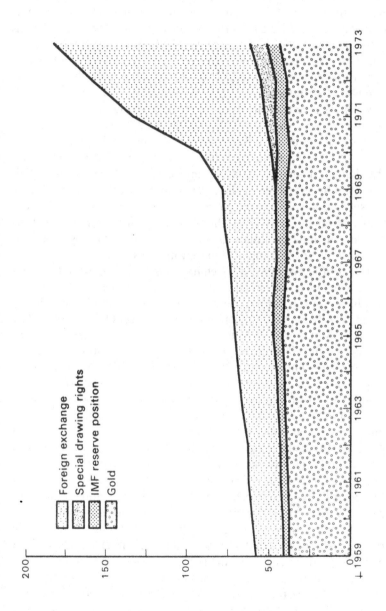

system operating through the Eurodollar market. In this context of 'monetary debauchery' reform became urgent, not as a means of guarding against an anticipated deflation, but as a means of eliminating the ability of the US to evade the normal balance of payments constraints and impose its deficits upon the strong. These negotiations took place in the Committee of 20 (C-20) appointed by the IMF to consider reforms which should include the creation of a multilateral substitute for the dollar which would be based upon the economic strength of all of the surplus countries. Since the SDR already existed, it was inevitable that this aspect of the debate would focus around the possibility of extending its role and turning it into the primary international currency. A fully developed international money, as envisaged by Keynes, would eliminate the special privileges derived from the dollar exchange system but ensure fair treatment to the deficit countries by guaranteeing them access to the savings accumulated by the surplus ones. While the problem was never directly posed in these terms during the early 1970s, this is what was ultimately at issue. Thus we can conclude the discussion of official intervention by looking at the reasons for the complete failure which ensured.

The conflicts of interest which had inhibited progress in the 1960s were now much intensified. The inflated dollar balances held by the surplus countries turned them into hostages to the US which had freed itself from any firm commitment to redeem them at par. They could only hope to redeem them, or at least to guarantee their stability, if the US could be persuaded to move into surplus or, at the very least, exhibit a real capacity to control its deficit. Yet the US was now involved in the closing stages of a costly and losing war so that it could not afford to incur the further unpopularity that would have resulted from a substantial reduction in imports. Even less could it undertake to raise the resources required to redeem any significant portion of its overseas debts. Yet this, of course, was exactly the price which the surplus countries were asking in exchange for their cooperation. Technically this was expressed in a demand for 'asset settlement', a euphemism for a process which would force the reserve currency country to accept a loss of reserve assets when it ran a deficit, rather than allowing it to finance it through a 'change in reserve liabilities'[67] – that is to say by increasing its external debt. This part of the debate was conducted at the most esoteric level, well documented in Williamson,[68] but in essence it involved the demand by the surplus countries that the 'normal disciplines exerted by reserve changes' be extended to the reserve centres.[69] The US therefore consistently opposed asset settlement (on the grounds that it would 'deprive the system of a useful element of elasticity'[70]) and thereby made it virtually impossible for agreement to be reached with the surplus countries. At the same time, now perhaps in a context where it was less concerned to find a solution to a problem which brought it such direct benefits, it also took a much less positive attitude to the problems of the LDCs and was entirely opposed to the link,[71] a position which it shared with Germany though not with the rest of the Europeans.[72]

So far as the surplus countries were concerned, the major concession which they would have had to offer was some clear indication of their willingness to move into deficit either directly, or by allowing the SDR to be used to externalise a significant portion of their foreign exchange reserves. Yet at no point during the decade is there any evidence that they took the former possibility seriously, presumably for the entirely adequate reason that to have done so would have meant limiting the ability of their exporters to sell abroad or creating conditions in their own markets which would have increased imports. The former would have lost them the critical advantages to be derived from the scale economies stemming from maximum penetration of the world market; the latter might have been possible without reducing domestic output through an expansion in demand, but this was strongly resisted by German capital concerned about its possible inflationary effects.[73] The strong countries constantly resisted pressures to revalue their currencies and only did so under the most intense pressure even when they were obviously overvalued until floating was introduced, and it is only now that the Germans have moved into deficit against their will and because of circumstances outside their control. Perhaps most important, even if the surplus countries had expanded domestic demand (and their economies *were* subjected to externally induced inflationary pressures from the late 1960s onwards as we have seen) the greater part of this would have been satisfied by domestic producers as a result of their competitive advantages arising from their exploitation of scale economies. Thus we can see that the underlying reason for the failure to secure an agreement was not the technical failures or lack of political will identified by Williamson, and other orthodox commentators,[74] but the objective contradictions arising out of the process of uneven development examined in Chapter 3. During these negotiations the LDCs continued to press their demand for a link,[75] and, although they managed to secure more support as we have seen, were again unsuccessful. While they could demonstrate the positive long-term benefits which might accrue from it for the system as a whole, they could not exert any effective influence because real resources were directly controlled by those whose short and medium-term interests stood in the way of any such solution.

The result was a complete failure on the part of the C-20:[76]

> There was no agreement on a set of rules for assigning adjustment responsibilities, no design of a viable adjustment mechanism, no introduction of an SDR standard, no substitution and no curb on the asymmetries.... The outcome of the C-20 was, in effect, a decision to learn to live with the non-system that had evolved out of a mixture of custom and crisis over the preceding year.[77]

No further SDRs were issued until 1978 since the continued growth in the dollar deficit, combined with the effect of the oil price increases of 1973/4 and 1978/9 on the savings of the OPEC countries, confronted the world with the most rapid growth in international reserves in human history. Subsequent attempts at reform failed to confront the neccessity for a fundamental restructuring since the conflicts of interest made this quite impossible. Instead a number of limited changes have occurred which have done little to alter the underlying problems. The monetary settlement in 1976 allowed central banks to trade in gold at the unofficial price, abolished its monetary uses in the IMF, and attempted to minimise its use as a reserve asset. Subsequent instabilities in the international monetary and political systems have led to extreme fluctuations in the gold price which reached a peak of $850 an ounce in early 1980 and now (early 1981) is less than $500.[78] Thus it can no longer serve as a stable measure of value (its price fluctuations are in fact an indictor of international insecurity and instability), and these fluctuations make it very difficult for it to be used 'as a monetary asset' to transfer resources between central banks because of the likelihood of one making a profit at the expense of the other, 'in clear conflict to their normal working relationships'.[79] Thus the central banks initially attempted to minimise the role of gold in their reserves by not valuing it at the official price, but have gradually valued it upwards, starting with France in 1975, as might be expected, but with even Germany following suit at the end of 1978, 'an important symbol of the reassessment of gold's role which has taken place'.[80] This change has produced an immense increase in the value of the reserves of the seven countries with significant gold holdings, the most important of which is the United States whose stock is still by far the largest. This change, largely the outcome of the entirely anarchic operation of the gold market, has, in fact, increased the ability of the US to deal with the dollar overhang, and must help at least temporarily to limit the further decline in the dollar. On the other hand the re-emergence of gold in preference to credit as the main component in international reserves is a clear indication of the failure to create the 'adequate form of international state' capable of ensuring a stable and expansionary form of international credit money.

As we have already seen, a limited attempt has also been made to increase the volume and utility of the SDR. A decision was made in 1978 to issue a further 12 billion over three years from the beginning of 1979, the interest rate was increased, the obligation to reconstitute (repay) was reduced from 30 per cent to 15 per cent, the valuation process was simplified, and the number of authorised holders was widened to include 'certain official financial institutions'.[81] These changes have dealt with some of the limitations in the usefulness of the SDR documented very effectively by Crystal,[82] and allowed a number of private banks to 'launch a new financial market in London, trading in certificates of deposit denominated in SDRs'.[83] The rationality of the decision to expand the volume of SDRs was questioned at the Fund meeting, given the growth in foreign dollar holdings, but was defended on the grounds that existing liquidity was neither properly distributed, nor based on a sound foundation, while the increase in SDRs would be 'modest'.[84] The new issue is indeed modest compared with the continuing growth in reserves, notably from the highly inflationary operation of the private Eurodollar market to be discussed in the next section. Yet it made no concession to the demand for the link from the poorer LDCs, so that its extension cannot have a significant redistributive effect, nor can it assuage the increasing pressures which continue to develop in the system as a whole. In the context of this growing instability most of the countries of Western Europe (with the UK a notable absentee) came together at the start of 1979 to form the European Monetary System in the hope of organising policies which would serve to insulate it from external instabilities and maintain relatively stable internal exchange rates; it has created a European Currency Unit, and has plans to form a European Monetary Fund.[85] While this may serve to strengthen the position of these countries, this change suggests the beginning of a return to a system of separate currency areas and a breakdown of the monetary unity secured through the IMF after World War II.

Between 1978 and 1980 discussions began again on the possibility of a new 'substitution account' in the IMF to make it possible for the

Fund to 'issue SDRs against US dollars delivered to it by the countries that held dollars in their reserves'.[86] This was to involve much less pressure on the US than the proposal discussed by the C-20 which was mainly concerned to use it to force asset settlement on it, and which failed as a result. It was hoped that the new proposal would be workable since it was believed that the US had accepted the obligations of asset settlement 'since November 1, 1978' and also 'the need for monetary policies that would protect the exchange rate' though 'not in a legally binding way'.[87] But the scheme nevertheless failed, partly because it would have involved a diversion of part of the Fund's gold to defend it against a part of the possible losses, and this was rejected by the LDCs who had 'only a secondary interest in the account'; the US was unwilling to seek 'an advance congressional commitment' to share in the possible losses; nor did it seem that dollar holders would be willing to make use of it on any significant scale if they also had to bear some of the risk 'in certain contingencies'.[88] Thus the conflicts of interest continue and the possibility of a workable system of international monetary management becomes ever more impossible to achieve on a voluntary basis.

The SDR/liquidity debate was conducted between highly cautious central bankers and Finance Ministers obsessed with the need for 'discipline' in deficit countries and with the need to control inflationary balance of payments financing. These fears greatly inhibited the development of an official credit structure capable of dealing with the deficit problem in a reflationary and redistributive yet orderly way, and imposed such severe limits on the growth of official liquidity there can be little doubt that serious deflationary pressures would have begun to emerge in the late 1960s if their preferences had been translated into action. Yet the actual development of the system itself was to take an entirely opposite form with the emergence of forces outside their direct control which undermined the basis for most of the disciplines which they were seeking to impose. We have already seen how the 'indiscipline' of the Vietnamese peasantry forced the US into highly inflationary deficit financing from the late 1960s onwards, despite verbal commitments to the contrary; we have now to consider the equally undisciplined growth of the private international banking system which, fed directly by resources from the central banks of the surplus countries themselves, presided over a recycling process of an immense size from the late 1960s onwards. Here we had an example of the sort of credit mechanism which Keynes had in mind, but one which was to operate on purely commercial principles and entirely free of official constraints. The resulting growth in inequality and potential instability will be considered in the next section.

Private Recycling and the International Banks[89]

By the start of the 1980s it was evident that the private Eurocurrency market operated by the major international banks had assumed the role identified by Keynes of recycling savings from surplus to deficit countries, and were doing so on an ever expanding scale. For all but the weakest countries reltively easy access to foreign credit was now available, leading to a significant alteration in the operation of the system. J.J. Polak of the IMF described the broad results as follows:

> The development of international bank credit available to a wide range of countries, including many developing countries, has reduced the difference between the US, on the one hand, and many other countries, on the other hand as regards their ability to finance balance of payments deficits. At present, it is not only the US that can finance deficits by issuing liabilities expressed in US dollars – most other countries can do the same, by using the credit facilities of the world banking system.[90]

This statement greatly underestimates the difference in obligations between borrowers from private banks as opposed to the US government with respect to its foreign liabilities, but it nevertheless is probably correct in asserting that its effect has been to mitigate 'the asymmetry in the system ... not by the imposition of asset settlement on the US but by relieving many other countries from the strict rules of asset settlement'. What we have now to consider, therefore, is the extent to which the growth of this market has in fact significantly offset the tendencies towards uneven development set out in the theoretical part of this book and whether it is based upon relationships whose stability can be guaranteed over the long term.

The nature and growth of the Eurocurrency market

The Eurocurrency system is an 'offshore' market in externally held currencies (mainly dollars) in which 'banks resident in country A accept deposits and make loans in the currencies of countries B, C, D, and so on, and borrowers are often non-residents'.[91] It is concentrated in an international network of the largest US, European and Japanese banks and is able to operate almost entirely outside the regulations enforced on domestic banking practices by national governments. Its scale and the distribution of its lending can be derived from the Tables 6.5–6.7.

Table 6.5 External claims of Eurocurrency banks ($ billion)

	1969	1970	1971	1972	1973	1974	1975	1976	1977	1978	1979	1980
Gross total	58.1	78.2	100.1	131.8	187.6	215.1	441.7	548.0	689.7	892.7	1110.9	1323.1
Total net of double-counting	44	57	71	91	132	177	205	330	405	540	665	810.0

Source: Summarised from BIS *Annual Reports*.

Table 6.6 Geographical breakdown of external positions of Eurocurrency banks ($ billion)

	1975	1976	1977	1978	1979	1980
G-10 Countries	235.1	269.5	349.9	466.9	587.9	704.0
Offshore Banking Centres	61.9	83.5	98.9	123.5	155.6	187.5
Rest of Western Europe	31.8	42.7	40.8	50.4	58.7	70.1
Australia, New Zealand, South Africa	9.0	11.8	14.7	13.5	13.7	15.5
Eastern Europe	21.6	28.8	38.3	47.5	55.9	59.8
Oil Exporters	14.3	24.1	39.1	56.4	64.1	70.0
Non-Oil Developing Countries	63.0	80.9	98.7	121.7	158.8	195.0
Unallocated	5.0	6.7	9.3	12.8	16.2	21.2
TOTAL	441.7	548.0	689.7	892.7	1110.9	1323.1

Source: As for Table 6.5.

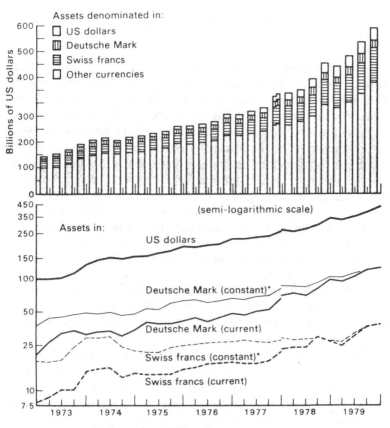

* At constant end-December 1979 exchange rates

Table 6.7   Distribution of NODC borrowing ($ billion)

	1975	1976	1977	1978	1979	1980
Latin America	43.5	57.4	65.9	79.9	103.5	130.2
Middle East	3.3	4.4	5.2	6.5	8.2	9.8
Other Asia	12.9	14.7	20.5	24.3	33.1	38.9
Other Africa	3.3	4.4	7.1	11.0	14.0	16.1
TOTAL	63.0	80.9	98.7	121.7	158.8	195.0

Source: As for Table 6.5.

The Eurocurrency market has been in existence since World War II when the Soviet Union lent its accumulated dollar balances through British banks for fear of confiscation by the US,[92] but the foregoing figures demonstrate that it was only at the end of the 1960s that its expansion really began. Now it is probable that a substantial source of liquidity must be the private corporate sector; this is not documented in the Bank for International Settlements (BIS) figures which are the primary source of information, although they do indicate at times that the weakening of investment activity during the recession has led 'the non-bank sectors' in the leading industrial countries to put their surpluses into the international banking sector.[93] But the major sources identified in these reports are the dollar deficit incurred by the US on the one hand, the oil surpluses of the OPEC countries on the other. The effect of the dollar deficit predominated from the late 1960s to 1973, and again from 1977 to 1979; the oil surpluses from 1974 to 1976 and from the latter part of 1979 to the present.[94] It is not clear how much of the growth of this market derives from pure credit creation and how much of it is the outcome of a growth in investible surpluses hoarded for want of profitable investment opportunities.[95] There seems to be little doubt, however, that the rate of growth has been predominantly supply-determined since the first oil price increase because the banks have been involved in intense competition since then for creditworthy customers and have cut interest rates and extended maturities to the point where 'increasing concern' has been expressed about their 'international risk exposure' in official circles.[96] Thus, whether the banks are actualy creating additional liquidity through the multiplier or not, there can be no doubt that they are playing an immensely important role in recycling surpluses on a global basis.

The Eurocurrency market operates on a wholesale basis, and will therefore lend directly only to large corporations and only indirectly to small firms through the domestic banking system.[97] The BIS reports suggest relatively limited use of the market by large corporate borrowers in the industrial countries from 1972/3 onwards as a result of the 'weakness in industrial activity' there.[98] Thus a very large proportion of the funds will have gone into official balance of payments financing, together with investments in public utilities and state services. Table 6.6 shows that more than half of this will have gone to the Group of 10 countries, but LDC borrowing has grown at least as quickly (as a substantial proportion of the lending through offshore centres will have gone to LDCs) and could now constitute 30 per cent of the total. Both lending and borrowing is highly concentrated. The petrodollar component of bank deposits is highly concentrated in the hands of a few OPEC countries; lending is concentrated in the hands of a relatively small number of the largest banks (thirteen leading US banks control two-thirds of US foreign bank lending); while eleven countries account for about 75 per cent of all third world debt, with more than 60 per cent of that borrowed by Brazil and Mexico. For the leading international banks these foreign operations are a very important component of their business – between 1970 and 1976 profits from this area increased from 16.7 per cent to 49 per cent of total profits for the thirteen largest US banks, with Citibank and Chase Manhattan earning 72 per cent and 78 per cent respectively.[99]

The Eurocurrency market has therefore transferred a very substantial quantity of real resources from surplus to deficit countries during the 1970s, and built up a huge banking structure to do so in the process. To examine its costs, benefits and risks it is necessary to look at the way interest rates and repayment schedules are organised since these determine the nature of the relationship which prevails between borrowers and lenders. The borrowers secure a once-for-all increase in resources from a Eurocurrency loan, followed by a more or less extended period of repayment at a variable rate of interest in most cases. Interest rates are usually calculated in relation to the London Inter-Bank Offer Rate (LIBOR) which is the weighted average of the official interest rates of the leading industrial countries and represents the cost of money to the bank itself. The return to the bank will therefore be determined by the 'margin' or 'spread' above LIBOR which can be secured from the customer in the competitive market situation. This will also determine the period over which the loan has to be repaid (its 'maturity'), since longer maturities will both reduce the real cost of borrowing (because of inflation) and increase the risk to the bank which will almost always have borrowed on much shorter maturities than it is lending.

Since 1975 the instability in the international economic system and the adoption of dear money policies in the attempt to reduce inflation has led to unstable but generally rising interest rates in the advanced countries. Thus three-month Eurodollar bid rates in London were 5 per cent at the end of 1976, 7.2 per cent in 1977, 11.7 per cent in 1978, 14.4 per cent in 1979, 19.7 per cent in March 1980, 9.7 per cent in June, and 15.4 per cent in October when they were still rising as a result of the restrictive monetary policies being followed in the United States.[100] Thus the cost of borrowing has fluctuated widely and unexpectedly, but has also substantially increased despite the supply dominated state of the market. On the other hand inter-bank competition has been so intense that spreads have been kept very low – at the end of 1979 prime borrowers like Belgium and Sweden were able to raise loans at $^3/_8$ per cent and Argentina at ½ per cent,[101] and some 'public-sector entities' in OECD countries at 0.375 per cent.[102] Thus while the borrowers might be paying more than 20 per cent for their money (with earlier credits acquired at lower rates constantly renegotiated to the higher figure), the banks could be receiving less than ½ per cent which might be hardly enough to cover overall costs. A good deal of bank income is in fact derived from the charges imposed for arranging loans. But loans are normally 'syndicated' (shared among a consortium of banks) and arranged by the leading bank in the group which will take all of the payments. These services are normally provided by the largest banks in the system, so many of the smaller banks concerned have to survive on the increasingly limited income derived from their margins. Further, the political and other uncertainties involved in the system are now making smaller banks more cautious, leading to an even greater concentration in the hands of the large banks and a corresponding 'narrowing of the market's lending base'.[103] While interest rates have been narrowing, maturities on the other hand have been lengthening since the early 1970s, with the exception of 1974 and 1975 after a number of important bank failures. Thus borrowers are in the situation where their ultimate repayments are likely to be made in substantially depreciated currencies, thus reducing the pressure on their own resources. On the other hand this tendency greatly increases bank risk exposure and raises serious 'prudential questions' about the stability of the system as a whole which will be considered in the final section.

The viability of the Eurocurrency market
There can be no doubt that this growth in the private banking system has made an important contribution to the recycling problem and created a powerful mechanism which has offset some of the otherwise highly deflationary implications of the uneven growth in producitve capacity in the world economy. Some bankers are willing to discount the risks involved in its further development,[104] while both bankers and academic commentators such as McKinnon[105] attributed its growth and efficiency to the freedom from regulation within which it operates, its scale and its intense competitiveness. Yet it is no longer possible to take these assertions at face value, for even the most conservative official banking circles are now very worried by the 'prudential' problems emerging as uncontrolled growth continues.[106] Two potentially critical problems now exist – on the one hand a recurrence of the bank crisis of 1930/1 whose effects 'contributed decisively to monetary contraction and depression in the US and other countries'[107] at the time; on the other that the increasingly overextended nature of the system will make it impossible for it to continue to perform its present role and thereby worsen the current recession.

A valid appraisal of the system must go beyond the sphere of exchange and money itself and consider the nature of the relationship between the production structures of all of the pariticipants involved. Any banking system which bankrupts its customers must bankrupt itself, so that the problem that we have to consider is the extent to which the resources provided by the banks to the deficit countries are actually being invested in the productive capacity needed to increase output and thereby to cover the costs of debt servicing without reductions in future consumption. Here a clear possibility of the emergence of what may be termed 'national bankruptcy' (which we can define for present purposes as an objective inability to repay or even reschedule existing debts) can exist as the result of a situation in which imports could only be financed through borrowing, borrowing only serviced by further borrowing, 'so that [a country] gradually surrendered an ever-increasing share of its assets to foreign control'.[108] Here it is important to note that because borrowing occurs in foreign currencies, payments must take the same form, so that the stability of the system depends not merely on the ability to increase domestic output, but upon an increase in *export* earning, that is to say of *internationally* competitive production, a far more difficult task. Thus while the long-term stability of the system might not depend on a 'clear prospect of [a country] moving back into surplus,' since debts can be sustained and rolled over, what is required is 'a clear prospect that indebtedness will not grow faster than debt servicing capacity'.[109] How far, then, does an examination of the relationship between import costs (including the costs of foreign debt) and export earning suggest that a stable relationship of this kind can be sustained?

If we look at the overall development of international balance of payments since the first oil price increase we can see that there has been a progressive worsening in the position of the non-oil developing countries and the weaker industrial countries. While the first oil price increase produced a general problem which was rapidly surmounted in the leading countries and much less adequately in the weaker ones, NODC deficits increased sharply in 1978 despite the fact that the relative price of oil and the OPEC surpluses had fallen; with the renewed increases in oil prices all deficits have now risen sharply after a prolonged period of heavy borrowing for the weaker countries. These movements, and the increase in debt in the developing countries can be seen in Tables 6.8 and 6.9

These figures considerably understate the real totals since they do not include short-term credits (in which there was 'a sharp rise' in 1980[110]) nor a substantial amount of debt which is usually kept confidential. They do, nevertheless, indicate a rapid growth in indebtedness with a reltively slow growth in official and a much more rapid growth in commercial debt, reflecting the stagnation in official aid flows and the growth of the Eurocurrency market in the 1970s. This change has produced an important change in the distribution, since 71 per cent of low income country debt was from official concessional sources, but 94 per cent of private debt has been held by middle income countries.[111] Thus we can see that the reflationary effects of the Eurocurrency system have been confined to a small number of the wealthier LDCs (and weaker industrial countries) so that the deflationary problem induced by the balance of payments crisis indicated in Table 6.8 is already a critical one for all of the poorest countries in which a very large percentage of the world's population lives. What we have now to consider, however, is the 'successful' portion of the system which has both sustained levels of activity in the middle income LDCs and, by doing so, also assisted the advanced countries for whom they have been important export markets.

A number of problems arise in this area, not all of them considered in the optimistic evaluations of bankers and internationl officials with a vested interest in maintaining the confidence on which the survival

Table 6.8 Payments balances on current account, 1973–80* (US $ billion)

	1973	1974	1975	1976	1977	1978	1979	1980**
Industrial countries	19.3	−11.6	17.9	−0.5	−4.1	33.4	−9.8	−50
Seven larger countries	14.1	−3.8	23.0	9.0	9.3	36.1	2.9	−29
Other countries	5.2	−7.8	−5.1	−9.6	−13.4	−2.7	−12.7	−21
Developing countries								
Oil exporting countries	6.6	67.8	35.0	40.0	31.9	5.0	68.4	115
Non-oil developing countries	−11.5	−36.9	−45.9	−32.9	−28.6	−35.8	−52.9	−70
By area								
Africa	−2.1	−4.8	−9.1	−8.2	−6.2	−7.0	−4.9	...
Asia	−2.6	−9.9	−8.8	−3.4	−1.5	−5.6	−13.5	...
Europe	0.3	−4.4	−4.8	−4.2	−7.5	−5.1	−9.3	...
Middle East	−2.3	−4.4	−6.6	−5.3	−4.9	−5.7	−7.9	...
Western Hemisphere	−4.8	−13.3	−16.5	−11.8	−8.5	−12.4	−17.4	...
TOTAL†	14.4	19.3	7.0	6.6	−0.8	2.6	5.7	−5

* On goods, services, and private transfers.
** Fund staff projections.
† Reflects errors, omissions, and asymmetries in reported balance of payments statistics; plus balance of listed groups with other countries.
Source: IMF, *Annual Reports.*

Table 6.9   Public and private debt of the developing countries
($ billion)

	End 1970	End 1974	End 1977	End 1978	End 1979
Disbursed debt outstanding					
Official	35.11	63.74	102.35	121.14	138.00
Private	29.03	78.20	155.20	197.25	238.00
TOTAL	64.14	141.94	257.56	318.39	376.00
	1970	1974	1977	1978	1979
Debt service					
Official	2.53	4.66	7.49	9.14	12.00
Private	5.74	16.25	30.37	43.11	57.00
TOTAL	8.27	20.91	37.86	52.25	69.00
Net disbursements					
Official	3.85	8.25	13.13	14.30	16.00
Private	4.81	17.51	28.69	37.72	35.00
TOTAL	8.67	25.75	41.82	52.02	51.00

Source: World Bank, *Annual Report*, 1980, p. 21.

of the system depends. On the one hand we have to consider the 'productivity of the investments financed by foreign as well as by domestic savings',[112] in the main borrowing countries, on the other the stability of the lending banks themselves where irresponsible external lending or problems in other areas of their domestic or foreign business could induce weaknesses which might lead to a crisis of confidence and a 1930s style collapse.

Sustaining the productivity of the debtor countries depends upon changes in the terms of trade and upon the quality of domestic investment opportunities, that is to say upon the domestic rate of profit. From a banking point of view the key indicator through which success or failure is to be measured must be the debt service ratio which must ultimately indicate whether the resources available to cover the costs of borrowing are growing or contracting;[113] thus while we have to look at terms of trade and investment problems to determine likely future movements, we can evaluate past tendencies in relation to movements in the debt service ratio.

The key third world borrowers are mainly newly industrialising countries (NICs) with relatively good growth records over the 1970s, at least partially based upon a diversification in their exports from an almost exclusive reliance on commodities to include manufactures,[114] although they are all still heavily dependent on raw material exports as well. It was this success which gave them the credit ratings which enabled them to borrow on a large scale on the international market. What must now be considered is the likelihood of their being able to continue to expand rapidly enough to offset the growth in their external liabilities without having to reduce their imports of essential producer goods.

On the import side these countries have had to contend with a continuous increase in the prices of manufactures during the 1970s offset by relatively similar increases in raw material prices; on the other hand they have suffered the dramatic increase in their energy costs which produced the large increases in deficits in 1974/5 and 1979/80. It is important to notice, however, that the substantial increase in deficits which took place in 1978 occurred during a period of falling real energy prices, so that it would be a mistake to attribute the whole of their balance of payments difficulties to this factor however important it may have been. So far as the future is concerned, it is relatively difficult to predict the likely movements in oil prices because surplus production might emerge if demand goes on falling and output could be increased from potential large producers (Iran, Iraq and Mexico), while shortages could just as easily intensify if further political instabilities were to affect other key producers, notably Saudi Arabia. If oil prices should decline then the pressure on the system would be relieved, but only if they were accompanied by a relatively stable balance in raw material as opposed to manufactured goods prices and by a continuous growth in the access of third world manufactures to the markets of the industrial countries. Given the nature of the present recession the latter seems to be highly unlikely so that we can expect a further worsening in the external positions of these countries in the near future.

While it is possible that manufactured export prices from the industrial countries will not rise very dramatically (since competition is intense and monetarist policies are tending to bring down inflation rates), it seems very probable that there will now be a real decline in raw material imports and prices. During the 1930s these fell much more rapidly than manufactures (producing a major debt servicing crisis for many LDCs), and it is generally expected that they will continue the decline which started in the early part of 1980. Further, while falling prices are likely to reduce export earnings from commodities, increasing protectionism in industrial country markets (and the balance of payments crisis in poor LDC markets are almost certain to reduce the growth in NIC manufactured exports which have been critical to their recent good performances. Thus two IMF writers noted that in the 1970s 'even small volumes of exports of manufactures by developing countries became subject to protectionist action almost as soon as they entered industrialised country markets',[115] and there can be little doubt that this trend will intensify as unemployment grows in the developed countries.

This analysis suggests that the emerging problems in the financial system are a direct outcome of the contradictions in the operation of the capitalist world economy set out in Chapter 4, and not simply the result of short-term variations in the price of oil. Thus, while we have seen how it is the decline of investment opportunities in the industrialised countries which have forced the banks to lend to third world customers at rates of interest they would never have considered in more prosperous times, we can also see that the absence of growth in the industrial countries now makes it impossible for them to absorb the increased exports which the borrowers *have* to produce in order to meet the costs of their loans. Thus the combination of overproduction and under-consumption takes on an international dimension, is expanded to extreme limits through the operation of the credit mechanism, and finally results in a situation in which borrowers have to export or bankrupt the western banking system, while western countries have to exclude those same exports or bankrupt large sections of their own manufacturing industry.

If this argument holds then even relatively successful processes of internal development must soon run up against external constraints, more especially if energy prices continue to rise. Yet even the relatively successful growth processes of the 1970s now seem increasingly unattainable given the increasingly intractable nature of a number of internal problems. First, inflation is far more rapid in these countries than in the industrialised countries, being 9.3 per cent for all Non-Oil Less Developed Countries between 1967 and 1972, but rising from 20.4 per cent in 1973 to 29.4 per cent in 1979,[116] while it has risen from 46 per cent in 1978 to approximately 60 per cent in the first three quarters of 1980 in the leading Latin American countries.[117] This suggests great difficulty in sustaining an investment process and the possibility that at least some of the increased liquidity derived from official borrowing will have gone into unproductive consumption rather than production. Secondly, monetarist policies followed in order to reduce deficits and inflation are likely to reduce domestic demand and push up units costs, thereby making it particularly difficult to maintain the rate of profit and encourage new investment for all of the reasons given in Chapter 4. Thirdly, bank exposure in the most heavily indebted countries could reduce the willingness to lend; in the present context a larger and larger percentage of new lending is going to repay old debts rather than into productive capacity. Any decline in new lending must therefore have dramatic effects upon the ability to maintain the supply of new productive equipment and spare parts and threaten domestic capacity and export production as well.

Finally, the repressive policies followed in pursuit of monetarist orthodoxy in the context of an increasingly unfavourable external situation must exacerbate political tensions and create the possibility of major upheavals which will threaten the state systems responsible for guaranteeing the loans. The Iranian crisis produced major problems for the international banking system at the end of 1979 when the US blocked Iranian deposits in retaliation against the occupation of the American embassy. This led to a wave of judicial proceedings between the various banks concerned as each attempted to appropriate Iranian assets in order to cover their own loan exposure to Iran. In this case the problem was mainly the tensions created within the banking system itself, since external Iranian assets were sufficient to cover outstanding liabilities, although it did raise serious questions about the political neutrality of the banking system and probably encouraged the movement of a good deal of money into gold.[118] But a far more serious problem would arise if a major political crisis erupted in one of the major debtors – most notably in Brazil – where debts could not be covered, a possibility which can never be excluded, however repressive the regime and extensive the activities of the CIA. A major city was occupied by workers and students in South Korea in 1980; large-scale political violence is escalating in Turkey where the military regime is absolutely incapable of developing a workable economic strategy and will have to rely more and more directly on terror to keep order. Any major crisis in any of these countries would immediately raise questions about all the rest, produce a real crisis of confidence among depositors and threaten a major withdrawal of funds. (The first serious political crisis in a major debtor has now – January 1982 – occurred in Poland.)

The effect of the unfavourable developments of the late 1970s has been a serious worsening of the debt service ratio for all of the main borrowers. These figures are difficult to obtain and, of course, enormously variable, depending as they do directly upon movements in the international interest rate and commodity prices. According to Citibank the ratio worsened from 11.5 per cent to 20.5 per cent between 1974 and 1978 for the leading eleven borrowers, and this figure must have deteriorated further since then given the effect of the new oil crisis.[119] Recent figures given by Michael Lipton from an apparently reliable but 'non-attributable' source, put the ratios for Brazil at 66.5 per cent, Chile 42.6 per cent, Peru 41.8 per cent, Bolivia 37.9 per cent, Mexico 31.4 per cent, and Argentina 25.5 per cent at the end of 1979.[120] If these figures are in any way accurate (and the fact that they are so difficult to establish may be connected with the problems of confidence which they are likely to create), then the situation has clearly reached its outer limits and it is impossible to imagine that further extensions of commercial credit can do any more than delay the crisis by making it far more serious when it finally arrives.

The crisis of control in international banking

One side of the recycling problem has to do with the capacity to sustain growth in the deficit countries, and hence in the world economy as a whole; the other with the viability of the financial institutions which now perform this task. Both have to be solved simultaneously if the system is to survive. Since difficulties are now emerging in the main deficit countries as we have just seen, even more now hangs upon the strength of the banks themselves than would be the case were the balance of payments problem less acute. What conditions must be met if they are to survive? What mechanisms exist to provide them with assistance if difficulties arise? Is their situation likely to become better or worse as the recession develops? A great deal more than the fate of some very rich institutions hangs upon the answer to these questions.

In May 1931 Austria's largest commercial bank closed immediately after a wave of US bank failures, leading to 'a chain reaction of deposit withdrawals, runs on banks, moratoria, exchange panics and devaluations' on an international scale which 'contributed decisively to monetary contraction and depression in the US and other countries'.[121] The suddenness, extent and interconnected nature of these events stems directly from the nature of banking itself – its integration, its internationlisation, and its heavy dependence upon public confidence in its activities. No bank is ever likely to be in a position to meet all of its outstanding short-term claims at short notice, but depends upon the stability of its borrowers and the confidence of its depositors to guarantee that it will never have to do so. For as long as its major borrowers remain solvent and its own organisational and financial structure is beyond question, no problems will arise even where a relatively unfavourable ratio exists between its cash reserves and short-term liabilities and the maturities of its assets in comparison with its liabilities. Once either its major borrowers or its own structure comes into question, however, confidence can disappear very rapidly and an otherwise manageable situation deteriorate into major crisis.

Prior to the Great Crash relatively few constraints were imposed upon the banks which were ultimately disciplined by market competition. Because of the immense social and political costs of the crash a substantial degree of state regulation was considered justified so that legal limits were imposed upon the ratio between reserves and liabilities, and central banks accepted a greater role in guaranteeing loans as 'lender of last resort'. Further, the growth of the interventionist state after World War II effectively provided a *social* guarantee that no major bankruptcies would be allowed, thus apparently guaranteeing conditions within which the banks would never be faced with very substantial bad debts. Thus Citibank claimed that the history of the 1930s could not be repeated because no central bank would now apply 'stiff monetary restraints even in the depths of a recession', and that they would also rescue commercial banks that were at risk.[122] Thus we can see that the success of the banking system, like that of the monetary system of which it is a part, depends directly upon the adequacy of the state system which serves both to regulate it, and to provide it with resources when market failures occur, and thereby to guarantee the confidence which ensures that it will not suffer a crisis such as that which occurred in 1931. Thus any consideration of the banking system must also incorporate an examination of that of the state structures within which it operates.

A number of important bank failures occurred during the mid-1970s recession which provide us with some important insights into the way in which problems can arise and the difficulties involved in dealing with them. In 1974 a major British secondary bank, London and County Securities had to be rescued, a 'wave of panic' then swept through the markets, and affected the 'sterling market' which is 'identical to the Euromarket in its organisation' though much smaller.

> Because of the failure of that one bank, every small bank in London, though perhaps perfectly sound, quite suddenly found it could not go back to the money market to roll over its loans. The good suffered with the bad. Banks had to be rescued, and then the banks which had rescued them had to be rescued.... It was only by the Bank of England's rallying of the clearing banks to the rescue of these fringe banks that the London sterling market was saved from disaster.[123]

In this case the crisis began with a collapse of the British property market which had been the scene of some highly marginal banking activities; the outcome was a serious threat to an international operation run by the same banks where the loss of confidence meant an inability to hold short-term deposits required to cover long-term liabilities. In the same year the Herstatt Bank of Germany failed as a result of risky foreign exchange dealings which had been concealed through false accounting practices; the German authorities closed the bank in the middle of the day imposing tens of millions of dollars worth of losses on other banks from which Herstatt had borrowed.[124] In the same year Franklin National, a medium-sized New York bank also collapsed; it had also been heavily involved in risky (and illegal) foreign exchange dealings and had made further losses through risky domestic lending to a number of companies which then went bankrupt in the recession. It had also recently entered the Eurocurrency market where its liabilities had increased to almost a billion dollars in less than two years. Although this business was initially profitable, once confidence came to be eroded deposits were withdrawn and it had to pay more and more to cover its positions and was soon making losses on this account as well; a very large withdrawal from its foreign branches then took place which effectively destroyed it. It was rescued by the Federal Reserve Bank (with Bank of England assistance) in May 1974 at a cost of more than $1.7 billion, but finally went bankrupt in October imposing heavy losses on both depositors and other banks.[125] Finally, an indication that these problems remain very much in evidence – First Pennsylvania, the twenty-third largest US bank was on the verge of collapse in April 1980 because of losses on its holdings of long-term Government securities, again worsened by an outflow of $300 billion of foreign deposits in the six weeks before a $1.5 billion rescue package could be assembled.[126]

Some general insights can be drawn from these cases. Firstly, losses incurred in one sphere, whether domestic or foreign, will quickly intensify weaknesses in others, especially where maturity transformations are very unfavourable as they are in the Eurocurrency market because of its intensely competitive nature. In the Franklin case the average maturity of its foreign loans was 5½ years, its financing was short-term, uninsured borrowing varying 'from overnight European placements to 30- to 90-day certificates of deposit'.[127] Secondly, that even large and apparently respectable institutions are prepared to withhold information from the authorities in order to conceal situations that might lead to a loss of confidence – a problem which is not confined to the smaller banks as we will note below. Thirdly, that very serious esclations of the banking problem were only avoided through large-scale central bank interventions which nevertheless left the banking system as a whole carrying very substantial losses.

The problem of maturity transformation noted above is exacerbated by the small number of OPEC depositors responsible for a very large proportion of total Eurocurrency assets. Normally banks are safeguarded from large short-term fluctuations in deposits by 'the law of large numbers' (of depositors) which should guarantee a stable deposit base. In present circumstances, however, a substantial withdrawal or shift of funds by even one or two of the major lenders 'might not only render illiquid individual or whole groups of Eurobanks but would pose a very serious threat to international monetary stability in general'.[128] With the recession intensifying in the industrial countries, bankrupting thousands of small and medium sized companies and threatening even giants such as Chrysler and Ford whose debts run into billions, there can be little doubt that the domestic problems in 1974 must be reappearing. We have already considered the marginality of their lending to deficit countries where countries in arrears on debt obligations or required rescheduling 'rose from 4 to 20' between 1974 and 1979.[129] High interest rates have tended to inflate profits in the larger clearing banks since a good deal of ther money comes from non-interest bearing current accounts, which has sheltered the giants from some of these pressures, but it now seems that even some of these are getting into difficulties. In West Germany the second and third largest banks have had to cut dividends and sell off assets to offset 'enormous pressure on margins'; in the US Citibank, one of the big five, has found its fourth quarter profits dramatically reduced,[130] probably as the result of a misjudgement on interest rate movements. The cases cited earlier were related to small or medium sized banks whose losses could relatively easily be absorbed by the official and large commercial banks which have immense reserves of capital, official support and public confidence to back them. Yet when large multinationals are threatened with closure as several now are, and when governments such as those of Reagan and Thatcher are elected which explicitly deny the obligation to avoid 'monetary restraints in a depression' which Citibank sees as the ultimate guarantee against a crisis, then we can no longer assume that the system rests on solid foundations.

In favourable conditions banks, like other capitalist enterprises, find little use for state regulation or intervention and assume that market competition alone will serve to guarantee the efficiency, stability and legitimacy of their operations. Thus Citibank in 1978 attacked the 'fairness and relevance' of the laws and regulations controlling their domestic activities and called for 'a sharp turn towards truly liberal ideals in which government is a silent partner in the relationship among individuals'.[131] Once equilibrium is threatened, however, only the adequacy of the state structures supporting the system can save it from collapse, as we have seen, and the whole capitalist class will expect them to provide both the resources and the guarantees necessary to solve the problems which they have created. Yet when we consider the adequacy of the state structures surrounding the Eurocurrency market we find the same indeterminacies which inhibit the development of an adequate form of control over the international monetary system itself. The Eurocurrency system is an *offshore* market dealing in foreign currencies largely outside the sphere of domestic banking regulations and controls. To what extent is this system capable of guaranteeing an adherence to sound banking practices and that there will be a lender of last resort should a major crisis occur?

The bulk of international banking operates out of specialised off-shore banking centres such as London, the Bahamas and the Caymen Islands which have attracted business by eliminating virtually all of the 'prudential' regulations which govern much domestic banking activity. While much of the business from London will be carried out through fully fledged domestic banks or foreign subsidiaries, a great deal in smaller centres will be performed through 'shell' branches which merely register transactions which are in fact carried out in New York or elsewhere. A major impetus to the development of this system has in fact been given by the highly restrictive regulations on American domestic banking; its effect has been to give the major foreign operators an entirely free hand in their overseas operations and a substantial competitive advantage over small domestic banks. Within this framework, the existence of internationalised operations and the ability to move money from one currency zone to another almost instantaneously has also made it possible for the leading banks to 'transfer price' their foreign exchange activities in order to minimise their tax liabilities, and also to evade the domestic controls which countries have attempted to impose upon their activities. The extent and implications of this process were clearly exposed in a recent case involving a Citibank employee who lost his job after challenging the legality of some of its foreign exchange operations which involved the transferrals 'of net foriegn exchange positions' between international branches[132] at administered prices in order to transfer profits to the lowest taxed location. The official auditor's report commissioned by Citibank itself to investigate the claims agreed that their operations in Switzerland raised serious 'questions of a possible evasion of law' with respect to exchange controls, the maintenance of reserves and to 'Swiss principles of taxation'.[133] This report also showed that the bank used an internal accounting system (the Management Information System) intended to keep track of the real contribution made by particular units to the corporation where its public figures had to be set out in terms of the administered prices used for their transfer pricing operations.[134] This information came to light only because a particular executive lost his sense of 'corporate loyalty' and found himself without a job as a result. It would be surprising if other banks were not behaving in the same way and thus using the freedom given to them at the international level by the existence of an essentially open monetary and unregulated banking system to maximise short-term profits (or perhaps minimise possible losses) without serious consideration of the risks to themselves and the system as a whole.

These developments suggest that competitive pressures and the search for profit have pushed the banks into acitivities which are dangerously risky and entirely out of any form of responsible social control. The London, Franklin and Pennsylvania cases all demonstrated the critical importance of the role of central banks as lender of last resort, and the willingness of the banks in the leading countries to attempt to deal with problems incurred as a result of irresponsible overseas activities of their national banks.[135] Yet these cases were very small compared with what would be involved in the failure of a major bank with tens of billions of dollars of liabilities in the Euro-currency system. Dealing with the problem on this scale would put intense pressure on even the US Federal Reserve Bank even if it could be contained within the limits of a single bank and did not precipitate a run on the banking system as a whole. The legal responsibilities of both parent bank and national central bank for losses incurred by overseas subsidiaries are by no means clear cut; where huge losses were incurred real instability could not be avoided.

The leading national central bankers, operating mainly through the Bank for International Settlements are fully aware of the dangers of the situation arising out of 'the prudential aspects of international banking',[136] including the problem of exercising responsible control 'over bank's foreign subsidiaries', growing risk exposure in deficit countries, especially 'certain developing countries', and the competitive pressures leading to squeezed margins and 'an increase in the degree of maturity transformation'. They also indicate clearly that the future is not necessarily going to mirror the past and that:

> as a result of the relatively good loss record of the international banking system in recent years some banks may have come to underestimate the risks involved in this part of their business, at any rate until last year's events in Iran.[137]

Given the seriousness of the situation they decided to act in 1980, announcing their intention to improve arrangements for monitoring the economic effects of banking development, to improve the supervision of bank's international operations, and to reduce the 'various biases in official regulations and policies that have favoured the growth of banks' international lending'.[138] Yet their capacity to control the growth and management of this immense private edifice is seriously open to question. We have already seen that important banks will use falsified accounts to conceal information, can use administered prices to transfer resources and are more and more dependent on the goodwill of tiny number of depositors and the success of larger and larger operations to maintain their stability. More significant, it is almost impossible to persuade the governments of offshore centres to impose rigorous controls on banks which are providing them with substantial earnings on their invisible account and which may well be far more powerful than the country itself. It is equally difficult to persuade industrial countries to reduce the level of domestic regulation (which in any event would only intensify the 'prudential problem') because, as BIS concedes, these are deeply rooted in national traditions and will raise 'questions about the harmonisation of countries' basic instruments of monetary control'.[139]

Perhaps the most substantial contribution which could be made to stabilise the situation is a massive increase in the level of concessional official lending to the main deficit countries through national aid programmes and the World-Bank and IMF. The banks themselves see this perfectly clearly and now strongly support initiatives of this kind.[140] Thus while the banks insist that the state serve as 'silent partner in the exchanges between individuals' for as long as money is there to be made, they are equally insistent on their right to direct assistance when the inherent instability of the system they operate threatens both their existence and the well-being of the societies which depend upon their activities. Yet here we also see the critical nature of the fundamental contradiction identified in Chapter 1 and considered in some detail in the first part of this one. The call to rescue the international banking system must go out to an internationalised state system, and this has only been allowed to develop in the most limited form because of the conflicts of interest which have constantly precluded the creation of an official means of recycling surpluses from strong to weak countries and thereby offsetting the crises emerging out of the uneven development of the capitalist world economy. Thus the institutions which are being asked to rescue the banks have only the most limited resources at their disposal and virtually no power to impose responsible behaviour on the banks or the surplus countries (though they can force the debtors into deflation and poverty) and thus ensure an equitable and expansionary solution to the problem which now threatens to engulf us all.

During the last thirty years capital has made immense gains by escaping state controls imposed on its actions at the national level by internationalising both its operations and its structures. As a result it now confronts the new crisis which it has created without the support of the interventionist and redistributive mechanisms which the most advanced nation states have created to deal with these problems in the past. Unless the international capitalist class can now produce a major political initiative at the international level, and there is little evidence that they will be able to sink their differences enough to even begin to do so, then it is evident that the existing level of international co-operation and exchange cannot be sustained and the system must regress to less extensive forms of organisation with major loses of productive capacity and well-being in the process.

Notes

1. R. Triffin, *The world money maze*, New Haven, Yale University Press, 1966, p. 288.
2. Ibid., p. 290.

3. Note here the evidence of union representatives on the negative effects of overseas investment by multinational on domestic employment opportunities. (US Senate, Committee on Foreign Relations, Subcommittee on Multinational Corporations, *Multinational Corporations in the dollar devaluation crisis*, Washington, Government Printing Office, 1975).

4. Could this be an exemplification of Stalin's dictum – 'When I hang the last capitalist will he sell me the rope?'

5. This inability can only be adequately understood through a development of G. Lukacs' conceptualisation of the 'dialectical false consciousness of the bourgeoisie', which cannot be developed here. (*History and class consciousness*, London, Merlin, 1971, pp. 61ff).

6. See J.K. Horsefield, ed., *The International Monetary Fund*, Vol. I, *Chronicle*, Washington, IMF, 1969, esp. Chapters 2 and 3.

7. Since representation on the Executive Board is also determined (though not on a one-to-one basis) by quotas, this also reduced third world influence on policy-making. In 1981 nine out of twenty-one directors came from LDCs.

8. For further details see 'Background notes on the IMF', *Development Dialogue*, No. 2, 1980, pp. 107ff.

9. IMF, *Annual Report*, 1980, p. 78.

10. For an official statement see J. deLarosiere, 'The Fund's new approach', *IMF Survey*, 13 October 1980, pp. 311ff.

11. R.F. Micksell, 'The emergence of the World Bank as a development institution', in A. Acheson et al., *Bretton Woods revisited*, London, Macmillan, 1972, p. 70; Micksell, a member of the American delegation, attributes this decision to Keynes.

12. E.S. Mason and R.E. Asher, *The World Bank since Bretton Woods*, Washington, Brookings, 1973, p. 125.

13. World Bank, 'Policy Memorandum 204', cited in T. Hayter, *Aid as imperialism*, Harmondsworth, Penguin, 1971, p. 31.

14. E.H. Rotberg (World Bank Treasurer), 'The World Bank – a financial appraisal: II', *Finance and Development*, Vol. 13, no. 4, 1976, p. 38.

15. For details of the Bank's new approach to deficit financing see E.P. Wright, 'World Bank lending for structural adjustment', *Finance and Development*, Vol. 17, no. 3, 1980.

16. On the IMF see *Development Dialogue*, op. cit., and E.A. Brett. 'The IMF, the international monetary system and the periphery', *IFDA Dossier*, Vol. 5, 1979; C. Payer, *The debt trap*, Harmondsworth, Penguin, 1974 deals with both IMF and World Bank interventions.

17. Notably in the statement by Amir Jamal, chairman of the 1980 Annual Meeting itself, who, as finance Minister of Tanzania had spent the preceding two years in acrimonious struggles with the IMF over their attempts to divert Tanzanian policy away from its socialist objectives, and the first week of July as an active member of the Arusha Conference which produced the critique referred to elsewhere. See Amir Jamal 'Challenge from the Chairman', *IMF Survey*, 13 October 1980; Julius Nyerere, 'No to IMF meddling', *Development Dialogue*, Vol. 2, 1980.

18. deLarosiere, op.cit., p. 314.

19. Ibid.

20. Notably B. Belassa, *Reforming the system of incentives in developing countries*, Bank Staff Working Paper no. 203, Washington, World Bank, 1975.

21. Notably H. Chenery et al., *Redistribution with growth*, London, Oxford University Press, 1974.
22. See in particular M. Bienefeld, 'The informal sector and peripheral capital: the case of Tanzania', *IDS Bulletin*, Vol. 6, no. 3, 1975; C. Leys, 'The politics of redistribution with growth', *IDS Bulletin* Vol. 7, no. 2, 1975; and *Underdevelopment in Kenya*, London, Heinemann Educational Books, 1975, pp. 267ff.
23. The seriousness of this problem was emphasised at the time by Per Jacobsson, *International monetary problems, 1957–1963*, Washington, IMF , 1964, p. 260; and also Bank for International Settlements, *Annual Report*, 1961/62, pp. 144–5.
24. Belgium, Canada, France, West Germany, Italy, Japan, Netherlands, Sweden, United Kingdom and the United States. Switzerland, a non-member of the IMF, associated itself with it in 1964, so that the group should in fact be one of 11.
25. R. Solomon, *The international monetary system, 1945–76*, New York, Harper and Row, 1977, p. 40.
26. IMF, *Annual Report*, 1980, p. 82.
27. Cited in Horsefield, op.cit., Vol. I, p. 511.
28. Williamson, op. cit., p. 28; see also S. Strange, *International monetary relations*, London, RIIA, pp. 115–6, 231.
29. Solomon, op. cit., p. 43.
30. Horsefield, op. cit., p. 509.
31. IMF, *Annual Report*, 1980, p. 82.
32. J.M. Keynes, 'The International Monetary Fund', speech to the House of Lords, 23 May, 1944, cited in S.E. Harris, *The new economics*, New York, Knopf, 1950, p. 373.
33. By the General Manager of the Fund, IMF, *Summary of proceedings*, 1969, p. 250.
34. M. de Vries, *The International Monetary Fund, 1966–71*, Vol. I, Washington, IMF, 1976, p. 177.
35. The rate was originally set at 1½ per cent, it fluctuated between 4 and 5 per cent from 1974 to 1978 and reached a peak of 10 per cent in the middle of 1980; see IMF, *Annual Report*, 1980, p. 84.
36. Composed and weighted as follows (September 1980): '$42 per cent, DM 19 per cent, Fr francs 13 per cent, Yen 13 per cent, £ 13 per cent. At the end of 1980 $1 = approximately SDR 1.3'.
37. Details of the recent modifications in its operation are given in the IMF's 1980 Annual Report, op. cit., pp. 90–1.
38. The position of the UK was perhaps most analagous to that of the US, but because of its secondary and weakening position in the system it became no more than an , 'anxious – and obviously interested – but silent bystander' (Strange, op. cit., p. 231).
39. The formulation of the Group of Experts appointed to consider the problem in 1965 by UNCTAD on behalf of third world countries when they were being excluded from the G–10 discussions. (UNCTAD, *International Monetary issues and the developing countries*, New York, UN, 1965, (TD/B/32), p. 9).
40. Strange, op. cit., p. 233.
41. Williamson's summary of Triffin's argument: Williamson, op. cit., p. 18.
42. B. Tew, *The evolution of the international monetary system, 1945–77*, London, Hutchinson, 1977, p. 144.
43. S. Cohen *International monetary reform, 1964–1969*, New York, Praeger, 1970, p. 53.

44. Strange, op. cit., p. 233 citing Karl Blessing of the German Bundesbank.
45. Statement by President Kennedy at the end of 1960, cited in Strange, op.cit., p. 208.
46. W. Wisley, *A tool of power: the political history of money*, New York, Wiley, 1977, p. 246
47. Group of 10, *Communique of Ministers and Governors and Report of Deputies*, July 1966, 1st page.
48. Ibid., p. 3.
49. Ibid., p. 4.
50. Ibid., outside cover.
51. Group of 10, *Report of a study group on the creation of reserve assets*, (Ossola Report), 1965, pp. 58–9.
52. Ibid.
53. Ibid., pp. 69–70.
54. Strange, op. cit., p. 218 sets out the basis of their position very clearly in relation to the debate on the first reform proposal, the Composite Reserve Unit (CRU).
55. Ibid., p. 218.
56. Ossola Report, op. cit., p. 56.
57. Ibid., p. 57.
58. Cohen, op. cit., p. 38.
59. Strange, op. cit., p. 237; see also Cohen, op. cit., p. 97.
60. de Vries, op. cit., p. 79, she also strongly emphasises the vote of the Fund in pushing for this inclusion.
61. de Vries contains a useful account of their position in the negotiations (Ibid., esp. p. 107).
62. See especially Cohen, op. cit., p. 125.
63. Here see Solomon, op. cit., Chapter 9.
64. See Cohen, op. cit., p. 154.
65. Solomon, op.cit., p. 149.
66. BIS, *Annual Report*, 1972/3, p. 122.
67. Williamson, op. cit., p. 63. His account benefits from the fact that he was a member of the C–20 at the time.
68. Ibid.
69. Ibid., p. 63.
70. Ibid., p. 107.
71. Ibid., p 83.
72. Ibid., p 84.
73. See for example the response of the Bonn-based Industry and Trade Association and West German Banking Federations cited in the *Guardian*, 14 February 1978. The later claimed that 'One cannot hitch the German economy before world business as a locomotive and at the same time worsen the [German] competitive position.'
74. Williamson, pp. 173–4, who here also cites Jeremy Morse (of the Bank of England) and Fred Hirsch.
75. See in particular Inter-American Committee on the Alliance for Progress, *Latin America and the reform of the International Monetary System*, Washington, OAS, 1972; UNCTAD, *Money, finance and development: papers on international monetary reform*, UN, NY, 1974.

76. The official reference is IMF, *International monetary reform: documents of the Committee of 20*, IMF, Washington, 1974.
77. Williamson, op. cit., p. 73.
78. The degree of instability involved can be established from the fact that the price increased by $200 between 14 and 21 January and decreased by the same amount over the following two days. (Bank for International Settlements, *Annual Report*, 1979–80, p. 148).
79. T. de Vries, 'Reforming international monetary relations', *Finance and Development*, Vol. 13, no. 3, 1976, p. 12.
80. *Financial Times*, 'A monetary renaissance', 12 June 1979; note how this reappearance of gold, and the increases in its price, confirm Marx's prediction that 'as soon as credit is shaken ... all the real wealth is suddenly transformed into money, into gold and silver – a mad demand, which, however, grows necessarily out of the system itself'. (K. Marx, *Capital*, Vol. III, London, Lawrence and Wishart, 1972, p. 574).
81. IMF, *Annual Report*, 1980, p. 91.
82. K.A. Crystal, *International money and the future of the SDR*, Princeton, Princeton University Press, 1978.
83. *The Guardian*, 8 January 1981.
84. Statement by IMF General Manager at press conference, *IMF Survey*, 2 October 1978, pp. 310, 312.
85. There is a brief description in IMF, *Annual Report*, 1980, pp. 45ff.
86. J.J. Polak, 'Hope for Substitution Account ...', *IMF Survey*, 27 October 1980, p. 337.
87. Ibid.
88. Ibid.
89. I am heavily indebted in this section to Sarah Bartlett for ideas and material.
90. Ibid., p. 337.
91. R.I. McKinnon, *The Eurocurrency market*, Princeton, Princeton University Press, 1977, p. 2.
92. US Congress, *Financial institutions and the nation's economy*, Part 4, (FINE report), Washington, Government Printing Office, 1976, p. 804.
93. For example, BIS, *Annual Report*, 1977/8, p. 89.
94. Information from BIS Annual Reports.
95. For an extensive debate on the nature and extent of the credit creating capacity of the Eurocurrency market see C.H. Stem et al., eds., *Eurocurrencies and the international monetary system*, Washington, American Enterprise Institute, 1976.
96. BIS, *Annual Report*, 1979/80, p. 110. Similar comments can be found in virtually every report since 1972/3.
97. An indication of their lending structure in the first half of the 1970s can be derived from the FINE Report, op. cit.
98. BIS, op. cit., 1972/3, p. 155; 1975/6, p. 100; 1977/8, p. 89; 1978/9, p. 107; only for 1979 did they report quite strong expansion in investment (1979/80, p. 111), though this had come to an end by the end of the year.
99. US Senate, Committee on Foreign Relations, Sub-Committee on Foreign Economic Policy, *International debt, the banks, and US foreign policy*, Washington, Government Printing Office, 1976, p. 11.

100. Data from Morgan Guaranty Trust Company, *World Financial Markets, 1976–1981*.
101. *Euromoney*, December 1979, p. 42.
102. BIS, *Annual Report*, 1979/80, p. 111.
103. Ibid., p. 112.
104. See for example the Per Jacobsson lecture by the Chairman of the Hanover Trust Company. (*Finance and Development*, Vol. 15, no. 4, 1978, p. 8; Citibank, *Monthly Economic Letter*, March 1980).
105. McKinnon, op. cit.
106. BIS, op. cit., p. 114–7.
107. J. Williamson, 'The international financial system', in E.R. Fried and C.L. Schultze, eds., *Higher oil prices and the world economy*, Washington, Brookings, 1975, p. 200.
108. Ibid., pp. 207–8.
109. Ibid.
110. IMF, *Annual Report*, 1980, p. 31.
111. J.A. Katz, *Capital flows and less developed country debt*, Washington, World Bank, 1979, p. 44.
112. E.W. Robichek, 'Official borrowing abroad: some reflections', *Finance and Development*, Vol. 17, no. 1, 1980, p. 17.
113. While conceding Robichek's (a senior IMF official) argument that using the conventional debt-service ratio 'implies a bias in favour of export promotion and against import substitution' (Ibid., p. 15). I would nevertheless assert that this will only be significant from the bankers' point of view if it produces a balance between debt service and export returns which is manageable in the long term.
114. For statistics see B. Nowzad, *The rise in protectionism*, Washington, IMF, 1978, p. 39ff; H. Hughes and G. Ohlin, 'Adjustment to the changing international structure of production', *Finance and Development*, Vol. 17, no. 2, 1980, p. 23.
115. Hughes and Ohlin, op. cit., p. 22.
116. G. von Furstenberg, 'Double-digit inflation: a wasteful tax', *Finance and Development*, Vol. 17, no. 3, 1980, p. 29.
117. *The Amex Bank Review*, Vol. 8, no. 1, 1981, p. 5.
118. For some details see *The Guardian*, 26 November 1979; 3 December 1979; 28 January 1980.
119. Citibank, *Monthly Economic Letter*, March 1980, p. 10.
120. M. Lipton, 'World depression by third world default', to be published in *IDS Bulletin*, 1981.
121. Citibank, 'Why the tragic scenario of the 1930's can't be replayed', *Money International*, Vol. 2, no. 8, 1974.
122. Ibid.
123. H. McRae, 'Commentary' in Stem, op. cit., p. 334.
124. US Senate, International debt, op. cit., p. 25.
125. Details from J.E. Spero, *The failure of Franklin National Bank*, New York, Colombia University Press, 1980.
126. *Financial Times*, 30 April 80; 2 May 80; 9 May 80.
127. Spero, op. cit., p. 92.
128. H. Meyer, 'Commentary' in Stem, op. cit. p. 341. This intervention contains an excellent summary of the overall problem.

129. B. Nowzad, 'Managing external debt in developing countries', *Finance and Development*, Vol. 17, no. 3, 1980, p. 25.
130. *The Guardian*, 22 January 1981.
131. Citibank, *Annual Report*, 1978, pp. 5 and 12.
132. Sherman and Sterling and Peat, Marwick and Mitchell, *Citibank report by audit committee*, New York, mimeo, 1978, p. 63.
133. Ibid., pp. 119, 123.
134. Ibid., p. 68.
135. Both Spero and McRae, op. cit., give details of the arrangements which emerged after the 1974 problems.
136. BIS, *Annual Report*, 1979/80, p. 117.
137. Ibid., p. 116.
138. Ibid., p 117.
139. Ibid.
140. See for example Amex Bank Review, op. cit.

7 Beyond Breakdown

In sum, the decade of the 1970s was not just a disturbing period in which severe economic problems emerged. It marked the end of an era, a great divide in economic history. The old 'world economic order' had crumbled. The profound problems that had emerged would require structural solutions – which would inevitably come – so that the latter part of the twentieth century was clearly going to be very different from anything that had gone before.

M.G. de Vries, Official Historian to the IMF. *IMF Survey*, 7 January 1980.

When a big enterprise [plans production and distribution for] tens of capitalism. This in itself determines its place in history, for monopoly that grows out of the soil of free competition, and precisely out of free competition, is the transition from the capitalist system to a higher socio-economic order.

When a big enterprise [plans production and distribution for] tens of millions of people ... then it becomes evident that we have socialisation of production, and not mere 'interlocking'; that private economic and private property relations constitute a shell which no longer fits its contents, a shell which must inevitably decay if its removal is aritificially delayed, a shell which may remain in a state of decay for a fairly long period ... but which will inevitably be removed.

V.I. Lenin, *Imperialism*, 1916.

Writing during World War I, Lenin identified the structure of the international division of labour as a form of imperialism which depended upon the first phase of the monopoly stage of capitalism. During this phase the most powerful producers in Europe, America and, increasingly, Japan, had centralised the crucial areas of production in a series of cartels which depended in turn upon organic links with finance capital itself organised upon a monopoly basis. This process, generating an enormous increase in productive capacity, had created both the possibility (through the improvements in communications, military capacity and social organisation), and the necessity (in order to dispose of ever-growing surpluses and to acquire raw materials) of an expansion into the markets of the as yet pre-capitalist regions of the rest of the world. At this stage, given the backward development of the forces and relations of production in those areas, and the corresponding inability to sustain forms of social and political organisation which corresponded to the economic needs of the monopolies, imperialism required the creation of the colonial system with its imposition of external control on indigenous populations through armed force. Thus the 'progressive' role of monopoly capitalism which Lenin identified was circumscribed within severe limitations – it required colonial subjugation and all of the deformations that invariably accompany coercive relations of that kind, including autocratic government, racist ideologies and, monopolistic forms of economic exploitation. It implied the intensification of imperialistic competition for markets and sources of supply and laid the foundation for wars which now moved from a national to a global scale; locally it implied the subordination of peripheral economies to the needs of the metropolitan ones and the possibility in the metropolitan countries of creating a parasitic rentier class and a labour aristocracy, bribed out of expropriated surpluses, and therefore detached from a full commitment to the struggle for socialism. Lenin clearly located the emergence of reformist or 'opportunist' social democracy in this process and saw it leading to the possible penetration of the working class by imperialist ideology.

Writing in 1916 amidst the carnage generated by the contradictions of this first phase of monopoly capitalism, Lenin could be excused for believing that the system had developed all the productive forces of which it was capable, had become a 'shell which no longer fitted its contents' and was faced with imminent collapse. Indeed, the transition from capitalism to an alternative form of organisation in Russia itself (whatever character one wishes to bestow upon that system) was a clear indication that monopoly capitalism in its existing form had lost a part of its hegemonic authority. Further, the experience of the following thirty years – of depression, fascism, autarchy and world war, can only be treated as another validation of his position. Although the bourgeoisie retained their hold over the producitve and coercive apparatuses, they had lost the ideological initiative and had more and more to resort to repression to retain their control over power.

Thus the debate at the end of World War II about the creation of a new international economic order which would provide a basis for harmonious expansion for the whole of the capitalist system constituted a last ditch attempt to resurrect a dying structure quite literally from its own ashes. With the obliteration of Hiroshima it became oppressively obvious that the world faced a real choice between social reorganisation and a barbarism whose effects now encompassed the possibility of the destruction not of a particular social system, but of mankind itself. For capitalism this message was then reinforced by the further expansion of Soviet influence into Eastern Europe up to 1947, and the decisive victory of the Chinese Communist Party in 1949. A huge sphere had been detached from capitalist control, and the intensification of socialist and nationalist struggles everywhere made it clear that the political offensive had not come to an end.

Faced with this fundamental challenge to its authority, there can be little doubt that monopoly capitalism was able to find new resources within itself, and to push its level of social organisation beyond its previous limits to levels which Lenin himself had clearly not anticipated. The organisation of the international monetary system through the IMF and the dollar was a central feature of this departure, but by no means the only one. Associated with and made possible by it was an evolution in the form and organisation of the international firm which created the possibility for a real process of industrialisation to begin, not merely in the previously strong centres, but even in some favoured areas in the periphery as well. Within the metropolitan countries, and indeed in the industrialised enclaves in the periphery, the massive increases in productivity secured through these innovations made it possible to further incorporate strata of the working class within capitalism, not merely on the basis of appropriating surpluses from colonial plunder, but through real improvements in the social productivity of labour. And this in turn made reformist social democracy a real and in some cases hegemonic influence within the structure of the state; the 'adequate form of capitalist state' in the post-war period was, indeed, the social democratic rather than the *laissez-faire* variant as it had been during the earlier phase. This transition, in turn, created the administrative apparatuses required to sustain a limited form of interventionist planning which has modified the operation of the law of value by giving the state power to transfer substantial quantities of real resources between uses without immediate reference to market criteria, and developing in the process large bureaucratic apparatuses capable of providing a number of services themselves (communication, education, health, etc.) and of modifying some of the most dislocative effects of market competition.

These developments depended upon the great increases in productivity resulting from the further expansion of monopoly capitalism and were simultaneously necessary to provide it with the inputs, stable environment and expansion in demand which it now required. No equivalent form of state could be developed at the international level (although the EEC must be seen as a partial exception to this), but these advances in productive and administrative capacity nevertheless made their effects felt at that level as well by providing the basis for the large expansion in international organisational competence which occurred. Thus the viability of the various UN agencies on the one side, and of the economic and military agencies of the 'western alliance' (IMF, GATT, World Bank, OECD, NATO) on the other, depended directly upon these broader developments. Thus the institutional innovations which occurred after World War II did represent a real extension of the capacity for international control over and planning of production. Further, however limited and deformed the economic revolution induced within the colonies by imperialism, this did transform their pre-capitalist structures and integrate them directly and irrevocably into the international division of labour. This, in turn, produced indigenous classes capable of organising nationalist resistance to direct political domination, and of providing the basis for a transition from colonial to semi-colonial status.

The formal subjection of colonial territories is only necessary for the most backward elements within the international capitalist class; the progressive elements can rely for their continued access on making themselves financially and technologically indispensable. Thus the transition to independence made it possible to eliminate some of the most regressive forms of external domination and to rely upon indigenous elements to guarantee the necessary conditions for extended reproduction in exchange for access to the capital goods required to initiate a process of local industrialisation, and to the military hardware required to guarantee their political security. Thus a continuous process of de-colonisation could occur which was almost completed by the early 1960s. Hence the international political order could now not only command a significant administrative and ideological capacity, but also take on the form of a free association of independent states. Thus, to the extent that the rather unwieldy machinery could be held together, it could present its agreements and interventions as the outcome of free discussion and voluntary compliance. This is nowhere more evident than in the monetary field where virtually the whole capitalist world – and certain of the smaller socialist countries too – are party to the IMF's Articles of Agreement, and where its interventions to organise 'adjustment' programmes to restore balance of payments stability in the interests of international financial stability (and more directly of the large banks whose loans have to be repaid) take on a very different aspect from the old exercises in 'gunboat diplomacy' or the more direct expropriations imposed by colonial powers. Given this continuous record of progress from 1947 to the early 1960s the bourgeoisie – and, indeed, the broad strata of the working class as well – could be excused for believing that the capitalist 'shell' had an infinite capacity for expansion and that the 'end of ideology' was therefore at hand.

   Looking somewhat deeper than the superficial manifestations of this process of expansion, we can see that it rested upon a series of compromises between a variety of disparate elements in the inter-national political system. Each of these implied a pattern of reciprocal obligation which depended, in the last analysis, upon the possibility of continuous economic expansion. At the apex of the system, American monopoly capital had essentially agreed to underwrite the costs of defence against socialist incursions, and thereby created the basis for a firm alliance with the strongest elements in the old indus-trial centres. This exchange then allowed the huge expansion in productive capacity in western Europe and Japan, and the further internationalisation of the monopoly sectors of American, and to a lesser degree, British capital. This expansion, in turn, provided the basis for a reformist social democratic compromise to be sustained between capital and labour in these centres based upon full employ-ment, high wages and improved social services. In exchange, the bulk of the working class deserted any form of revolutionary socialist ideology and its political and economic organisations and became deeply incorporated into the fortifications surrounding the existing power structure. In the periphery, on the other hand, a rather different compromise was established. Here monopoly capital attempted to guarantee the financial and technical resources required for the rapid establishment of a productive base adequate to sustain a full transition to the developed form of the social democratic state already in existence in the west. Aid, trade and private capital flows, combined with a local planning capacity was expected to result in a rapid growth of opportunities for the indigenous *petite bourgeoisie*, and of well paid wage employment for those in the subsistence sector who could not raise the productive capacity of their own land, skills or technology. Here the creation of an alliance between monopoly capital and a nationalist movement for 'modernisation' could be expected to eliminate the necessity for class struggle and unite local and foreign elements around a programme where technocratic planning could be substituted for political and economic competition over the direction and content of resource allocation. For as long as this alliance held the local bourgeoisie could be relied on to sustain the repressive apparatus required to control the pressures from those dispossessed during the process of primitive accumulation which followed, and thus to deflect political opposition away from international capital and the international political structures upon which it had come to rest.

Fifteen years into this process, therefore, all seemed to be well. The US and IMF interventions after Suez had both demonstrated that old-fashioned methods would no longer work, and that international agencies could provide the resources required to stabilise financial relationships where necessary. The establishment of convertibility at the end of the 1960s meant that the leading industrial countries could relate to each other with much greater flexibility and openness than ever before, and this was constantly complemented through the reduction of tariff barriers through GATT regulations. The establishment of the EEC provided a basis for a massive free trade area, and integrated a number of countries whose conflicts had disrupted development incessantly for centuries. The revelations at the Twentieth Party Congress in the Soviet Union, combined with the intervention in Hungary, served to discredit socialism more effectively than years of work by the CIA, and it seemed that Soviet expansionism could now be contained. Although the process was not as fast as had been hoped, rapid growth in manufacturing capacity began to occur throughout the periphery organised and directed through a body of modernising theory which had decisively rejected all varieties of the Marxist critique.

Yet this whole superstructure had been erected upon sand. None of these compromises could be sustained over the long-term because all of them involved serious conflicts of interest which the capitalist mode of production could moderate but never bring under effective control. Thus the growth of American defence spending had eliminated its own productive dominance and with it the basis for the whole apparatus by the early 1960s when the 'dollar overhang' first appeared on the scene to herald the storms ahead. The growing power of the new strong centres could not be controlled and generated growing hoards of foreign currency which exerted a deflationary effect on the whole system, just as the American surplus had done before the war. Given the continued dominance of foreign monopoly capital, the whole growth process in the periphery was distorted, leading to the creation of small islands of advanced capitalist industrialisation within seas of intensifying backwardness and marginalisation. The intensified repression required to sustain this division, together with the backward forms of state intervention created to integrate monopoly capitalism into backward social structures led to rapid degeneration. Incompetence, corruption and coercion expanded and with it the flow of resources out of these countries into monopoly profits, private bank accounts and luxury consumption. Apparently progressive regimes – notably those associated with the ECLA 'import substitution' strategy – collapsed and were succeeded by dictatorship that relied directly upon external assistance to stay in power. A few centres such as Taiwan, Korea and Brazil succeeded in continuing the expansion and are hailed as examples for the rest, without any understanding of the extent to which their expansion is based upon their capacity to compete effectively in the surrounding areas and thus to undermine the productive efforts which are needed there.

While the dollar overhang symbolised the bankruptcy of the larger monetary structure, the Vietnam war symbolised that of the development strategy in the periphery. During the 1960s and early 1970s the expansionistic tendency in the industrialised centres has been powerful enough to contain the pressures which were coming to be felt by the working class as the rate of profit began to fall. In the periphery, however, the marginalisation of the semi-proletariat proceeded apace and created the basis for mass resistance which brought the Americans face to face with their future in the wars of South-east Asia. Suddenly monopoly capital no longer appeared in the guise of the aid agency providing capital goods and equipment for hospitals and schools, but as an army of mechanised locusts laying waste villages, fields and forests with fire, chemicals and high explosive. The shell no longer fitted, and a new period of degeneration had emerged but now with a much greater potential for destruction than before given the growth in military capacity which had taken place since World War II and which had been partly instrumental in making it possible for the system to expand at all. Since then the crisis has intensified across the periphery with a rapid escalation into violence which the ruling class finds it increasingly difficult to control. Samoza of Nicaragua and the

Shah of Iran symbolize yet another failure, that of the relationship between monopoly capital and an indigenous *petite bourgeoisie* seeking a common path to modernisation and collapsing in an orgy of torture, mass murder and ideological bankruptcy.

Although the crisis does not take on the same forms in the metropolitan countries which have long been insulated from the worst effects of capitalism through their favoured access to scale economies and therefore to international markets, it began to appear there as well at the end of the 1960s, and to undermine the basis for the social democratic compromise. In Britain the Labour government was forced to give up both its commitment to a reformist programme and to the fixed parity system in the face of the balance of payments deficit which produced an austerity programme, devaluation in 1967 and the loss of the election in 1970. In France the riots of 1968 indicated that the process of radicalisation initiated by the Vietnam war could easily influence the working class if continuous progress could not be sustained. In the United States the student movement, responding mainly to the war, demonstrated that the costs of imperialism could not be imposed exclusively on foreign populations, while the subsequent loss of the war and moral collapse of the presidency demonstrated that powerlessness and corruption, too, were not foreign monopolies. In Portugal de-colonisation led to the verge of a socialist revolution on European soil; in Spain democratisation could lead to a renewed emergence of radicalism; in Italy the Communist Party is now indispensable to the regime in power and threatens to become the first such party to win a place in the government of a NATO power; in France a Socialist regime has now been elected.

Underlying all of these tendencies is the experience of a working class which can no longer be provided with an automatic increase in its wages, services and security each year. The process of uneven development occurs not merely between the North and the South, but within the OECD countries themselves. Thus countries such as Portugal, Italy, Spain and Britain find their own productive capacity undermined by the power of the stronger centres in Germany and Japan, while within each country we find areas of underdevelopment emerging as a result of the further process of centralisation. Thus Brittany in France, the South in Italy, the Basque region in Spain and Northern Ireland, Wales and Scotland in Britain become focuses for resistance to the established system and even a threat to the unity of the nation state itself. Perhaps more important in the long term, the crisis has forced a process of restructuring upon even the strongest industrialised centres which had involved an intensification of exploitation and insecurity for the working class.

Generally presented in its 'monetarist' guise, the new policy package requires the reimposition of market criteria during a period of intensified competition as well as a reduction in all social services that can be classified as 'non-productive' and therefore expendable in the general struggle to raise the rate of profit to acceptable levels. What is actually going on here is a struggle to determine which components of the world's productive capacity are going to be closed down to get rid of the surplus capacity which had emerged at the end of the long boom by the middle of the 1970s. Given that there is no means of organising this productive capacity rationally to provide for the millions who are living on the verge of subsistence, this process can only be carried out through an international struggle for existence which in the past had led directly to war. At one level this process presents itself as a struggle between national fractions of capital in which each attempts to secure its future by increasing its international sales and thereby exporting its difficulties to the countries which cannot resist them. This international conflict is very real, and is leading to a resurgence of protectionism and economic war. But it is important at the same time to recognise that the international capitalist system nevertheless remains an integrated whole, and that the most important elements of monopoly capitalism now operate on the international as opposed to the national level alone. This may account for the relative weakness of the protectionist impulse as yet, since powerful interests even in weak centres such as Britain, are more concerned about maximising their international profits than those that they derive from what used to be called their 'home' market. It is the working class rather than the monopoly capitalist class which is primarily dependent upon the productivity of any particular nation and it is this class which gave up its ability to resist the control of monopoly capitalism with its adoption of reformist social democracy in the 1940s and 1950s.

Thus, while each small or large capitalist which falls by the wayside has to be seen as a victim of the competitive process, it is important to recognise that the real price for restructuring is being paid by the working class of the weaker centres. The deepest effects of the crisis manifest themselves concretely in the constant intensification of labour processes and the corresponding pressures for 'demanning'; in struggle for wage increases which barely keep pace with inflation but which nevertheless appear to be more and more unreasonable as output shrinks; in the growth of unemployment and its cynical manipulation as a means of reimposing the labour disciplines which have been relaxed during the golden days now long gone; in the attack on services for the young, the old, the helpless and the infirm; and in the growth of sectarian and racist ideologies which are increasingly resorted to as a means of concealing the true nature of the problem which now confronts us all.

For the moment the working class response to this has been limited and fragmented. Spontaneous resistance develops at each point where the pressure is intensified – strikes, sit-ins, occupations, demonstrations are used to counter falling wages, redundancies and cuts in services. But there is as yet no real recognition that the problem is a problem of the totality. Given that the whole structure is crumbling, the attempt to increase this or that wage, save this or that job, or restore this or that service cannot resolve any of the fundamental difficulties. The bourgeoisie recognises this clearly and has returned to its classical roots with the reassertion of the old verities – a day's work for a day's pay, no subsidies to the incompetent, the re-establishment of the reserve army of labour to limit the power of those who remain in work. Without a decisive intervention at the centres of power there is no real alternative to these prescriptions as every reformist government which has attempted to bypass them – of which Allende, Wilson/Callaghan and Manley as merely leading examples – have found out to their cost. Reformist social democracy has now got to respond to this challenge by producing a means of organising social production in order to eliminate this inherent tendency towards dislocation and breakdown. Given the internationalisation of the capitalist class it is difficult to discover even the terrain on which the battles have to be fought, but there is no doubt that any failure to begin will lead to a period of dissolution which will have devastating effects upon everything which has been created over the past generation.

This book has merely attempted to demonstrate the existence of a structural problem and to identify the nature of the processes which have brought it to the surface and refuse to be stilled. It can specify the broad requirements for a solution without being in a position to spell out the detailed prescriptions which might serve as the basis for a programme of rebuilding led by the need to integrate the western working class into a rational and equitable social order which can make full use of the most advanced technology without being driven into exhausting the world's resources or immiserising the periphery.

In the periphery the need is for a programme of mobilisation in which the existing technological advances can be harnessed for the benefit of the mass of the poor without requiring the intensification of inequality and the structural dislocations that must accompany a growth strategy presided over by the dominant influence of monopoly capitalism. Twice before the world capitalist order has reached its limits and been unable to push beyond them without the intervention of a global war. We have clearly reached a similar impasse, but now a time when the growth of our creativity has created along with it the imminent possibility of a nuclear holocaust. If we do not solve this problem without war we will solve no others.

Index

Printed in the United States
by Baker & Taylor Publisher Services